THE MODERN METROPOLIS

Hans Blumenfeld, fall 1965, Washington, D.C.
(photo by Rose-Hélène Spreiregen)

THE MODERN METROPOLIS
Its Origins, Growth, Characteristics, and Planning

Selected Essays by

HANS BLUMENFELD

Edited by Paul D. Spreiregen

THE M.I.T. PRESS

Massachusetts Institute of Technology
Cambridge, Massachusetts, and London, England

Foreword

In 1949, Hans Blumenfeld and I spent some time in Germany as Visiting Experts in City Planning for the U.S. Department of Defense. Among other things, we were supposed to consult with and advise city officials, planners, and others on the problems of city reconstruction. I suspect that in our time together I learned a great deal more from him than others did from me.

I recall the way in which Blumenfeld and his ideas were received: the warm respect shown by the older architects and planners, who knew him personally, and the avid following of his words by the new, younger group of professionals, who knew something of him by repute. I recall especially the visit we made together to Hamburg, which was a kind of homecoming for him, and the revealing account he gave of the history and planning of the city.

His knowledge of people and their work, current and earlier—despite his absence from Germany—his perception of what needed to be done and the possibilities that lay ahead, his clear exposition of problems and programs presented in his quiet way, almost reticent yet with grace, humor, and a characteristic twinkle, reflected what I had come to know as one of the most profound, penetrating, creative minds in planning of our time.

More of this I came to know later when I gave a civil service examination for the City of Philadelphia which Hans Blumenfeld took for a top position with the Philadelphia Planning Commission. I wish that the oral part of this examination had been recorded and included among his papers. His terse and pointed briefs on the planning needs and directions of the city were jeweled by fresh and sparkling ideas and concepts. He displayed not only vast knowledge and understanding but that great gift of expressing simply and clearly the insights that make the complex and the new seem obvious and familiar.

From time to time, one would meet Hans Blumenfeld at a professional planning meeting, conversing casually in the halls or lobby, following intently a more formal paper, responding with a shrewd observation or question, giving point to the very essence of the matter. It is, I suppose, the combination of the clarity of his views and the ever-stimulating freshness of idea that permeates his work and his writing that makes us all his students.

A graduate in architecture from the Polytechnic Institute of Darmstadt, he had studied architecture previously at Munich and Karlsruhe and the history of city planning with Dr. A. E. Brinckman. In his earlier days he practiced as an architect — once with Adolf Loos — but from the 1930's on he has been almost wholly involved in planning both with governmental agencies and as a private consultant. Never far from educating himself and others, he has been identified with Columbia University and the University of Pennsylvania and most recently with M.I.T. and the University of Toronto. He has thought as well as practiced.

The great range of his mind and work from theory and analysis to civic design, from the region and metropolis to the neighborhood, from transportation to urban renewal, gives in his writing a grand conspectus of the modern metropolis. With a quiet inner conviction, yet without rigidity, he presents planning without pedantry. One cannot be with him for long and see his smile, sometimes wistful, sometimes sardonic, yet always with a crinkly twinkle in his eyes, without realizing that his writing — serious, broad-visioned, and lucid — is very much the man.

San Antonio, Texas   S. B. ZISMAN, AIA, AIP
August 1966

Preface

About five years ago I started to read the essays of Hans Blumenfeld. My enthusiasm for his work led to a search for additional material. Perhaps a year later I met Mr. Blumenfeld in Toronto. With his help I began in earnest to assemble the seventy or so essays from which selections were made for this book.

In the course of assembly, selection, and editing I often spoke to colleagues about Mr. Blumenfeld's writings. Without exception the proposal to publish his work as a collection was enthusiastically met. Every serious student of the modern city knows at least a few of his articles. Even more telling, however, is the range of professionals who hold these essays in high esteem. Indeed, that range extends far beyond the world of the professional, for we are all necessarily students of the modern city.

Collections such as this one sometimes suffer from their very breadth, from their original modeling to suit diverse audiences. This book should prove an exception to that generality. The range of interests and outlooks that Mr. Blumenfeld addresses are the very basis for his wide professional audience. That appeal is furthered by his clarity, his intellect, and his humanity.

Today the literature of the city multiplies torrentially. Much of it is beyond the mental grasp of laymen and even some professionals. One would hope that Mr. Blumenfeld's ability to illuminate the obscure, to clarify the complex, and to see always as a human being would guide our growing understanding. Whatever directions that may take, Mr. Blumenfeld's thoughts will serve as an ample base for further exploration. For it well may prove easier to build upon Mr. Blumenfeld's thoughts than to broaden them.

The essays of this book were selected to serve as a broad and solid base of understanding. Appendix B lists other essays not included but of complementary interest. The only exceptions to the general appeal of these essays are a few pieces on planning methodology in the book's final section.

Obviously, the rewards of the effort spent in preparing this work lie in helping to give this gift of knowledge to others. On a more personal basis the friendship with Mr. Blumenfeld—the opportunity to know so great an intellect combined with so great a heart—is much beyond the realm of personal reward.

Washington, D.C.   Paul D. Spreiregen, AIA
August 1966

A Word to the Reader

The thirty-three papers assembled in this volume, including nine not previously published, have been written during the past quarter of a century at various times and directed to various audiences. Inevitably, many of them repeat the same thoughts. I had therefore been hesitant to put them side by side into one book. Paul Spreiregen as editor, in addition to translating my poor sketches and faded photos into clear line drawings, has done his best to eliminate these annoying repetitions. However, many could not be cut out without destroying the meaning of the texts; and in rereading these now consecutively, I feel embarrassed to encounter the same thoughts expressed over and over again, sometimes in identical words.

If I present them nevertheless in this form, I excuse myself by two rationalizations. First, most readers of a book like this one are likely to pick and choose those articles which appear to be of interest to them, and skip the rest. Few will read the book from cover to cover—and they have only themselves to blame.

Second, I recall that there exists a musical form called *tema con variazione* and that many lovers of music, including myself, listen to such works not only patiently but with thorough enjoyment.

So—if I may use the language of the Victorian Age, in which I grew up—I beg to hope that you, my gracious reader, may also welcome this *tema con variazione*.

Toronto, Canada   HANS BLUMENFELD
November 1966

Contents

II. METROPOLITAN AND REGIONAL PLANNING

III. TRANSPORTATION

VI. METHODOLOGY OF PLANNING

I

THE MODERN METROPOLIS:
Its Origins,
Growth,
and Form

1

Form and Function in Urban Communities

The infinite variety of form manifested by cities and towns has always appealed to the imagination of men. To us the contrast between the confused ugliness of most modern cities and the ordered beauty of old ones poses the question of origins. Were these communities designed as a church or a palace is designed, or did they develop as trees or flowers grow?

Some scholars have tried to distinguish two types of cities: "grown" and "planned." But this dogmatic distinction is hardly valid, for all cities are created by men acting purposefully. The choice of site is always an important act of planning and involves a decision that may be made by either a group or an individual. The same holds true for every other element constituting the city. The question is therefore: Who planned this or that element; what was planned by this or that individual or group; and, most of all, why did they plan it so?

Whoever made the decision was ultimately controlled by the needs that the settlement was intended to satisfy. Its functions determined its form. The difference lies in the degree of consciousness of the city builders. Did they anticipate all their needs and provide for them immediately, or did they have to learn the hard way, being forced gradually to adapt the framework of their community to their way of living?

Between these two extremes, there exists a series of intermediate solutions. At one end we find a swarm of squatters, each building where, when, and how he pleases; at the other, the military camp predetermined to the last doorknob. Neither of these is a city.

WHAT IS A CITY? In primitive human settlements, such as the "longhouses" of American Indians or Polynesians, or the "pueblos" of cliff dwellers, there can hardly be a question whether they were "planned" by the group or "just growed" out of a sequence of unrelated individual actions. In primitive clans, the individual is not yet differentiated from the group.

At a later stage, in the early Middle Ages of Northern Europe, we find two main forms of human settlement: villages and castles. But neither of these may yet be called a city or town. As in the "longhouse," the inhabitants of the castle all belonged to one household, although they were divided by rank and occupation. Villagers, on the other hand, like members of a clan, were equals, but they lived in individual, relatively independent households. Only where the plurality of social units of the village is combined with the social and functional differentiation found in the castle can we talk of a city.

Often the town's difference from the village has been ascribed to the division of industrial and agricultural labor. But in most ages and lands, city dwellers have also been tillers or owners of the soil; and industrial villages have flourished from the remote past to our day.

It was division of class, not work, that separated the city from the village. The testimony of the past is unmistakable on that point. In the medieval city, citizens within the walls enjoyed military, political, or economic power, and legal privileges, especially monopoly of trade and personal liberty.

Likewise, in antiquity the Greek word "polis" denoted public authority. In Homer's day "polis" meant castle, such as that seen in the powerful ruins of Tiryns. The common people lived in scattered villages. Later, one of these villages enjoying a particularly favorable location became the concentration point of the local aristocracy and assumed dominion over the entire surrounding territory. As merchants and crafts-men rose in power and finally overthrew the big landowners, *they* became the "polis," controlling the countryside and ex-ploiting the fields increasingly by slave labor. Now the entire settlement was enclosed by walls. The former castle became the "acropolis," its walls either demolished or incorporated in the new enclosure of the city. Finally, in the fourth century B.C., when new cities were founded, they often lacked either castle or acropolis. At Priene, for example, the city occupied the slope of a hill. The towering peak above, though enclosed within the city wall, was uninhabited except for an occasional garrison in its fort. The relation is exactly the reverse from that at Tiryns.

In Italy the development differed somewhat. Here the politi-cal unit had never been the village, but always the *pagus,* the region inhabited by the tribe. In normal times its members lived scattered over the countryside, but when danger ap-proached, they all took refuge with their herds in a walled place, usually located on a mountaintop. Remnants of similar camps of refuge (the *Fluchtburgen* of the German scholars) are also to be found in other European countries, often dating back to neolithic times. In Italy, the *oppida* became the capi-tals and sanctuaries of their tribes. Their center, the *templum,* magically bound to the four cardinal points, was the ideal center of the *pagus,* bound to it by the two main streets and the four gates. Here, in the very center of the enclosure, was the forum, a meeting place of the tribe. The Greek agora, in contrast, lay outside the gate of the original polis. Soon the priests and magistrates became permanent inhabitants of the place. Again the city had evolved as the seat of a privileged class, with common folk scattered over the adjoining country-side.

Apparently, the result was the same as in Greece, but the different origin made itself permanently felt. The city had started as the recognized center of a territory. Its sacred walls remained. The patricians were rarely displaced or subdued by the plebs. There was usually no duality of acropolis and lower city, no moving down the slope. Even today, many of these towns crown the hills of Italy, filled with the palaces of pro-vincial landlords who thus look out over their tenants in the valleys.

This characteristic situation is rarely found north of the Alps. Here the development sprang, not from the refuge of the tribe, but from the castle of count or bishop—or from a monastery. Peasants brought their *dime* to the gate of their lord's court. Here, too, they exchanged some of their products with each other, with craftsmen working for the lord, or with traveling merchants. If the location was convenient, a market developed. Its place is always the same, before the gate—as it had been in Greece, and in Palestine still earlier. The Bible leaves no doubt that the gate was all in all: market, meeting place, courthouse, and town hall. As the medieval market developed, a special town hall was erected before the gate. The older German towns, especially in Westphalia, invariably show this sequence: castle, town hall, market.

Because they stemmed from the market, not from the camp of refuge, these North European towns usually developed, not on hilltops, but in valleys. The market might stretch out along a street leading to the gate, or on a road perpendicular to it. Whatever its shape, roads from the surrounding countryside tended to converge on it.

As soon as merchants and craftsmen felt strong enough, they turned against the lord of the "burg." If successful, *they* became the "burghers" and at once started to build wall and moat. However, they did not succeed in suppressing the barons as completely as their Greek predecessors had done. At best, they drove the nobles from the immediate neighborhood, but the lords still continued to rule the countryside from their rural castles. The burghers now formed a secondary class, well above the common peasant folk and used their newly won power principally to monopolize trade within their walls. Merchants' and craftsmen's guilds grew. While the larger houses of the merchants clustered around the market, each craft guild settled in its own street. Organization of space reflected organization of function.

With increasing prosperity, the market could accommodate only a portion of the trade. Peasants were forced to park their beasts and carts before the city gates, and new markets for horses, cattle, or wood developed outside the walls. Once more roads converged toward these points, once more merchants and tradesmen settled along these roads, once more the "outs" rebelled against the "ins" until a new wall took them in also, making new burghers out of inhabitants of the old "faux-bourg." The familiar "radial-concentric" plan of many old European cities shows the result of these developments.

PLANNING FROM INSIDE OUT AND FROM OUTSIDE IN

While suburbs might be included within city walls and while neighboring towns might merge into a single community, the founding of new cities remained the privilege of the secular and ecclesiastic lords. They made ample use of it. Between the twelfth and fourteenth centuries, hundreds of towns were founded throughout western and central Europe, especially in southern France, northern Germany, Bohemia, and Poland.

We should expect the plan of these new towns to follow the radial-concentric scheme, which was beginning to evolve in their predecessors, but there is not a single example of such a plan. The majority of these creations show what we call a "gridiron" scheme.

We usually regard city plans mainly as street plans and think only of traffic needs wherever we see a street following a straight line. But the *locatores* of the medieval towns were concerned, not with traffic, but with parceling out land to settlers. They allotted town plots according to the same method that they used to allot parcels of land to tillers of fields.

In northern Europe, village lands were divided into fields, each cultivated according to the three-year crop-rotation system. Each field was divided into long narrow "hides" of equal width, one for each plowman. Cities in these lands show the same sort of subdivision, with long narrow lots running from street to town wall or to the next street. Only later were these strips cut in half and houses built on both ends.

In Latin countries, with their vineyards and olive groves and with a different technique of plowing—plowing crosswise or both ways—land was divided into squares of equal size. The same unit is to be found in Roman cities: a square block, normally divided into four square lots.

The universal influence of agriculture on city planning was reflected by the important role played by the plow in the founding rites of cities. These rites show curious similarities at points as far apart as ancient Etruria, medieval Bohemia, India, Siam, and the Sudan.

In the great valleys of the Indus, Nile, Tigris, and Hwang Ho, civilization had grown as marshy plains were drained by systems of ditches and dikes. The newly won land was allotted to tillers of the soil. "Sesostris," says Herodotus, "divided the land, . . . giving to every man an equal square of ground." As far back as 3000 B.C., geometry, the art of land measuring, determined the layout of huge cities built in these plains. Five thousand years later, compare the division of all land west of the Ohio River into square-mile units that controlled the layout of a large number of nineteenth-century American cities.

In all these cases, allotment of a piece of ground to the individual user was the guiding principle; and wherever this consideration determines the plan, the rectangular pattern prevails. The lots add up to blocks, the blocks add up to a city. It is growth *from the inside out, by addition, with a definite interior pattern, but with indefinite outer limits.*

As such, it is the direct opposite of the radial-concentric plan, which starts from the enclosure. Within it the main radial streets divide the enclosed territory into major blocks, which are in turn more or less arbitrarily subdivided by lesser ways into minor blocks and individual lots. Hence, growth is determined from the *outside in, by division, with a definite outer limit, and in an irregular interior pattern.*

These two contradictory tendencies may be traced in every city plan, combined in various ways. The first represents the element that the city has in common with the village: that of being the sum of many social units. The second stems from the element that the city shares with the castle: that of being a single corporate unit, a center of power that controls the surrounding territory politically by the strength of its walls and economically by the tentacles of roads leading to its market.

Only where both of these elements are present, may we talk of cities or towns. A group of houses is not a city; nor, at the other extreme, is any settlement subject only to a single will, as is a palace, an estate, or a monastery. Co-ordination of many social units within one larger unit is the specific task of city planning. The inherent contradiction is ever present. Today, we talk of the "superblock" and of the "neighborhood" as units of planning. The superblock is determined from the outside in, by the surrounding major traffic arteries that serve the city; the "neighborhood" is determined from the inside out, by the community activities of the inhabitants. The two are not necessarily identical or coextensive.

Only in the irrigated plains where land was subdivided into square acres have cities from the earliest days been laid out on rectangular plans. In hilly Greece, where boundaries of fields and vineyards followed the irregular pattern traced by nature, the arrangement of early towns showed no rational pattern. Streets and alleys were simply the residue left between houses and courts. When rectangular patterns came to be adopted for new cities, resulting probably from experience in colonizing, dimensions of the blocks were carefully determined as multiples of a basic "module," but street widths were not controlled by any definite rule. The secondary character of the streets is clearly visible from the way the "agora," the public place, was arranged. It was always treated as a separate structure, a court surrounded by a U-shaped colonnade, built on one side of a street. The building on the other side of the street was not treated as part of the enclosure of the market place. The "stoa" at Priene, for instance, extends farther along the street than does the colonnade of the agora facing it.

It was different in Italy. There two main streets, meeting at the forum, were the primary elements. They were always broad and straight, even though the blocks were often somewhat irregular. As the Roman Empire came to dominate the peoples of the world, these main streets came to represent its power. They were dominated by some monumental building as a *point de vue,* and the center of the forum was strongly emphasized. Wherever men have desired to symbolize authority, whether in monarchic Versailles or in republican Washington, they have adopted this Roman principle of axiality.

Sometimes Roman city builders further emphasized monumental perspectives by lining both sides of the street with colonnades. This application of a uniform design to the walls of a street or a place, regardless of the variety in building plans behind these façades, reflects faithfully the division between public and private spheres of life in ancient Palmyra as in Napoleonic Paris.

The Greeks knew nothing of this, for they had no conception of the state or law as abstract powers differing from citizens and their decisions. Their buildings on the agora, as

VICISSITUDES OF THE RECTANGULAR PATTERN

in the sacred precinct of the gods, were never related to any axis, but to man, especially to the person entering the precinct through the propylon, the entrance gate. With them, the rectangular pattern had an entirely different origin and purpose; yet the resulting straight streets lent themselves well to the Roman purpose of axial organization.

The medieval towns cared nothing for such abstract formality, but they adopted the rectangular pattern because it facilitated subdivision. Never were streets emphasized by monumental *points de vue;* nor were places arranged symmetrically to streets. Where a market place was needed, one or more blocks were left open. If their streets were sometimes fairly straight and wide, it was hardly because of traffic needs but because they served an important function as firebreaks. In later periods, for instance, in the replanning of Russian cities during the eighteenth century, it was mainly for this reason that a checkerboard pattern of very broad streets was generally adopted.

The right-angled net of streets, so convenient for the surveyor, was found to be equally opportune for the builder. Bricks or paving blocks, boards or tiles, crossings of rails, or connections for an ever increasing number of pipes—everything was made to fit this most universal of standards. Finally, when traffic increased in speed and volume, straight streets were found eminently fit for rapid movement, and rectangular crossings the most practical for traffic regulation by red and green lights. Thus, the checkerboard pattern, originally developed for a now obsolete function—the division of acres for plowing—was again and again successfully adapted to new purposes.

VICISSITUDES OF THE CONCENTRIC PLAN   This persistence of form despite changing functions is even more noticeable with the opposite type, the town plan determined by the circular form of the enclosure.

This type of plan can claim an ancestry no less venerable. If the rectangular division of land goes back to the plowman, the first round enclosure was the herdsman's pen. Today, in the Hottentot kraal, huts are built along the inside of the circular fence, with an open space for the herds in the center. The Scythians, in their camps, parked their wagons in the same way. Villages of the Western Slavs were similarly arranged, with huts in a wide circle around the central commons and pond.

The circle, shortest line of enclosure, was as appropriate to keep the enemy out as it was to keep the cattle in. Walls of castles of refuge and later of cities were skillfully adapted to use natural defenses, and consequently their outline usually only roughly approximated a circle. But, wherever the city is viewed primarily as a fortress, the circle is regarded as the ideal form. This is evidenced not only by written and painted testimony but also by occasional realizations of the perfect circular wall, as in the ancient Hittite capital of Sendjirli, or in medieval towns, like Bergues in French Flanders, and Madrigal in Spain.

Whether the outline is mathematically exact or not, the circular pattern becomes more blurred as we approach the center. This is a visible expression of the fact that the plan originated with the enclosure and developed from the outside in.

It has been said that walls influence the city plan more profoundly after they have been torn down than when standing. Frequently, fortifications have been transformed into promenades surrounding the city or into a green belt. Because markets developed outside of several of the gates, it was felt necessary to connect these centers of trade with each other by circular streets. When railways appeared, their terminals were located at the edge of the densely built-up core of the old cities. The circular road following the old enclosure of this core gained added importance as a connecting link between these railroad terminals. Sometimes even a circular railroad was built along the line of the former enclosure. Hardly ever have these encircling belts been entirely obliterated.

Such is the tenacity of these simple geometrical forms, the circle, the straight line, and the right angle. They survive because of their adaptability. Forms more specifically adapted to their functions perish as soon as those functions become obsolete. The carefully calculated polygons of Vauban's fortifications have had to be destroyed at great cost, leaving no trace, while the primitive circles drawn by the medieval builder still have their use as voids, just as once they were used as solids. "Transposed" crossings, cleverly invented by city planners less than a generation ago were made obsolete by the introduction of traffic lights; but these same traffic lights fitted perfectly into the old-fashioned rectangular street crossing. What will happen to our beautiful cloverleaves once our present system of motor traffic will have had its day?

PLANNERS ARE ALWAYS LATE   Faced with an ever-changing world, the planner's task is not an easy one. How did the planners of old acquit themselves?

We have mentioned the fact that medieval city planners thought primarily of allotting parcels to settlers, a consideration that usually resulted in a pattern of roughly rectangular blocks. Their concept of the town as an agglomeration of residences for farmers and merchants, protected by a wall, reflected the social structures of the early Middle Ages when traveling craftsmen worked in the houses of their clients. In China, where guilds have always remained weak, this is still largely the case; and it is hardly an accident that Chinese cities show a similar pattern, though often on a much larger scale. But even in medieval cities, planned in the thirteenth and fourteenth centuries at a time when the guilds had become powerful and crafts could be practiced only in the shops of their members, there is nothing in the plans of our towns to indicate that streets were differentiated according to trade or profession, or that streets were designed to serve the traffic moving to and from the market.

Only in the Renaissance period did city planners develop a new concept. The city was to be surrounded by a polygonal wall, with radial streets converging toward the central market with a tower or castle in the middle. The radial streets were connected by secondary streets forming a series of rings concentric with the wall. The central market was to be reserved for the most valuable commodities, and secondary market places, distributed symmetrically halfway between the center and the periphery, were assigned to other commodities. A separate street was to be allotted to each trade. All of these traits were to be found in existing medieval cities, but the new scheme rationalized the type that had developed spontaneously. After 300 years, theory had caught up with practice.

The concept of the city as a complex entity now controlled every detail of the plan. Symmetrical places and streets were carefully designed, sometimes even at the expense of a reasonable shape of the building lots. Few cities were actually built following *in toto* this elaborate scheme, but many of its elements were embodied in cities built during the following centuries. Especially did the central place with streets radiating from the castle become a favorite motif in many European capitals. Lord Baltimore's cavaliers transplanted it to our shores in their beautiful capital, Annapolis.

At the time when Renaissance architects were designing their "ideal" cities, the economic basis of the medieval city was already beginning to crumble. Craftsmen's guilds no longer monopolized the local market. Division of labor between cities was developing. Rich merchants, favored by princes, set peasants to work on industrial products. Factories and mills sprang up in the countryside. Alongside the merchants, a new upper class of civil and military officers and professional men appeared. As guilds decayed and free trade came into being, weaver's row and tinsmith's alley became mere names. Both the number and the size of trade establishments were constantly shifting. The importance of the market place decreased as permanent commercial shops handled an increasing share of business. The city wall, now of little avail against heavy artillery, was still a serious obstacle to expansion.

The old pattern, with its elaborate, carefully balanced specialization, had become obsolete. What was needed now was a city of a more uniform character. To most inhabitants — the merchants, the civil and military officers, the professional people — the house was now mainly a residence. Industrial activity was carried on largely outside of the city at the sources of waterpower. The needs of the remainder were so undifferentiated that all they asked for was the right to buy, sell, divide, and combine lots as the need might arise.

City planning ideas at the end of the eighteenth century reflected these simplified needs. As in the primitive agricultural town, the city was once more mainly an undifferentiated agglomeration of residences and was once more planned as an assemblage of rectangular blocks. Since no function was localized, there was no center, and there were no streets leading toward a center. All streets were about equally important and, therefore, were made equally wide. Sometimes diagonals were introduced, but as there was no particular spot to which they should lead, they were distributed according to an arbitrary geometrical pattern.

Schematic as this plan seems to be, it was quite well suited to city life as it existed at the time, lacking as it did any clear differentiation of function. But even while these plans were being translated into brick and stone, a new differentiation arose, more fundamental than anything previously known. For the first time in history, separation of residence and work place became general. More people now were drawn into the business center than had ever been attracted by the market. Huge industrial enterprises could no longer be fitted into the small blocks; railroads cut through the established street pattern; smoke and noise drove inhabitants toward the outskirts. Enormous agglomerations clustered around the centers of water-borne and railroad traffic and around the sources of raw materials and energy.

Throughout the Industrial Revolution, city planners had continued to extend their gridiron schemes, but at last a new pattern evolved in response to the new needs. As the residential city of the eighteenth century had resembled the primitive agricultural town with its rectangular pattern, so the localization of functions in the modern metropolis seems to reproduce on a gigantic scale the radial-concentric organism of the medieval city. Rapid-transit lines radiate from the central business district, just as streets had radiated from the central market. Freight terminals for bulky goods have taken the place of the markets formerly at the gates. Industries have been placed in separate zones, just as medieval craftsmen were allotted special quarters. The city wall has disappeared, but the modern city's services stop at the invisible city line, just as formerly protection had stopped at the wall.

Now, however, people live far removed from their work. White-collar workers employed in the business center live in suburbs made easily accessible by rapid transit. Some workers, enjoying reasonably permanent employment, settle around factories on the outskirts, in satellite towns, but the bulk of the workers' families prefer to be closer to the center in a location that allows them maximum mobility in seeking jobs both at the center and on the periphery.

With better understanding of the basic structure of the big city, we have invented new techniques to control it: land-use planning; use, height, and density zoning; protective green belts; green wedges and parkways; superhighways; integrated systems of transportation; satellite towns; neighborhood planning; etc. While we are, here and there, beginning to use these tools to transform metropolises into livable places, their economic bases are shifting once again. With energy coming to be widely distributed by high-tension networks, sources of energy cease to be centers of attraction. As chemistry discovers uses for everything and makes "waste" an obsolete concept, nearness to sources of raw materials loses its compulsion. With intricate nets of railroads and highways, transportation acts to decentralize as well as to centralize.

As the majority of the population no longer lives on the land, cities begin to lose their age-old distinctive character as seats of the privileged. Industrial villages have grown into communities containing more inhabitants than many of the most famous ancient cities ever had. The old difference between town and countryside is beginning to disappear, and a new unit of human settlement is emerging: the industrial region.

But again the spiral is reversing. Within the region as a whole, functions are not yet localized. In many places throughout this superunit, industrial, business, residential, and even agricultural sections may appear. But the individual units, as well as the entire region, are on a vastly larger scale than anything previously known.

In retrospect, city planning does not seem to have been very successful. Almost invariably, the planners thought of one or two functions, forgetting others that soon became important. The rectangular plan was useful in many ways; but its basic concept of the city as an addition of individual units impaired any functional differentiation and hindered the development of definite centers.

The circular plan proved even more adaptable to various uses, but its basic concept of the city as a definite unit stood in the way of gradual growth. These cities could grow only by leaps and bounds. Until they had gathered enough strength for the leap, they almost suffocated in their enclosures. Nor has removal of the walls entirely overcome this hindrance. The broad boulevards, the parks, or the railroads that have taken their place still act as barriers. While on Manhattan's gridiron the shopping center shifts gradually northward on Fifth Avenue, in Vienna shops still hesitate to move outside the "Ring."

Yet, there were and are many old cities that are clear and beautifully articulated organisms, perfectly adapted to their functions and to their natural settings; but, with few exceptions, these are cities where the original plan has been all but obliterated by gradual change. We have objected to the concept of the "grown" city, but it must be admitted that the process has much in common with organic growth. It follows the line of least resistance; natural selection is at work. If a street is not used, neighbors encroach on it. Farmers driving to market avoid steep slopes, and the wheels of their wagons trace a street following the contours. There are community decisions also. A street is widened, or a new one is broken through to connect two important sites; a public building is erected in a conspicuous place; swamps are transformed into lakes or parks. There may even be undertakings of great scope, such as a system of superhighways or a central railroad station replacing a confused muddle of terminals and tracks. But all these decisions are made to answer problems as they come up; they are not necessarily part of any preconceived, comprehensive plan.

If the results of gradual adaptation have in the past been so much better than the results of most preconceived plans, should we not follow this method exclusively?

The old cities we admire today took a long time to reach their present perfection. Social changes were slow, and physical decay was rapid. Most buildings were constructed of wood or clay, and most streets were only dirt roads. The process of weeding out the unfit had time to run its course. "Organic" growth was possible. Today social changes are rapid, and our buildings and streets are made of solid brick, steel, and concrete. They remain intact long after they have outlived their usefulness.

Therefore, we can no longer wait for nature to take her course. *We* must take *her* course. We must learn to plan a city in the way it would have grown if it had not been planned — if it could have had the time to grow. This is not the prevailing concept of city planning. Most city planners of the past have approached the design of a city in the same way architects design an individual building or a garden. But the difference between an individual building and a city is not merely quantitative. The individual building provides for one social unit, even though it may be a large corporation. In contrast, the city consists of a multitude of social units with ever-changing relations.

It is the task of the city planner to anticipate the needs of all these units and to co-ordinate the means of satisfying them. This he can do only if he is able to grasp not merely the changing intentions of men, but also the basic trends that determine these changes. He must be able to understand the ever-changing relations of social forces and of the physical environment in which these forces operate. Essentially, this is a historical approach. Although the city planner does not have to be a historian, he should be historically minded, for it is doubtful whether he can acquire this fundamental understanding without a knowledge of history, especially the history of his own field, the history of cities.

The city builder of old, in creating the framework for the life of his contemporaries, visualized his city as a three-dimensional organization of space and mass. When he designed places and streets, he saw clearly the simple spatial relations of the paved surfaces and the walls of the surrounding buildings. When he traced the city walls following the contours, he visualized the towers and gates crowning the hill. There was no hiatus between the technical and the artistic side of his work. Because his creation *was* clear and logical, it *appeared* clear and logical. Because it sprang from human imagination, it can, to this day, be perceived and enjoyed by human imagination.

Increasing division of labor has destroyed this natural unity of function and form. Street plans are drawn without any conception of the buildings that are going to line them. Every element of the city is treated separately, without visualizing its environment.

Today we must regain, by conscious effort, the essential unity of function and form. It is not a question of inventing a "city beautiful." It is a question of discovering the forms that will most clearly give expression to the functions of our cities, as the form of the old towns reflected their way of living. The social life of men is the specific side of nature that the city builder's art reflects. His task is the same as any artist's; as Albrecht Dürer put it: "For, verily, art is inherent in nature; he who can extract it therefrom will hold it."

2

Theory of City Form, Past and Present

Physical city planning—as distinguished from socioeconomic planning—designs the spatial framework for the life of urban society. It requires the abilities of the architect and engineer. But is this work identical with the work of the architect who designs an individual building; does it differ only in scale? Is city planning or city building a fine art?

Architects have usually and normally approached city planning from the aesthetic side. Impressed by the beauty of old towns, as contrasted with the ugliness of most modern cities, they have tried to learn their secret. The more they studied, the more they were puzzled by the question: Is this really the beauty of a work of art, consciously designed, or is it rather the beauty of an organic product of nature?

Some students of the subject have made a distinction between "planned" and "grown" cities. The validity of this distinction is very relative: there are some elements of planning in every city, and none has ever for any length of time followed the original design in every detail. It is a question of the degree of consciousness: which needs have been foreseen; which elements have been planned beforehand; and which elements

The rows of stands, paralleling the edges of the square, show a city in the process of growth. Frequently such temporary rows become permanent streets. Without having been "planned," they follow a logical pattern.

Figure 1
Puri, India,
market place.

have been adapted to unforeseen needs by a slow process of trial and error (Fig. 1)?

The extreme cases fall outside the sphere of city planning. On one side, we find complexes such as an Egyptian temple, a Roman villa, a castle, or a monastery that are indeed designed by the same process as is a smaller individual building; they are large corporate units, conceived as a whole and divided into functionally different parts. The "ideal" fortress cities of the Renaissance, like Palma Nuova, are close to this extreme (Fig. 2a). On the other hand, we find settlements where each settler built his house where he pleased, without thought of other buildings, the sum of undifferentiated individual farms adding up to a village. Countless villages on all continents represent this type; they have indeed grown like products of nature. Cities have been built that differ from such villages merely in size, as some cities in the Islamic Orient. They consist of an agglomeration of individual houses in garden compounds surrounded by mud walls. Only enough is left open between these walls to provide an access lane to every court so that these lanes form a pattern reminiscent of the small blood vessels feeding a piece of tissue (Fig. 2b).

THEORY OF CITY FORM, PAST AND PRESENT 19

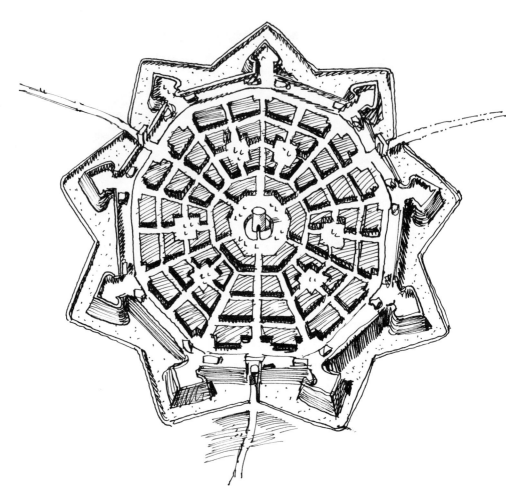

Figure 2a
Extreme example of
a "planned" city.

Palma Nuova, Italy. Some cities, like this sixteenth-century fortress town, have been designed and built as units planned in every detail, in the same way as individual buildings are planned and built.

Theory has tended to emphasize one of the two poles: either the city as a whole, as one big unit, or the city as a sum of many small units. "A city is an organism where nothing counts before the *collective* interest expressed by its law," says Pierre Lavedan, eminent authority on the history of city planning. But the "Town-planning Chart of the C.I.A.M. (Congrès International d'Architecture Moderne)," leading organization of modern architects, proclaims: "The point of departure for all town planning should be the cell represented by a single

Namangan, Central Asia. Other cities have grown like products of organic life; in this Oriental town the streets and lanes form a pattern reminiscent of blood vessels feeding a piece of tissue.

Figure 2b
Extreme example of a "grown city."

dwelling, conceived together with similar cells so as to form a neighborhood unit. . . ."

Both sentences, while true, are incomplete; only when taken together do they define the specific nature of the town. Historically, the city was the seat of power where the ruling aristocracy was concentrated; from here it dominated the surrounding countryside, entrenched behind the city walls. The Greeks had a word for this process of concentration; they described the founding of Athens by Theseus, and of many other cities, as *synoikismos*, or "together-housing." An exact parallel to the mythical feat of Theseus is graphically described in a saga of a different people, living at a different time and on a different continent, but of a comparable stage of cultural development, the Soninke on the Upper Niger. The saga says: "All the 80 princes and many knights came to Annalya Tu-Bari and stayed in her city. Annalya Tu-Bari's city grew and grew. Annalya Tu-Bari ruled over all princes and knights of the wide country around her town."

Military reasons, such as security against attack, were also originally the strongest factor in the first conscious act in the formation of a city, the selection of a site, which in turn becomes one of the main determinants of the shape of the city. Hilltops are often selected, like the Acropolis of Athens or the Palatine of Rome; or islands, as at Tyre, Paris, or Mexico City. Even more typical is what has been aptly described as a "cape situation": a piece of land protected by water or by steep slopes on three sides but connected with its "hinterland" on the fourth. New York and Boston originated that way, as did Lyon and Hamburg in the Old World.

Security remained a prime consideration. But as cities grew stronger and the art of fortification developed, security became less dependent on natural conditions. Instead of retreating from the highways of the world into the inaccessibility of the mountaintop, the city approached them in order to dominate them. Islands and capes served this purpose well; other sites were selected because they dominated land or water ways, especially the crossing of two such ways, a ford or a bridge. Out of these typical situations developed typical forms. Towns built on a riverbank, as far apart as medieval London, Bilbao, and Danzig, show the same pattern, consisting of a number of long narrow blocks between parallel streets perpendicular to a broad embankment.

When at a later time considerations of security receded into the background, accessibility remained a prime consideration in the selection of a site; but again the very development of man-made means of transportation diminished the importance of natural routes. Instead of the caravan routes and rivers determining the location of the city, the cities determine the net of highways, canals, railroads, and airports. Other factors, such as natural resources, health, and convenience, may determine the choice of the site. Water and food, for instance, have always been important in selecting a site; sacred spots have produced towns like Olympia, Lhasa, or Lourdes. In mining towns or in health resorts, typical sites give rise to typical forms.

With this interaction of site and function, towns may survive and grow long after their original reason for existence has disappeared or been destroyed — often destroyed by their very growth. Moscow was originally built in a typical "cape" situation at the confluence of the Neglinnaya Creek and the Moscow River. Under the protection of this triangular fortress — the Kreml — merchants settled at the river crossing. Roads converged toward this city; the princes, drawing wealth and power from the growing trade, gradually extended their rule over all of Russia. The capital became the center of a net of railroads, and the center of railroads attracted industries. Finally canals were built to connect the great industrial city with the sea. Long has the Neglinnaya Creek been covered, and the visitor will look in vain for the "cape" that prompted people to select this site, but the city they founded has lived on and created and re-created its own preferential site.

Manchester gained importance as the seat of the textile industry. As such it attracted the textile trade and factories building textile machines. Soon the textile industry could not compete with the wages paid by these new sources of employment and moved out into the villages of Lancashire. The very growth of the city had destroyed its original reason for existence, but the city, once established, had created a new function.

This interaction of site and function determines ultimately the form of the city. In the endless variety of existing forms two basic schemes stand out: the radiocentric and the gridiron. Both have a long and varied history.

The circle, as the shortest line enclosing a given area, is the logical form where security is paramount and natural boundaries are lacking. The circular form, sanctioned by religion as an image of the cosmos, is praised in literary descriptions of Ecbatana, Jerusalem, and Baghdad, and sometimes, as in the Hittite capital of Sendjirli, the wall actually describes a perfect circle.

As the cities dominate the surrounding countryside, important roads converge toward their gates. Transportation is added to security as a second element determining the form of the city. The combination of city wall and converging streets creates the radiocentric plan.

Inclined as we are today to think of speeding traffic wherever we see a straight street, we read all gridiron plans as street plans. There is plenty of evidence, however, to show that most of them originated as block plans. In ancient Crete and early Greece the streets and alleys were simply what was left over between the houses, and it was only the roughly rectangular shape of the houses that gave some element of regularity to their pattern. In the strictly rectangular scheme, which the later Greeks regarded as an invention of the philosopher Hippodamos, the blocks have definite proportions, but the streets have not. The way squares are laid out also shows that the streets were not regarded as the determining elements of the plan. Never in classical Greece do squares have any axial relation to streets. The agora, or market, of Priene is a colonnaded horseshoe built on one side of the main street like an individual building (Fig. 3). On the other side of the street is another public building that is longer than the agora. In medie-

Figure 3
Priene,
Asia Minor,
300 B.C.

In classical Greece the buildings, not the streets, were the dominant elements of the city plan. Therefore the squares have no axial relations to the streets. The agora, or market, of Priene, is a colonnaded horseshoe built on one side of the main street, asymmetrical to the hall that flanks the other side of the street.

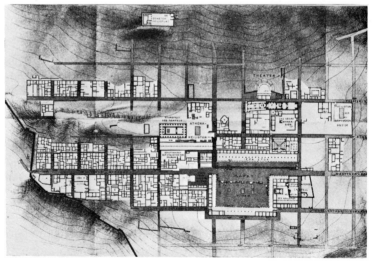

val cities the squares are also never centered on streets but are formed either by widening a street or by leaving a block unbuilt (Figs. 5a, 5b).

In some cases, however, not the lot but the street has been the originator of the plan. Even in the elementary village form both types go side by side. In the European Middle Ages, when virgin soil was settled, each settler was allotted an equal width at the edge of the forest or on the bank of the river and could extend his property in depth as far as he could cultivate the land. Similarly, in early medieval towns, the houses were built on the street, and the lots stretched out back of them through the whole depth of the block. In our country the founders of Detroit followed the same procedure, extending their property inland from the waterfront in parallel strips.

Alongside this type of "row village" are to be found "street villages." In these the houses are built close together on both sides of a broad street that serves as a commons, while the acres are scattered over the village lands. Sometimes around such a street there would grow a town; and if it was crossed by a similar street, a gridiron pattern might develop spontaneously.

The principle of axiality, heritage of Imperial Rome, has dominated Western city planning since the Renaissance. The spires of the two churches flanking the entrance of the Corso in Rome are symmetrical to the street, not to their churches.

Figure 4
Rome,
Piazza del Popolo,
1600.

It is, however, the street endowed with a spiritual significance that has acted most powerfully as a generator of the city plan. The broad processional street leading up to the temple in ancient Egypt became the backbone of the city; so did the *cardo* and *decumanus* of the Roman city leading from the *templum,* the point where the priest had founded the city, to the four cardinal points. This cross dominates the city plan;

 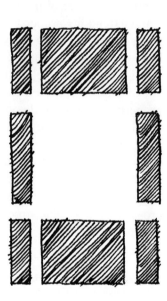

a. Neustadt in Bavaria, Germany, thirteenth century.

b. Sauveterre de Guyenne, France, thirteenth century.

Figure 5 Two methods of forming squares. *In the medieval city, as in classical Greece, the city plan is essentially a block plan. Squares are formed either by a setback of blocks (a) or by leaving one or more blocks vacant (b).*

the unity and dignity of these dominating streets are later emphasized by uniform colonnades and by triumphal arches as *points de vue,* as in Palmyra. The same principle of axiality shapes the symmetrical plazas.

This concept has dominated Western city planning since the Renaissance, monumentality again serving, as in Imperial Rome, to express the unity and majesty of the state. The street fronts are related more to the streets they enclose than to the buildings they shelter. On the Piazza del Popolo in Rome the entrance to the main street, the "Corso," is flanked by two churches; their bell towers are symmetrical, not to the churches, but to the "Corso" (Figs. 4, 5c, 5d).

In the modern gridiron the distinction between block plan and street plan is pointless. The right angle and the straight line, convenient for the division of land, are equally convenient for the erection of buildings, for the laying of pipes

c. Livorno
(Leghorn), Italy,
seventeenth century.

d. Kalinin
(Tver), Russia,
eighteenth century.

In all cities following the Renaissance pattern, as in Imperial Rome, the city plan is essentially a street plan. Squares and monuments are axially related to the streets in a simple (c) or sophisticated (d) pattern.

and rails, and for the regulation of traffic by traffic lights. As was the case with the radiocentric scheme, simple geometric forms have justified themselves as a permanent framework for varying functions.

The original function, however, has permanently determined the basic character of the scheme. In the radiocentric city, conceived as a common enclosure subsequently divided into parts and developed from the outside in, the outer contour is clearly defined, while the interior street pattern is indefinite

Figure 6
Middelburg,
Netherlands.

The radiocentric city plan starts from the common enclosure of the city territory, which is thereafter subdivided into blocks and lots. Consistent with this development from the outside in, the outer contour is clearly defined, while the interior pattern is indefinite.

Figure 7
Verona, Italy.

The gridiron plan starts with the individual lots that add up to blocks; the blocks, in turn, add up to the city. Consistent with this development from the inside out, the interior pattern is clearly defined, but the city contour is indefinite.

(Fig. 6). In the gridiron city, conceived as a sum of individual lots adding up to a city, developing from the inside out, the interior pattern is clearly designed, but the city contour is indefinite (Fig. 7).

This contrast is visible also in the aesthetic concept of the city as evidenced in paintings. Medieval painters conceive the image of the fortress city as a collective unit presenting its silhouette as seen from outside, enhanced by its isolated location on top of a hill or surrounded by water (Fig. 8a). The painters of Pompeii, like those of the Renaissance, look from inside the city at individual streets and squares (Fig. 8b).

The nineteenth-century gridiron plan of our cities was designed without any mental image of the body of the city, and the buildings were constructed without relation to any design of the city as a whole. No one could guess from a map of Manhattan from which field on this checkerboard rises the fantastic silhouette of the city's skyscrapers.

Yet it is possible to discern a definite pattern of the modern city that has gradually superimposed itself on the ubiquitous gridiron. This pattern is essentially a product of the growth of transportation, which at different stages developed centralizing and decentralizing tendencies.

In the first stage interurban traffic was revolutionized by steamships and railroads. Where they met, and only there, could modern industry assemble the masses of coal—its driving power—and of raw materials and food that it needed. And only from these points could it easily ship its products to distant markets. Factories attracted workers, and the presence of many workers of various skills created favorable conditions for more factories.

But while steamships and railroads carried huge masses of goods and passengers to and from the far corners of the earth, traffic within the city moved, as of old, on foot or by horse and buggy; and while the telegraph carried news around the globe within a few seconds, communications within the city were still carried by messengers. So factories and offices and dwellings all tried to be close to the center of the city, crowding each other.

Only after several decades did the technical revolution reach the interior communications of the city. Suburban railroads, streetcars, elevated trains, subways, buses, automobiles, and

Figure 8 *Two different functional concepts of the city find their contrasting visual expression in these two paintings, both works of artists in fifteenth-century Italy.*

a. Francesco Pesellino.

The city as a fortress, conceived as a collective unit, presents its silhouette as seen from outside, enhanced by its isolated position on top of a hill.

b. Gentile Bellini.

The city as a place of habitation, conceived as the sum of its buildings, is seen from the inside as a sequence of streets and squares, spreading out over the plain.

the telephone overcame the distances within the urban area—
as steamships, railroads, and telegraph had already succeeded
in overcoming distances between cities. While interurban
traffic continues to act as a centralizing force, concentrating
business and population in metropolitan areas, intraurban
traffic acts as a decentralizing force within the limits of these
areas. The densely crowded agglomeration of the nineteenth
century with its concomitant, the fantastic skyrocketing of
urban land values, turns out to have been a short-lived passing
phenomenon necessitated by the time lag between the transformation of interurban and intraurban traffic, respectively; it
was bound to disperse once this lag was overcome.

Though it would disperse, it would not dissolve. Sources
of power, raw materials, and markets may be equally accessible also outside the metropolitan area, but it is only here that
employees and employers have a wide range of mutual choice,
as skills become ever more varied and specialized. The modern
metropolitan area is primarily a labor market; it extends only
as far as people can commute daily to and from work.

Within this area growth proceeds in three dimensions: horizontal, vertical, and interstitial (Fig. 9). As long as intracity
traffic moved only by foot or hoof, possibilities of horizontal
and vertical expansion were strictly limited. Growth was
mainly interstitial, filling up every square yard of vacant land
left between buildings until the city became a solidly built-up
amorphous mass of brick. With the advent of the elevator and
the steel frame, the vertical growth of skyscrapers began,
leaving interstices of half-developed and vacant lots. Suburbs
spread out horizontally along streetcar and bus lines and
around suburban railroad stations, surrounded by wide-open
spaces. But with the development of the private automobile,
these interstices between the suburbs began to be filled in,
tending to make the outskirts as amorphous as the central area,
though less densely settled. In a more limited way, the story
of the opposite action of interurban and intraurban traffic was
repeated by the suburban nuclei: population concentrated
here when transportation between suburb and central city was
established, and it dispersed when transportation developed
within the suburban territory.

As the network of highways around the city grows denser,
superhighways are cut through and form the backbone of a

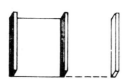

a. Horizontal growth;
area increased;
height and coverage
not changed.

b. Vertical growth;
height increased;
area and coverage
not changed.

c. Interstitial growth;
coverage increased;
area and height
not changed.

Figure 9   Three ways of city growth.

new linear development. Should commuting by airplane become general, we may see the development of new nuclei
around suburban airports.

Every new means of transportation brings about horizontal
(or vertical) growth and a greater differentiation between
developed and undeveloped parts; the city begins to look like
a unit divided into structurally distinct parts. But further
development of transportation then gradually fills the interstices, and the city seems to consist of the addition of many
identical elements. Foundation of new nuclei and accretion
to old ones alternate and supplement each other as they have
done through the entire history of city growth.

Any analysis of city form describes but a cross section
through this incessant flux at a given moment. Its present
structure resembles a sequence of concentric circles. It is
determined by the location of work and dwelling places, which
for the first time in history have become universally separated,
and is modified by the functions of recreation, servicing, and
transportation. At the core is the business center: offices for
the management of private and public business that have to
be close to each other and easily accessible to all inhabitants
of the area and to visitors from outside. Retail stores, places
of amusement, hotels, and apartments—serving the entire area
and places beyond—are to be found in or immediately adjacent
to this area. Surrounding this core is the older part of the city,
now inhabited by the lowest-income group, interspersed with
factories and warehouses. Subsequent widening concentric
rings, consisting of gradually newer and more spacious resi-

dential sections, are occupied by gradually wealthier groups. Somewhere beyond the belt inhabited largely by skilled workers new factories are built on ample cheap land. However, they rarely form a complete circle but tend to concentrate near to waterways and railroads on level sites. Inversely, the high-class residential sections prefer those parts of the periphery which are favored by natural beauty and are located to the windward of sources of smoke and dust. Toward these preferred residential sections the retail stores, hotels, etc., tend to stretch out from the business center, while wholesale business and warehouses grow toward the docks, railroads, and industries. Thus the concentric structure is modified by wedge-shaped developments.

Relation between place of residence and place of work within the metropolitan area is not determined by a simple relation of nearness but by the characteristic polarity between place of production and place of marketing. Dispersed production requires a central market where all producers meet; on the other hand, dispersed markets can be efficiently served only by centrally located producers. Thus in the Lancashire cotton district the weavers, who supply the great wholesalers in Manchester, are located in small towns on the periphery of the area; but the spinners, who supply the weavers, have their mills in a narrow belt around Manchester. Similarly, the white-collar workers, who can find a market for their skills exclusively in the business center, may choose their residence at any place on the outskirts from which they can commute; but the unskilled workers, who sell their labor at unsteady jobs in the factories anywhere on the outskirts, and occasionally in the center, must seek a central location from which any part of the area can be easily reached.

These tendencies are at work in all contemporary cities, but everywhere they clash with remnants of a physical shell built up under different conditions. The ensuing chaotic state with its numerous and serious evils has given rise to many proposals for an entirely new and different city pattern. As was the case with "ideal" cities of the past, these patterns are usually derived from the satisfaction of one or two functions, but with neglect of others.

When the electric streetcar began to carry city dwellers beyond the tight-packed agglomeration that was the nineteenth-century city, a Spanish engineer and businessman, Don Arturo Soria y Mata, proposed the *ciudad lineal,* or the "lineal city," consisting of rows of houses built in the open country on both sides of a trolley line that would take them to their place of work. A generation later, Russian architects based a similar scheme on the development of the automobile; these "disurbanists" visualized single-family houses on ample pieces of land along roads rambling through the countryside, their inhabitants driving to factories scattered here and there in suitable locations. Others, "urbanists" like Le Corbusier, believe that the automobile, in combination with the express elevator, makes possible a rational solution of the modern metropolis. Le Corbusier's "radiant city," with its skyscrapers in the center, elevator apartment houses in an inner belt, and lower houses on the periphery, is essentially a rationalization of the existing concentric pattern of the typical metropolis (Fig. 10).

While Le Corbusier's city is developed around the business center, with industry relegated somewhat casually to one side, Russian city planners during the period of rapid industrialization of their country conceived a scheme consisting exclusively of factories and workers' settlements and dismissed a commercial center as obsolete. Factories and settlements were grouped in parallel bands, with a protective green strip between them. Thus, workers normally live within walking distance of their place of work, while a railroad, running between the factory and the green zone, connects the various factory-settlement units. Growth by erection of new factories is possible by extension of the line, while growth of the individual factory and settlement may occur perpendicular to the line in opposite directions (Figs. 10 and 11).

Contrary to this growth by gradual accretion, Ebenezer Howard in England had proposed growth by deliberate planning in his book *Garden Cities of To-morrow.* Each garden city was to be a self-sufficient unit containing both residences and places of work, within walking distance from each other, and surrounded by a permanent agricultural belt. Each city was to be limited in size, like the cities of ancient Greece and the Middle Ages, and the need for expansion was to be satisfied by the foundation of new garden cities, even as the Greek cities expanded by founding colonies (Fig. 12).

Howard's ideal has found wide acceptance in somewhat

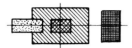

Figure 10
Scheme of concentric city.
Based on business center; industry not an organic part of scheme. Industry located on leeward side. Green areas on windward side and interspersed throughout city. Short or moderate distance to business center; long distance to industry. No provision for growth.

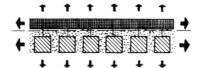

Figure 11
Scheme of ribbon city.
Based on industry; no provision for business center. Industry located on leeward side. Green areas between industry and residences and between residential neighborhood units. Short distance to industry. Growth both by accretion to existing industrial and neighborhood units and by foundation of additional units.

modified form as the "satellite city." Eliel Saarinen, for instance, advocates "organic decentralization" of the big city by gradual transfer of its industries and population into such satellite cities, each being a self-contained unit of definitely limited size, while the surrounding open country could easily accommodate whatever traffic arteries might be needed.

In its basic approach this idea is akin to both the concept of the early middle ages and that of the eighteenth century which created the gridiron plan. Again the city—or metropolitan area—is conceived as the sum of identical units with indefinite relations to each other; only these units are no longer city blocks but highly organized communities, with the open spaces between them taking the place of the simple streets of the old gridiron. Where it is not modified by topographical conditions, the completely decentralized city would assume a checkerboard pattern on a gigantic scale.

Actually, the unity of the metropolitan area, dominated by its center, asserts itself strongly; in practice, most garden or satellite cities are mainly "dormitories" for the central city. The basic idea of the garden city as a balanced and protected community has, however, deeply influenced plans for the reconstruction of existing cities by dividing them into a number of self-contained "neighborhoods." Modern planners try to break up the amorphous agglomeration of city blocks into units organized around the common institutions of daily life — school, playground, shopping facilities — and protected from

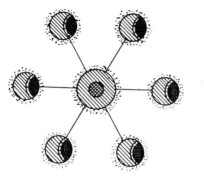

Figure 12
Scheme of central city
with satellite cities.
*Function of central city not
clearly defined; satellites based
on industry. Industry located on
leeward side of each satellite.
Green areas in each satellite
between residences and industry
and around each satellite. Short
distance to industry; long distance to central city. Growth
only by foundation of new satellites; no provision for growth
of business center.*

Figure 13
Star-shaped city.
*Based on business center and
industry. No relation to direction of prevailing winds. Green
areas between residences, industry, and business center. Short
or moderate distance to industry
and to city center. Growth of residential and industrial areas by
accretion; limited growth of city
center possible.*

through traffic. Such a unit, planned from the inside out, meets
with the concept of the "superblock" or "precinct," as the
English like to call it; the superblock, however, is planned
from the outside in, by dividing the entire city territory by
widely spaced high-speed traffic arteries, which are to replace
the dense net of narrow streets inherited from the horse-and-
buggy age.

Opposed to all these adherents of various theories of the
ideal city who believe that existing cities could and should be
gradually transformed in harmony with a preconceived pattern
is the school of "practical" planners who scoff at any attempt
at long-range comprehensive planning, convinced that human
foresight can never prevent the evils constantly produced by
the unpredictable city. They limit themselves to immediate
practical objectives, to the correction of evils that already have
become apparent.

This school of hindsight planners, ably and audibly represented by Mr. Robert Moses of New York City, might well

point out that most preconceived "planned" cities of the past have been failures and that the best historical examples of city planning have been created by gradual adaptation to ever-changing needs. However, conditions have changed. In the old days most buildings were constructed of wood or clay, and streets were just dirt roads; decay was rapid and physical change easy, while social change was slow. Today our buildings and our well-paved streets with their subterranean labyrinth of utilities are far more permanent than our rapidly changing social and economic conditions. Foresight is needed, and we have developed techniques, previously unknown, to measure trends of social change. Certainly a city plan cannot be a definite rigid scheme such as the architect designs for an individual building. It must be based on constant observation of ever-changing trends and on anticipation of their future strength and direction.

These trends seem to point toward a star-shaped pattern (Fig. 13), which may be regarded as a rationalization of the pattern of settlement that is evolving in metropolitan communities throughout the modern world. The difference between such a community and the city, as we have known it through history, is more than quantitative. The metropolitan community combines the traditional function of the city as the political, economic, and cultural leader with the age-old function of the countryside as the place where the world's work is done. Spatially it combines built-up areas and green open spaces. Formally, it can be perceived neither from the outside as a body circumscribed by its silhouette nor from the inside as a sequence of volumes of streets and plazas. As its function and its size transcend the city, so does its form transcend city form in a new concept of the urban landscape.

3

Alternative Solutions for Metropolitan Development

The evils plaguing our large urban centers have increasingly become the object of complaints, discussion, analysis, and proposals for reform. As one palliative after another is being tried and found wanting, more and more voices are heard condemning the concentration of millions of people in a contiguous urban settlement as basically and incurably unsound and demanding their dispersal into "garden cities" or "New Towns." A former chairman of the New York Regional Plan Association, Mr. Paul Windels, in a pamphlet entitled *At the Crossroads*, has advanced the proposal to accommodate the bulk of the future industrial and residential growth of that region in a series of about forty "self-contained towns," averaging around 60,000 inhabitants, and located at distances from 15 to 50 miles from Manhattan. Coming from the leading private planning organization in the country, this proposal deserves the greatest attention. Unquestionably, New York presents all problems of the metropolis in the most concentrated form. It is, after all, the world's biggest urban agglomeration or "conurbation," to use a term coined by Patrick Geddes. If the problems of New York can be solved, then the problems of any city can be solved.

The Association poses the alternative of "self-contained towns" versus "suburban sprawl." It accuses the latter of two basic faults: first, excessive demand for transportation and, second, lack of open space for recreation and also for expansion. It also claims that a dispersal of the population into self-contained towns is the only means to correct these as well as other evils of the big city.

It may be admitted that such "either-or" simplification is not only permissible but indispensable to stir up popular interest. However, in order to arrive at valid conclusions, it is not enough to describe graphically the obvious shortcomings of the present metropolitan pattern. It is necessary to analyze, one by one, the evils hidden under the sinister symbol of the octopus.

The evils of the big city and their remedies are dependent on four factors, which may operate in various combinations but must be dealt with separately. They are: (1) size, or the number of people in the conurbation; (2) functional structure, which is primarily the relation of places of residence to places of work; (3) interior structure of the residential communities; (4) over-all shape, or the relation of developed areas to open land. We might add as a fifth factor "unplanned or planned growth," but this is of importance only as it affects the other four factors.

The alternative of a cluster of satellite towns versus a compact city deals directly only with the fourth factor, and nothing more is expressed, or could be expressed, in the diagrams presented by the Regional Plan Association of New York. Of the "major consequences of development by sprawl" listed, the first, increased demand for transportation, is the result of size and of functional structure; if these remain unchanged, it would exist whatever the over-all shape of the conurbation. In fact, it would be worse in a cluster of satellites than in a compact city. On the other hand, there is nothing in the compact city shape *as such* that would make it impossible, or even more difficult than in other shapes, to distribute places of employment and residence so that everyone lives close to his place of work; as is well known, that was the rule in the compact cities of the preindustrial age. Conversely, the second point, the loss of open spaces for recreation and for expansion, is in no way connected with the functional structure; it depends on the size and over-all shape of the conurbation and also on the interior structure of the residential communities.

It is evident that loss of open spaces and many other urban evils can be prevented with more than one solution of the over-all shape of the conurbation. The specific reason for selecting the cluster of satellites as the most desirable over-all shape has been clearly stated by Mr. Windels. It is the desire to set a definite limit to the ultimate size of every unit and to isolate it from every other by complete greenbelts, in conformance with the ideas expressed by Ebenezer Howard in his book *Garden Cities of To-morrow*, the fiftieth birthday of which was celebrated in 1948 by the planners of England and America.

There is always something pathetic about celebrating the birthday of an idea: after 50 years tomorrow still has not become today. Howard was confident that once an example of the garden city had demonstrated its virtues, everybody would follow, and the existing overgrown cities would rapidly shrink. But they continued to exist and are continuing to grow beyond anything Howard could have visualized in his wildest dreams 50 years ago. Why?

It was certainly not because Howard's ideas were so new and unusual as to be unacceptable. Our European guests at the meeting of the American Society of Planning Officials, Gordon Stephenson of England and Gaston Bardet of France, each talking of his own country, have shown how these ideas had been prepared by a long line of predecessors, especially among the utopian socialists. But it was not only the socialists; liberal reformers were, if anything, even more insistent that the big city was responsible for the evils that distorted a basically sound economic system; and the conservatives condemned it as responsible for the disappearance of the good old days. All were and are sympathetic to the "garden city" idea. And yet the garden cities actually built are driblets compared to the torrents of building activities that are pouring out of our big cities all over the globe.

This failure cannot be attributed to any avoidable mistakes made in creating the first examples of garden cities. No better men could have been selected for the design of Letchworth than Raymond Unwin and Barry Parker. As examples of attractive housing and site planning, Letchworth and Welwyn are impressive; so is, or was, Hellerau in Germany and our own Greenbelt towns. But after 40 years, Letchworth has not yet grown to its planned size of 30,000 population; Welwyn is, for part of its families, a dormitory suburb of London, and Radburn and the Greenbelt towns have become and remained pure dormitories; and here we are coming closer to an answer to our question: *Why* is the big city?

Howard's "garden city" has often been called an invention; some have called it a discovery. I do not believe that any planner can invent the good city; it must be discovered as the adequate form of the existing and developing functions of society. It can only be developed by understanding the fundamental trends that determine our way of life. *Trends*, let us remember, are the composite results of human actions, born from human desires. These results are often very different from the goals that every individual is pursuing — people do not want a depression, yet they bring it about by their actions. The fact that people create the big city does not mean that the result is what they want. But before we thoroughly understand what desires make them live in the big city, we cannot say that these desires can be satisfied in a better way than they are now, nor what this better way may be.

A sarcastic Indian philosopher has characterized our American way of life as the strenuous accumulation of useless junk. Shorn of the sarcasm, this means that we want to have many things; and it follows that we want efficient mass production to make these things, as many as possible and as cheaply as possible; and we want an opportunity to make money, as much as possible and easily as possible, so that we can buy these things. In other words, we want to live in an industrial civilization. And wherever that industrial civilization exists, in widely varying socioeconomic and political forms, from capitalistic America through the mixed forms of Europe and Australia to socialistic Russia, it has certain characteristics. Because these are identical under so widely divergent conditions, we may assume that they are basic and relatively permanent. What are they? I shall try to spell them out.

1. Place of residence is separated from place of work; this is the most striking change from the preindustrial way of life.

2. Many places of work are large; this refers both to area and to employment.

3. The number and type of people in any one place of work varies; i.e., employment is relatively unstable.

4. Workers want to select the place of employment that offers the best opportunities; i.e., labor is mobile.

5. People live in families, in which frequently more than one person is working.

6. There is division of labor with ever-increasing specialization.

This last is perhaps the most basic factor. "Specialized division of labor forces workers to live in big cities," said the German economist Justus Moeser at the eve of the industrial age, more than 150 years ago. People seek in the big city, not primarily a way of living, but a way of *making a living.*

At the meeting of the American Institute of Planners, Lewis Mumford, in an inspiring address, described the physical environment necessary for "good living" for every age group, from the cradle to the grave. It is good that somebody reminds us planners of these basic needs; engrossed in the study of means, we are always in danger of forgetting the end.

But there can be no good living without making a living. People will leave the green and pleasant fields and crowd into the city slums if that is where they can make a living. That has been happening ever since the beginning of the Industrial Revolution. Up to that time, only a small minority had been living in the city, mainly the leading and ruling groups. The vast majority lived in the countryside, and it was there that the world's work was done.

Transportation was the main factor responsible for the reversal of this age-old relation. In the first stage, interurban traffic was revolutionized by steamships and railroads. Where they met, modern industry could assemble the huge quantities of raw materials, fuel, and food that it needed; and from these points of concentration it could easily ship its products to distant markets. Factories attracted workers, and the presence of many workers of various skills attracted more factories. The cycle fed on itself, and the city kept growing. But during the greater part of the nineteenth century, it could only grow within a very limited area because transportation and communication within the city were still, as of old, exclusively by foot or hoof. So they grew by filling every interstice in the already built-up area and by building higher and higher. Nobody ever desired to live under such crowded conditions, but the desire to make a living made people accept them.

Finally, shortly before and since the turn of the century, the technical revolution reached the second stage. The internal transportation and communication of the city were transformed by electric traction and the automobile, and by telephone, radio, and television. People could do what they had always wanted to do: live in more spacious surroundings with some green, some fresh air, and sunshine, but work and seek work in the great metropolitan labor market. They could improve their conditions of living without impairing their chances to make a living. The great exodus to the suburbs began and is still gathering momentum.

To listen to our urban redevelopers, there is something sinful in this trend toward decentralization that threatens the city's land values and tax base; it should be reversed! It is time for these modern King Canutes to understand that this trend will never be reversed and that anyone who tries to do so is bound to come to grief. The densely crowded agglomeration of the nineteenth century with its concomitant, the fantastic skyrocketing of urban land values, was a short-lived passing phenomenon caused by the time lag between the modernization of interurban and intraurban traffic; once this time lag was overcome, it was bound to disappear forever; and few will regret its passing.

If decentralization is to continue, how far can or should it go? Where is the limit? The answer is contained in the remark of a modern British planner: "The main reason for the drift into the cities . . . is mutual accessibility."[1] This means accessibility primarily from home to place of work but also to shopping, recreation, education, and perhaps more important, to friends and relatives. The "metropolitan area," or "conurbation," or whatever you want to call this new phenomenon that is neither city nor country extends as far as mutual accessibility is possible, and no farther. Thus, while within the metropolitan area the movement goes from the center to the periphery, there is no general trend to leave the metropolitan areas entirely in order to settle in new centers or in smaller centers in other

[1] R. B. Hounsfield in *Reference Sheet No. 12* (London: Association for Regional Reconstruction, August, 1948).

parts of the country. There is some confusion in our terminology between these two essentially different forms of movement. I should like to use the terms "concentration" and "dispersal" when discussing the relation of large urban centers to the country as a whole, and to speak of "centralization" and "decentralization" in reference to movements within an urbanized area. All factors that have worked for concentration since the beginning of the Industrial Revolution are still in full force; in fact, with the decreasing importance of nearness to raw materials or sources of energy as a factor determining the location of industry, the relative weight of nearness to labor force and to markets has grown. Both work in favor of the big metropolis, reinforcing each other.

Our conclusion is that the basic trends are toward *concentration and decentralization:* concentration from the country — in all countries — into relatively few metropolitan areas; and decentralization within these areas. Now this is the exact opposite from the basic and original goal of Howard and the advocates of "New Towns," who want not merely satellite towns around existing big cities but completely new and independent towns, and want them relatively compact, with a strict prohibition to "sprawl" beyond a preplanned limit; that is, they want *dispersal and recentralization.* There may be a few isolated cases where such genuine "New Towns" are possible. But the main task is to solve the problem of the metropolitan area, which is growing in population and spreading in area.

The New York Regional Plan Association has faced this problem; their plan assumes that more people will live in their region and that they will spread out over a much greater area. They have faced the fact that this event threatens to engulf the remaining open areas and will increase the demands on transportation. Certainly, if more and more people commute to work in Manhattan from greater and greater distances, traffic problems will become worse and worse. There can be no quarrel with their proposal to transfer as many places of employment as possible from Manhattan — and from other overgrown industrial districts — to outlying points within the region, so that more people can find work within easy distance from their homes. Which places of employment will have to remain in Manhattan?

I have emphasized that the metropolitan region is a new form of human settlement that is not only quantitatively but qualitatively different from the "city" as we have known it through 5,000 years of history. But the old function of the city as the seat of political, economic, and cultural leadership has by no means disappeared; on the contrary, in New York it has grown beyond anything previously known. Despite telephone and television, the people engaged in these activities need personal contact, and they concentrate in an area that, here as elsewhere, quite appropriately is called the "City" in a specific sense. This *specific* central-city employment amounts to hundreds of thousands of persons.

It has been suggested that these persons also should live close to their place of work. Specifically, the urban redevelopers propose that the well-to-do business and professional people, who now commute from the suburbs to the city, should replace the low-income inhabitants of the blighted areas, who should move elsewhere—just where, we are never told. I think that this mechanical concept of the relation of place of residence to place of work is wrong and that the labor force is subject to the same law of polarity as that which governs the relation of production and marketing of a commodity. Dispersed places of production require a central market; dispersed markets can be served only from a central point of production (or distribution). Farmers sell to a central produce market; but the Fuller Brush man can sell to thousands of households only by working out of a central office. Similarly, the white-collar workers who can find a market for their skills exclusively in the business center may choose their residence at any place on the outskirts from which they can commute; but the families of unskilled workers, in which several members sell their labor at frequently unsteady jobs anywhere at the outskirts as well as in the center, must seek a central location from which any part of the region can be easily reached.

This view is strongly supported by the results of a survey made in the Central South Side of Chicago.[2] The places of employment of those gainfully employed were almost evenly divided between those in the Central Business Center, or the Central South Side itself, and those located farther out, in all

[2] Supplements to *An Opportunity for Private and Public Investment in Rebuilding Chicago* (Chicago: Illinois Institute of Technology, 1946-1947).

directions. In 42.4 per cent of all families there were two or more workers. It is evident that most of these families would be severely handicapped if they were to live on the outskirts where they would have to spend a substantial part of their income for commuting to work.

From the point of view of employment opportunity, it is desirable to have short journeys to work but, at the same time, to be able to reach any place of employment anywhere in the region. The principle of "mutual accessibility" requires *a combination of minimum need for commuting with maximum opportunity for commuting*. Taken alone, these basic requirements for a metropolitan area suited to *making a living* would result in a compact city with an even distribution of places of employment. But they are modified by the requirements of *living*, which demand that the compact city be interspersed with green and open spaces at various scales. I am convinced that by far the most important are those on the smallest scale, the open space in your yard and the green before your window. On the next level, the interior structure of the residential communities should certainly provide for playgrounds and neighborhood parks. But I feel strongly that, on a still bigger scale, people need not only large parks but also access to real open country, to farms and forests. I feel it strongly, but I am somewhat at a loss to answer the questions: *Why* do they need it, and what do they do when they get there? I might answer that the kids should be able to see a cow without having to go to the zoo. But that again brings up the question of scale.

The satellite towns suggested by the Regional Planning Association have a radius of two miles; a child living near the center of such a town would hardly be able to walk out into the countryside. But once you *drive* on an uncongested road, is there really any difference between driving two or five miles? I do not know the answer to this question of the optimum or maximum distance to the open country; but I think we have to beware of reproducing, regardless of scale, a rigid pattern of open country, be it a greenbelt or a green wedge.

Whatever our decision as to the scale of the units of developed and open land that compose the over-all pattern of a metropolitan region, it is hard to see the advantage of having access to open country in all directions. A pattern composed of strips of limited width would enable the residents to reach the open country as easily, or more easily, than could the residents of a satellite town, and they would have far better mutual accessibility to all parts of the region. There certainly would be great economies in transportation time and cost, and probably also in utilities. The need for such economies cannot be obliterated by the establishment of a balance between population and employment in each part of the region, because people will, for many reasons, prefer to work at other places than those that happen to be next door; nor does continuity of development in any way preclude full development of local political, commercial, and cultural institutions.

I am personally inclined to visualize such strips of development as radiating from the city center, interlocking with green wedges extending from the open country into the heart of the city. That this shape is not very different from the "octopus" pattern, which our big cities tend to assume without benefit of planning, seems to me to confirm that this is a "discovery" rather than an "invention" and therefore an additional reason for, rather than against, such a pattern.

But maybe we should also study such theoretically possible patterns as a gigantic grid of one-mile strips of developed land at distances of, say, five miles. If somebody showed me such a plan on paper, I would certainly be horrified. I would be shocked by the idea of open country being enclosed on all four sides. But here again it is a question of scale. Do you feel enclosed in 25 square miles of farmland? If this "enclosure" is connected with its neighbors by parkways 1,000 feet wide, will the driver even notice that he is not in "open country"? Maybe we should approach this problem of the over-all shape of the metropolitan region with more critical analysis of its actual functions and with less emotional reaction to the visual appeal of the plan.

The satellite town appeals to us as an "organic entity." We all like to talk of "organic growth." Now growth in cities as in organic nature proceeds in two ways: by accretion of new cells to the individual and by procreation and birth of a new individual. In organic nature, an individual ceases to grow beyond a certain size; but if such a size exists for cities, we are forced to conclude that it has not yet been reached. We may well talk of a hardening of the arteries of our big cities, but even the biggest of these are still very much alive. In organic nature, birth is frequent and easy among lower organisms, less frequent and more painful among the higher ones. Is it an accident that the foundation and relocation of cities, so frequent in less developed cultures, have become so rare in our mature industrial civilization?

The British, who have seriously embarked on a program of building New Towns, have very clearly stated the problem: "The majority of people transfer individually to growing towns because industries and other businesses are there in which they can find employment; but new industries, or industries seeking new situations, more readily establish themselves in an area where there is already a pool of potential employees within easy traveling distance. Thus the flow of industries and [the flow] of working population to a town, once it is well established and regarded as a suitable center, support and reinforce each other. The special problem of a new town is how to get this process under way." And they add: "When the need for housing outpaces the transfer of industry . . . transport between the new town and the present places of employment . . . would be [a] regrettable necessity since it makes the new town to some extent a dormitory for the time being."[3]

So the New Town, planned to end all commuting, calls on commuting to serve as its midwife! And shall we really believe that once this close relation with the old town has been established, with the transportation facilities it involves, it will be broken by some future secession, so to speak, of the New Town?

But if it is hard to start the growth of a New Town, it is ten times harder to stop it. Letchworth and Welwyn have never grown to their planned size and therefore have never been put to this acid test. But another nation, equipped with far stronger legislative and administrative tools, has had ample experience with the attempt to limit the growth of cities. The planners of the Soviet Union always plan a definite size for their cities, both new and old. But I do not know of a single case where this planned size has not been increased if and when the gradual growth of the city pushed beyond the planned limit. It is not a question of legal tools but a question of motives. Do you really want to prohibit an industry in your town to expand?

[3] *Second Interim Report of the New Towns Committee,* presented by the Minister of Town and Country Planning, London, April 1946, pp. 8 and 9.

Or to prevent the new workers of this industry from building houses for themselves? You would not survive the next election.

If your new towns in the New York region prosper, they will certainly outgrow their planned size, and you had better plan, right away, where and how that growth is to take place. Growth by accretion will remain the rule, and growth by procreation the exception.

The fixation on the "New Town," it seems to me, is rooted in a conscious or unconscious desire to escape from the complexities of our rapidly changing times into a simpler and stabler world that probably never existed and certainly cannot exist today. This attitude was expressed with rare candor by a very thoughtful and well-informed writer reporting on the recent Decentralist meeting in Hershey.[4] Says the author: "It is absurd to spend millions of dollars for educating a people to understand an environment that is always changing and never understandable. But is it possible to establish institutions that are stable, knowable, and manageable? It is, the decentralist answers."

I thoroughly disagree. I do not think that it is possible. But if it were possible, I do not think it would be desirable. An unchanging environment certainly would be the negation of the very essence of our civilization. If education has any meaning, it must be education for change. I hope we shall never cease to educate ourselves to understand a changing world, to adjust ourselves to a changing world, and, most important of all, to do our share in changing the world.

[4]"The Fifth Conference of the National Decentralist Institute Meets at Hershey," *Commonwealth*, Vol. 11, No. 9 (State College, Pa.: Pennsylvania State College, August 1948).

James S. Hilander

4

The Urban Pattern

The Latin word *urbs* is related to *orbis*, the circle. Like the English "town" and the Slavic *gorod*, related to "yard" and "girdle," it denotes as the basic characteristic of the urban phenomenon the enclosure that separates it from the open country. This is the city as it has existed through recorded history: a static unit, confined and defined by its enclosing boundary, and with a definite pattern of its internal organization, in which each part has a stable and defined relation to the whole.

But the static concept of the city is no longer valid. It is constantly changing and growing, and, as it grows, it bursts its girdle and overflows into the countryside. The result is universally viewed with alarm as "urban sprawl," as being "neither city nor country."

In this fluctuating mass, the old static patterns dissolve. If any pattern can be discerned, it can only be the pattern of flux. This apparent chaos can no longer be grasped as formation but only as transformation, as historical process.

THE METROPOLIS AND ITS REGION For the purpose of this discussion I am defining the metropolis as an area in which at least half a million people live within a distance not exceeding 45 minutes' travel time from its center by means available to the majority of the population. With current North American technology, this means a radius of about 30 miles.

The essence and reason for existence of the metropolis is, as for its predecessor the city, mutual accessibility — primarily, though by no means exclusively, mutual accessibility of place of residence and place of work. The metropolis extends as far as widespread daily commuting extends, and no farther.

However, its influence extends over a wider area that may be defined as the "metropolitan region," generally up to a time distance of about two hours from the center of the metropolis. Here the influence is twofold. Because the metropolis is easily accessible as a supplier of goods and of business and consumer services and also as a market for their products, establishments and households prefer to settle in towns within these regions rather than in those remote from metropolitan centers. While isolated towns are losing population relatively and often absolutely, each metropolis is typically surrounded by a number of active and growing "satellite" towns, based generally on manufacturing plants, which are often branch plants of or migrants from the metropolis.

But the pattern of the region is determined not only by those functions which are served by the metropolis but also by those even more rapidly growing and wider-ranging ones which serve the recreational needs of the metropolitan population: summer cottages, lodges, motels, camps, picnic grounds, parks, and facilities for a growing variety of land and water sports, with a host of services to their users. The Stockholm regional planners define a vast "summer Stockholm" surrounding the "winter" metropolis, and a similar "summer metropolis" can be identified everywhere in America.

A strange reversal is taking place. For thousands of years, the countryside has been the main locus of production, while the city was largely a place of consumption. Now all activities but the immediate cultivation of the soil — even the raising and feeding of the new "animal" that draws the plow — have been specialized and transformed into "urban" activities. The same process, abetted by the same transportation technology that, at one pole, transformed the city into the giant metropolitan concentration, has, at the opposite pole, dissolved the village into ever fewer and more widely dispersed farms. But over wide areas, though not everywhere, the dwindling farm population is being replaced by a different group, those who "retire" to the countryside. The vast majority of these retire only for short periods, week ends or a few weeks of vacation, but a growing number are permanent residents. This is true not only of the insignificant numbers of gentlemen farmers but of many people of modest means, living on pensions, insurance, or other transfer payments, often supplemented by various services to tourists. No systematic research has explored this phenomenon, but casual observation indicates its growing significance. With the increase in leisure time, it may ultimately influence the pattern of the metropolis itself.

For the present we are dealing only with the latter, the area of regular daily commuting, and only with its most frequent form, the "mononuclear" metropolis. There exist other metropolitan areas that are "polynuclear," resulting from a process for which Patrick Geddes coined the term "conurbation," the growing together of several important independent cities. This has occurred in areas of old and dense urban developments that had already expanded rapidly during the early phases of the Industrial Revolution. The English Midlands, the "Randstad Holland," and the Rhine-Ruhr concentration are the three major examples. In other areas of equally old and dense urban development that, however, started their transformation only at a later stage of the Industrial Revolution, one city increasingly assumes a dominant central role. Cases are Stuttgart for Württemberg, Zurich for northwestern Switzerland, and Milan for Lombardy. They become increasingly similar to the metropolitan areas in younger countries that started out from a single big city such as Chicago or Melbourne.

Many observers believe that the process of conurbation is now repeating itself on an enlarged scale in the United States, notably along the Atlantic seaboard from Boston to Washington. However, analysis of available data shows that daily commuting between the metropolitan centers located on this axis is quite insignificant and that intervening areas show densities that are, on the average, very low compared to those within the major metropolitan areas. The following discussion will therefore deal only with the single monocentric commuting areas as the "archetype" of the metropolis, recognizing, however, that its boundary with the region is fluid and tends to expand.

The developing pattern of the transmutation of the traditional city into the metropolis can be understood best by identifying their essential differences.

1. The metropolis combines with the traditional city function of central leadership the traditional function of the countryside to provide the bulk of material production.

2. As a result, as a country reaches the "developed" level, the majority of its population is now, or soon will be, living in metropolitan areas or, at least, in metropolitan regions. The population of the individual metropolis is much larger than that of the city. The biggest metropolis, New York, contains ten times the population of the biggest preindustrial city, Imperial Rome.

3. This larger population is dispersed over a much larger territory. With a radius of 30 miles it comprises a hundred times more land than the area determined by the three-mile radius of even the biggest foot-and-hoof cities.

4. This vast territory contains not only "urban-developed" land but also extensive "open" areas, parks, golf courses, country clubs, institutional campuses, even farms and forests.

5. Places of work and places of residence are located in separate areas.

6. Residential areas are segregated according to class or income of their residents.

This last-named difference calls for some comment. At first sight, it seems paradoxical that democratic capitalism should have produced a pattern so contrary to democratic ideology. In preindustrial societies, a large part of the "lower" classes lived on the premises of their masters, as slaves or domestic servants. The alley dwellings of Washington and other Southern cities still reflect this older pattern. Elsewhere, as in Chinese cities, ambulant craftsmen worked and often slept in the compounds of their wealthy clients. Almost everywhere in preindustrial cities hovels are found next to or behind palaces. This did not disturb the "upper" classes. Their status was secured by family, title, rank, speech, manner, and clothing. In contemporary American society these no longer determine status. Only financial status remains and is documented by conspicuous consumption. The decisive status symbol is the residence in the "good neighborhood," legally protected by zoning and fiercely defended against any intrusion of non-conforming elements, structural or human.

7. Finally, and only fairly recently, there is another reversal of a historical trend. Previously, as manufacturing specialized out of the peasant village and proliferated, the old elite-service city had become the industrial city, with industrial workers forming the majority of its population. Now the same process of increasing productivity and specialization leads to a proliferation of mass services, business services specializing out of production for the market, and consumer services specializing out of households. Now industrial workers are predominant and growing in number primarily in the satellite towns of the metropolitan regions. In the metropolis itself, manufacturing employment is decreasing relatively and sometimes absolutely. Generally, two thirds or more of the labor force works in a great variety of tertiary or service industries.

PATTERN OF LAND USES   As a result of these transformations, four basic types of "land use" can be identified: central business, industrial, residential, and open areas.

The historical core of the metropolis, the original "city," tends to remain its center. With the main lines of the transportation system oriented to it, this center remains the point most accessible to all parts of the metropolis and therefore attracts all those functions which serve the entire area. Partly attracted by these, partly for historical reasons, all those functions which require mutual contact also concentrate here, typically in office buildings. These two basic central functions attract others that serve them, such as eating and drinking places and parking facilities.

The resulting competition for space, both within the center and on the transportation facilities leading to it, leads to a displacement from the center of all those uses which require relatively much space and can also function elsewhere. These uses are primarily those dealing with goods, manufacturing, and warehouses, but also retail stores, consumer services, and residences.

As the metropolitan population grows and spreads out, outlying sectors accommodate sufficient population and purchasing power to support "second order" services of their own, notably retail, but also most consumer and some business services. With continuing growth, the quality of the "second order" moves up, leaving a narrowing range of the "highest order" in the center. Similarly, second-order routine office functions also move out, leaving only the highest-order contact functions in the center. However, with the over-all growth of the metropolis, both types of highest-order functions are growing and are being augmented by others of still higher order that can exist only when the size of the total market has reached a higher threshold.

Thus, the center is undergoing a process of continuous selective adaptation to those functions for which it is uniquely suited. Surprisingly, this unending change in quality seems to produce stability of quantity. The number of persons entering the central areas of major American cities has remained constant over the last 30 years. During the last 12 years, the same constancy has been observed in Toronto, a younger and smaller metropolis. Congestion acts as the selective agent that maintains the balance. The center is always "choked" but never "chokes itself to death."

From the center outward, density of population and of all activities decreases with amazing regularity. The curve, representing population density in concentric circles, falls constantly toward the periphery. Over time, this curve undergoes two typical modifications: it becomes flatter, and it becomes smoother. The increasing smoothness seems to indicate that the center, despite its relative decrease in quantity, increasingly dominates the entire area, superseding the influence of other, pre-existing centers. The flattening results from a slow decrease of density in the inner and a rapid increase in the outer zones, each of which, however, finally stabilizes at a lower density than the previous one.

Within this basic pattern, modifications are brought about by topography and by transportation. Where expansion is possible in all directions, the original center tends to remain the point of gravity of the metropolitan population, and its growth confirms and strengthens its location. Where expansion in one or more directions is barred by a large body of water, as is the case in many North American cities that started as ports, the center of gravity moves constantly farther inland, away from the original center. The most spectacular example

MODIFICATION BY TOPOGRAPHY AND BY TRANSPORTATION

is the gradual shift of the office and retail center of Manhattan farther and farther "uptown" though, significantly, the financial center has remained "downtown" around Wall Street. On a lesser scale the same gradual movement "uptown" can be observed in many other cities such as Philadelphia, St. Louis, Toronto, and Montreal. However, it is not universal; it has, for instance, not occurred in Chicago.

More general has been the modification by transportation. Whenever individual transportation predominates, time distances tend to be proportional to straight-line distances, and the over-all form of the settlement tends to be circular. This was the case in the foot-and-hoof city. The development of suburban railroads brought a change, because the trips made by their passengers were performed by two means of radically different speeds: a train at 30 miles an hour and walking at 3 miles an hour. As the technology of steam railroads dictated few and widely spaced stations, a pattern of small circular dots developed, strung out over a considerable length of railroad line, with a small commercial center at each station.

With the electric streetcar, stops were far more frequent, and the speed was only about three times walking speed. So the dots merged into solid and shorter lines, with commercial concentrations at their intersections.

When the automobile brought about a sudden and unpredictable reversal of the secular trend from individual to collective transportation, the use of one means of transportation for the entire trip and at fairly uniform speed reproduced, on a vastly larger scale, the circular form of the foot-and-hoof city. The structured pattern of developed and open land, which had begun to emerge in the railroad and streetcar areas, was submerged in universal sprawl. "Developments" were scattered all over the metropolitan area, cutting up the open space into smaller and oddly shaped remnants.

The developments are of two major types: industrial and residential. The former, used for manufacturing, warehousing, and transportation, select relatively large areas of level land with good access to transportation by water, air, rail, and road.

THE RESIDENTIAL PATTERN   Residential areas are practically unrestricted in their choice of location and cover much more extensive areas. They are patterned by two factors: family composition and income.

Single adults and couples without children are more numerous in the inner zone, and families with children are more numerous in the outer zone. A recent survey of all nonsubsidized apartment houses in metropolitan Toronto showed that within each type—one-, two-, three-bedroom apartments—the percentage occupied by bachelors decreased and the percentage occupied by families with children increased from one concentric zone to the next one, from the center outward. This occurred despite the fact that, in the inner zones, the supply of one-bedroom apartments was higher and their vacancy rate lower than in the outer ones, and vice versa, for the two- and three-bedroom apartments.

This is easy to understand, since adults use the central city for work and many other purposes, but most of them have time and inclination for the use of open space only on week ends. Children hardly ever use the central city but use open space, private and public, at all hours of the day. The pattern of residential distribution by family type is entirely voluntary, deliberate, and rational. It is hard to defend the fashionable outcry "to bring the middle-class family back into the city."

There are, of course, in the inner areas, families with children, many children indeed. But most of them live there not by choice but by economic compulsion, which, in part, limits their use of transportation but more generally and powerfully their choice of housing. Normally, a poor family has four choices: to build a shack, to double up with another family, to be subsidized, or to buy or rent secondhand—or twenty-secondhand—housing. The first choice has been completely barred and the second has been largely barred by the exercise of the police power. Subsidized housing, strictly limited-access, has, after a quarter century, accommodated barely one per cent of American households. Only the last choice, constantly narrowed by slum clearance, remains.

At present, the pattern of segregation by income class is, in the United States, overlaid and obscured by race segregation. However, if and when colored citizens achieve full equality and the Negro middle class shares equally with the white middle class the right to segregate itself from the lower-income groups, the pattern will stand out clearly. The lower-income groups live exclusively in the inner zone, and most of the other income groups live in the outer zones.

PLANNING PROPOSALS   This is, in generalized terms, the "natural" pattern of the contemporary metropolis, as it develops without the benefit — or "malefit" — of planning. Is it "good"? How can it be improved?

The need for commuting can be minimized by providing employment in every part of the metropolitan area. This requires the reservation, by zoning or by creation of industrial "districts" or "estates," of land for industry. But, with a growing majority of the labor force employed in services, the location of these functions assumes even greater importance. Service employment outside of the central area is growing, but it is scattered. Much could be gained by concentrating into major subcenters or "secondary downtowns" the consumer, public, professional, and retail services. Probably manufacturing plants of those labor-intensive industries that can operate on small lots might be located in their proximity. Around and possibly also within these centers, housing at relatively high densities could be developed. The concentration would, in turn, make possible the establishment of higher-order services.

Such centers would also satisfy the criteria of variety and of integration of functions and would be identifiable focal points, continuous as to location and basic arrangements but changing in detail, of the districts that they serve. There is no certainty about the most desirable size of such districts. However, it is pertinent to note that the estimates of the minimum population required for a self-contained urban unit have been steadily going up. Ebenezer Howard thought of 20,000-30,000 for his "garden cities." The English "new town" program started with a limit of 50,000-60,000 but subsequently has raised it to 100,000 and more. American planners now talk of a quarter million. It may be that the half million, which we specified as the minimum population of a metropolis, is required to support a really vital and attractive secondary downtown.

The concentration of many potential trip destinations would reduce the number of trips and also make it possible to provide good public transportation. This is likely to result in substantial economics in transportation costs.

While such centers would also, to some extent, increase the choice of jobs, maximization of opportunity requires primarily a relative compactness of the entire metropolis that can be effectively served by an economical public transportation system.

Compactness also facilitates access to the metropolitan center. However, complete compactness would make access to open country very difficult. At the same time, the frequently advocated proposal to isolate each urban unit by a "green belt" would increase the distances to the center as well as to other units and would increase the cost of transportation and of public utilities. Increasing distances would also result from a "linear" scheme, which would line up its urban units along one axis.

It seems preferable to line up such units along a greater number of shorter lines, which would radiate from the metropolitan center. This would result in a "stellar" or "finger" scheme, with easily accessible wedges of open country between the fingers. It would, by its orientation to the metropolitan center, facilitate identification with the metropolis as a whole, while the centers of the districts, out of which the fingers are composed, would encourage identification with the district. Growth would be possible by adding new districts at the ends of the fingers, but it would be gradual, preserving continuity with the previous district.

It appears that some modification of the "natural" pattern **ENDS AND MEANS** of the metropolis could make it "better." However, such modifications are hardly possible without some fairly substantial institutional changes.

Deliberate modification of the pattern of the metropolis presupposes that its area is brought under one jurisdiction, by annexation, federation, or any other means — if there are others. Separate municipalities, each hard pressed to balance its budget and with the real-estate tax as the main source of income, must of necessity, like the private real-estate owner, attempt to get those land uses which produce the highest revenue and require the lowest operating cost — industry, commerce, and wealthy residents, preferably without children. They can hardly be expected to provide open space for the recreation of their neighbors or to house and educate workers to produce added value in the factories and spend their money in the stores of the next municipality.

A metropolitan government could, legally, implement a land-use pattern by zoning. But zoning transfers development rights from some property owners to others. If a strong secondary downtown is to be created, values from other sites that might be chosen by its occupiers would be transferred to its area. If an area is to be kept open, its development value is transferred to all sites in the development fingers. The blatant inequity of such a procedure makes it unfeasible. Substantial development rights can be shifted around only within the same ownership, which, in this case, means ownership by a metropolitan authority.

Such an authority could become the owner of all or most of the land within its boundaries only if it could tap the very substantial income generated within its boundaries far more effectively than our present three-level tax structure permits.

These three measures would make it possible to modify the general metropolitan pattern. They could not, however, deal with the most serious inadequacy of the present pattern, the exclusion of the low-income groups from the expanding outer zones of the metropolis. This could be accomplished only by assumption of public financial responsibility for standard housing. It is self-deception to talk of "socially balanced" new neighborhoods or "new towns" when one third of the population cannot possibly afford to live in them.

Metropolitan-wide governments with commensurate financial resources, public land ownership, housing financed, though not necessarily owned or managed, by and for the public, not token ghettos for the poor—these are all "radical" innovations in terms of current American thinking. However, in different forms and degrees, all of them have been adopted, singly or jointly, within the framework of democratic capitalism by the countries of northwestern Europe.

The American and Canadian people are faced with a dilemma. They want, and want badly, two things. They want to live in an efficient, convenient, healthy, and pleasant environment, and they want, as individuals and collectively as municipalities, to be able to make an honest dollar out of every piece of property they happen to own. The two are basically incompatible. Sooner or later they will have to decide which one is more important to them.

5

The Modern Metropolis

In speaking of urban revolution we refer today not to the "modern city" but rather to the "modern metropolis." This change of name reflects the fact that from its long, slow evolution the city has emerged into a revolutionary stage. It has undergone a qualitative change, so that it is no longer merely a larger version of the traditional city but a new and different form of human settlement.

There is some argument about the term. Lewis Mumford objects to "metropolis" (from the Greek words for "mother" and "city"), which historically had a very different meaning; he prefers the term "conurbation," coined by Patrick Geddes, the Scottish biologist who was a pioneer in city planning. This word, however, implies formation by the fusion of several pre-existing cities; most metropolises did not originate in that way. The term "megalopolis," coined by the French geographer Jean Gottmann, is generally applied to an urbanized region that contains several metropolitan areas, such as the region extending from Boston to Washington. On the whole it seems best to retain the term "metropolis," now common in many languages as the name of a major city center and its environs.

"Metropolitan area" can be defined in various ways; the U.S. Bureau of the Census, for instance, defines it as any area containing a nuclear city of at least 50,000 population. The new phenomenon we are considering, however, is a much bigger entity with a certain minimum critical size. In agreement with the German scholar Gerhard Isenberg, I shall define a metropolis as a concentration of at least 500,000 people living within an area in which the traveling time from the out-skirts to the center is no more than 40 minutes. Isenberg and I have both derived this definition from observations of the transformation of cities into metropolises during the first half of the twentieth century. At the present time—at least in North America—the critical mass that distinguishes a metrop-olis from the traditional city may be considerably larger—perhaps nearing one million population.

The emergence of a basically new form of human settlement is an extremely rare event in the history of mankind. For at least 5,000 years all civilizations have been characterized predominantly by just two well-marked types of settlement: the farm village and the city. Until recently the vast majority of the population lived in villages. They produced not only their own raw materials—food, fuel, and fiber—but also the manufactured goods and services they required. The cities were inhabited by only a small minority of the total population, generally less than 20 per cent. These people were the ruling elite—the religious, political, military, and commercial lead-ers—and the retinue of laborers, craftsmen, and professionals who served them. The elite drew their subsistence and power from the work of the villagers by collecting tithes, taxes, or rent. This system prevailed until the end of the eighteenth century, and its philosophy was well expressed by physio-crats of that time on both sides of the Atlantic, including Thomas Jefferson.

The Industrial Revolution dramatically reversed the distri-bution of population between village and city. A German contemporary of Jefferson's, Justus Moeser, foresaw at the very beginning of the revolution what was to come; he ob-served that "specialized division of labor forces workers to live in big cities." With increasing specialization there had to be increased co-operation of labor both within and between establishments. The division of labor and increased produc-tivity made concentration in cities possible, and the required co-operation of labor made it necessary, because the new system called for bringing together workers of many skills and diverse establishments that had to interchange goods and services.

The process fed on itself, growth inducing further growth. Many economists have noted that the rapid rise of productivity has been largely instrumental in bringing about a progressive shift of the main part of the labor force from the primary industry of raw-material production to the secondary industry of material processing and finally to the tertiary industry of services. Less attention has been paid to a related, equally important factor behind this shift, namely the "specializing out" of functions. The farmer's original functions of producing his own motive power (work animals), fuel (hay and oats), tools, building materials, and consumer goods have been specialized out to secondary industries that supply him with tractors, gasoline, and his other necessities. Today, in the tertiary stage, much of the work connected with secondary industry is being specialized out to purveyors of business services (accounting, control, selling, distribution). Even the functions of the household itself (personal services, housekeeping, repairs, shopping, recreation, education) are taken over by consumer-service industries.

The dual spur of specialization and co-operation of labor started a great wave of migration from country to city all over the globe. In the advanced countries the nineteenth-century development of long-distance transportation by steamship and railroad and of communication by the electric telegraph made it possible for cities to draw on large regions and grow to populations of millions. For a time their growth was limited by internal restrictions. Travel within the city still had to be by foot or by hoof. A New York businessman could communicate quickly with his partners in Shanghai by cablegram, but to deliver an order to an office a few blocks away he had to send a messenger. This situation limited cities to a radius of only about three miles from the center. In the absence of elevators the city was also limited in vertical expansion. The only possible growth was interstitial, by covering every square inch of available space. Residences, factories, shops, and offices all crowded close together around the center. The result was a fantastic rise in the price of city land compared with the cost of the structures that could be built on it.

This was only a transitory phase in the growth of the city, but its heritage is still with us, in structures, street patterns, institutions, and concepts. We still think and talk and act in terms of "city and country" and "city and suburb," although these concepts have lost meaning in the modern metropolis and its region. The transformation was set in motion toward the end of the nineteenth century and early in the twentieth with the invention of the telephone, the electric streetcar, the subway, and the powered elevator. Even more far-reaching was the impact on the city of the automobile and the truck. With the acquisition of these aids to communication and mobility, the city burst its eggshell and emerged as a metropolis. (It is worth noting that the telephone and the automobile had equally profound effects on rural life, fragmenting the old farm village and giving rise to huge, scattered farms.)

The centripetal migration from the country to the city continues unabated, but now there is an equally powerful centrifugal wave of migration from the city to the suburbs. Although on a national scale more and more of the population is becoming urban, within the urban areas there is increasing decentralization. The interaction of these two trends has produced the new form of settlement we call the metropolis. It is no longer a "city" as that institution has been understood in the past, but on the other hand it is certainly not "country" either. The fact that it is neither one nor the other has aroused nostalgic critics, who appeal for a return to "true urbanity" and to a "real countryside." But in view of the inexorable technological and economic trends that have created the metropolis, these terms also require a new and different interpretation.

It has become fashionable to describe the transformation of the city into the metropolis as an "explosion." The term is misleading on two counts. The change is not destroying the city, as "explosion" implies, nor is it a sudden, unheralded event. The movement of population from the center of the city outward to an ever-expanding periphery has been going on for at least a century. In the metropolitan region of New York, New Jersey, and Connecticut, where the average density of population within the cities and towns of the area increased steadily up to 1860, it began to drop after that date. The outward spread of the city was nearly as strong between 1860 and 1900 as it has been since 1900. In Philadelphia the population movement away from the center of the city was actually proportionately greater in the half century between 1860 and 1910 than in the period 1900 to 1950.

Analysis of the population density in the metropolitan area of Philadelphia and that of other cities shows that the centrifugal wave of movement to the suburbs has proceeded with amazing regularity. From the center of the city out to the periphery at any one time, there is a consistent decline in residential density from one zone to the next. As time has passed, the curve representing this decline has become less steep; that is, the center has lost or stood still in density while the outer areas have gained, so that the difference between them is less. Interestingly, the density gradient from the center to the periphery has also become smoother (that is, less lumped around outer towns), which seems to indicate that the center is actually strengthening its influence over the outer areas. In each zone the rise in density with time eventually flattens out, as if the density has reached a "saturation" level for that zone; this level is lower for each successive zone out to the periphery. With the passage of time the crest of the wave (the zone of fastest growth) moves outward in a regular fashion. The innermost zone at the center of the city seems to show an anomaly, in that its population density is lower than that of the surrounding area, but this merely reflects the fact that the center is occupied predominantly by stores and offices. If its daytime working population were included in the census, it would have a far higher density.

One can outline a "natural history" of the modern metropolis. The metropolis is characterized, first of all, by a certain measure of mutual accessibility among its various parts, which determines its total size. As I have mentioned, in most cases the area embraced by the metropolis has a radius represented by a traveling time of about 40 minutes in the principal vehicle of transportation (train or auto), or about 45 minutes from door to door. With improvement in the speed of transportation, the extent of the metropolis in miles can, of course, expand. In most metropolitan areas the average travel time to work for the working population as a whole is about half an hour. No more than 15 per cent of the workers spend more than 45 minutes in the daily journey to work.

This may sound surprising in view of the frequent complaints of commuters about the length of their journey. The complaints are not new. A century ago a German observer declared that the distance people on the outskirts of cities had to travel to work had reached the limit of what was bearable. Probably the range of travel times to work then was wider than it is in the metropolis today. There are strong indications, however, that the half-hour average has been more or less standard. In most American small towns, although a majority of the workers are employed within the town, a sizable minority do travel long distances to work in other communities, usually because they cannot find a job in the hometown and must seek work elsewhere but do not wish to change their home.

It is one of the great advantages of the metropolis that people can change jobs without moving their homes. Breadth of choice—for workers, for employers, and for consumers—is the essence of the metropolis. The worker has a choice of employers; the employer can find workers of a wide variety of skills, including professional and managerial. Even more important is the accessibility of a variety of goods and services on which any business enterprise depends. Only a metropolis can support the large inventories, transportation facilities, and specialized services—particularly those of a financial, legal, technical, and promotional nature—that are essential to modern business. Such services constitute the main source of economic strength of the metropolis—its true economic base. They are especially important to small, new, and experimental enterprises. The metropolis, in particular its central area, therefore serves as an incubator for such enterprises. Contrary to a common impression, the big city is most suitably a home for small industries rather than large industrial complexes. The big plant, being more nearly self-sufficient, may often be as well off in a small town. This fact is reflected in the statistics of employment: in most metropolises the number of people that are employed in manufacturing is decreasing, relatively and sometimes absolutely, while the number that are employed in services is increasing rapidly.

What is true of business services is also true of consumer services: the metropolis attracts the consumer because it offers a wide freedom of choice. Only the large population of a metropolis can support the great proliferation of special services found in the big city: large department stores, many specialty shops, opera houses, art galleries, theaters, sports stadia, special schools, large and well-equipped institutions for medical care and adult education, and a host of other necessities for the full life.

To sum up, the modern metropolis differs from the traditional city in several crucial respects: (1) it combines the function of central leadership with the functions of providing the main bulk of material production and services; (2) its population is up to 10 times larger than that of the biggest preindustrial city; (3) with modern fast transportation, which has increased its commuting radius about tenfold, it is up to 100 times larger in area than the biggest city of former times; (4) it is neither city nor country but a complex of urban districts and open areas; (5) its residential and work areas are no longer combined in one place but are located in separate districts; (6) its workers have high mobility in the choice of jobs.

The feedback cycle of metropolitan growth enlarging freedom of choice, and freedom of choice in turn attracting further growth, has given the metropolis amazing vitality and staying power. In the premetropolis era cities laid low by war, pestilence, or loss of prestige were often abandoned or reduced to weak shadows of their former glory. Even Rome became little more than a village after it lost its empire. In contrast, all the big cities destroyed in World War II have been rebuilt, most of them to beyond their prewar size. Particularly significant is the experience of Leningrad. During the Russian Revolution and again in World War II, it lost about half of its population. Moreover, the revolution ended its former role as the center of government and finance and deprived it of most of its markets and sources of supply. Yet the population of Leningrad is now 4,000,000 — four times what it was in 1921. This growth is especially remarkable in view of the Soviet government's policy of restricting the growth of major cities, a policy based on Karl Marx's condemnation of big cities because of their pollution of air, water, and soil. As a metropolis Leningrad is an outstanding testament to the viability of the species.

Attempts to halt the growth of the big city have been made ever since the phenomenon first appeared on the human scene. They have been singularly unsuccessful. Elizabeth I of England and, after her, Oliver Cromwell tried to limit the growth of London by circling it with an enforced greenbelt, but this method failed. In any case such a device, applied to a growing city, can lead only to overcrowding. To avoid big-city problems, nearly all countries today have embarked on programs of industrial decentralization, often with unsatisfactory results. In the Western nations the most far-reaching attempt at decentralization is Great Britain's "New Towns" plan. This program has been eminently successful in creating new centers of industry as "growth points," but it has not availed to stop the growth of London or to limit other cities, new or old, to their planned size. Significantly, all but one of the seventeen New Towns built in Britain since the war are satellite towns within previously existing metropolitan regions.

The Soviet Union, by virtue of centralized planning and ownership, has been able to carry out decentralization on a continental scale. Its program has been remarkably effective in slowing the growth of Moscow and promoting that of smaller cities. Between 1939 and 1959 the towns in the Soviet Union with populations of less than 200,000 grew by 84 per cent; those in the 200,000-500,000 class grew 63 per cent; those in the 500,000-1,000,000 class grew 48 per cent, and Moscow itself increased only 20 per cent in population. Moscow has, however, gone well beyond the limit of 5,000,000 that the government planned; it is now at 6,000,000, nearly four times the city's population in 1921.

In the United States, where the forces of the market rather than central planning determine industrial location, the growth rates in the decade 1950-1960 were 27 per cent in metropolitan areas of 50,000-500,000 population and 35 per cent in those of 500,000 population. In the metropolises with a population of more than 2,000,000, the average growth rate was smaller: 23 per cent. This average, however, was heavily weighted by the comparatively slow-growing centers of the Northeastern sector of the nation; in Los Angeles and San Francisco, the only two metropolises of this class outside the Northeast, the growth was far above the national average for all such areas.

There is no denying that the growth of the huge metropolises has brought serious problems, chief among which are traffic congestion and the pollution of air and water by smoke, household wastes, detergents, and gasoline fumes. Many critics also claim that the metropolis can exist only by draining the countryside of its economic, demographic, and social strength. These problems are not essentially unsolvable, however. Effective methods for control of pollution exist; they need to be applied. The economic and social complaints about the metropolis seem to have little substance today. The city now repays the country in full in economic terms, as we have noted, and with the improvement in sanitation and lowering of the high nineteenth-century urban death rate it contributes its share of the natural population increase.

The most persistent accusation against the metropolis is that it has dissolved the family and neighborhood ties that existed in the small town and has produced anomie: the absence of any values or standards of behavior. This is questionable. A number of sociological studies in metropolises of North America and Western Europe have shown that family ties remain very much alive and that much informal community organization can be found even in their slums.

In considering the future of the metropolis the central question is that of crowding. How much bigger can the metropolis grow? Will it eventually be "choked to death" by its own growth? Data are available for examining these questions.

It is widely believed that in a big metropolis there can be a choice only between crowding together at high densities or spending an excessive amount of time traveling to work. Actually, a reasonable travel radius from a central point takes in an amazing amount of territory. At an over-all travel rate of 20 miles per hour, typical for present rush-hour trips from the center to the periphery in the largest American metropolitan areas, a radius of one hour's travel describes a circle with a total area of about 1,250 square miles. No more than 312 square miles would be required to house 10,000,000 people if they lived in single-family houses on 30-by-100-foot lots. Including streets, schools, and other neighborhood facilities, the total area needed for residential use would amount to about 500 square miles. Commercial, industrial, and other nonresidential facilities could be accommodated amply on 150 square miles. There would be left, then, some 600 square miles, almost half of the total area within an hour's distance from the center for parks, golf courses, forests, and farms.

If the travel speed were increased to 30 miles per hour, quite feasible for both private and public transportation, the area within an hour's distance from the center could accommodate 15,000,000 people in single-family houses on 60-by-100-foot lots, take care of all business uses and leave 1,000 square miles of open land. It may be objected that an hour is an excessive time to spend in travel to work. In practice, however, the radius from the center to the periphery would not represent the traveling distance for most workers. Relatively few would live close to the periphery, and most of these would be working at places near home rather than in the center of the city. In a metropolis of such dimensions only a small minority would have to travel more than 45 minutes to their jobs.

Evidently, then, the modern metropolis does not inherently necessitate either very high residential densities or excessively long journeys to work. The problem in planning it therefore lies in achieving a rational distribution of its components and a suitable organization of transportation facilities to connect the components.

What are the major components of the metropolis? Basically there are four: (1) the central business complex, (2) manufacturing and its allied industries, (3) housing with the attendant services, and (4) open land. Let us examine each in turn.

The central area epitomizes the essence of the metropolis: mutual accessibility. It attracts particularly those functions that serve the metropolis as a whole and those that require a considerable amount of close interpersonal contact. The most conspicuous occupant of the center is diversified retail business: large department stores and specialty shops. It is surpassed in importance, however, by the closely interrelated complex of business services that occupy the giant office buildings characteristic of the central area of a metropolis: the headquarters of corporations, financial institutions, and public administration and the professionals who serve them, such as lawyers, accountants, and organizations engaged in promotion and public relations. Also grouped in the central area with these two categories of services are various supporting establishments, including eating and drinking places, hotels, job printers, and many others.

Surprisingly, surveys show that, in spite of the recent proliferation of new office skyscrapers in the center of cities, the size of the working population in the central areas of the largest American metropolises has not actually increased over the past 30 years. Toronto, a smaller and newer metropolis, shows the same constancy in the number of central workers during the past 13 years. The explanation lies simply in the fierce competition for and the rising cost of the limited space in the center; it has caused an outward movement of those functions that can conveniently relocate farther out. Housing in the main moved out long ago; manufacturing and warehousing have tended to follow suit; so has a considerable part of the retail trade, and some of the routine business services that do not require continuous contact with their clients have also moved to less expensive locations away from the center. Modern means of communication have made this spatial separation possible. Moreover, the growth of population and purchasing power in the peripheral areas has provided bases of support there for large shopping centers, including department stores, and for many business and consumer services.

All of this indicates that the central area is undergoing a qualitative change in the direction of concentration on "higher-order" functions and at the same time is maintaining stability in quantitative terms. The forces of the market act to control overcrowding of the center. There is not much basis for the widespread fear that the metropolis will choke itself to death by uncontrolled growth.

As for manufacturing and its satellite activities, the increasing volume of production and changing technology, with a consequent requirement for more space, have made their move out to the periphery of the metropolis imperative. This is true of factories, warehouses, railroad yards, truck terminals, airports, harbor facilities, and many other establishments. Three technical factors are at work: the increasing mechanization and automation of production, which calls for more floor area per worker; a switch from the traditional multistory loft building to the one-story plant, which demands more ground area; the new practice of providing open land around the plant for parking, landscaping, and plant expansion. The combined effect of these three factors has been to raise the amount of land per worker in the modern factory as much as 100 times over that occupied by the old loft building.

The next major category of land use in the metropolis — housing — accounts for the largest amount of occupied land. It also presents the greatest ills of the metropolis: slums and segregation of people by income and race.

In all metropolises the low-income families tend to be segregated in the older, high-density areas toward the center of the city. This is not by choice but because they cannot afford the prices or rents of the more spacious new homes in the outer areas. The alarming result of the centrifugal movement of new residences toward the periphery is an increasing segregation of the population by income, which in the United States is compounded (and partly obscured) by segregation by race. The situation is more disquieting in the metropolis than it was in the smaller city or town. There, although the poor lived in older, shabbier houses, they at least shared the schools and other public facilities with the higher-income groups. In the metropolis the people living in low-income districts, particularly the housewives and children, never even meet or come to know the rest of their fellow citizens.

Poor families are effectively prevented from moving to new housing in the suburbs not only by economic inability but also by deliberate policies of the suburban governments. Squeezed between rising expenses and inadequate tax resources, these governments have quite understandably used their power of zoning and other controls to keep out housing that does not pay its way in tax revenue. More recently the central cities have adopted policies that have much the same effect. Their programs of slum clearance and redevelopment, financed in the United States by the National Housing Act, have failed to replace the housing they have destroyed with sufficient new housing at rents the displaced families can afford. It should be obvious that housing conditions cannot be improved by decreasing the supply. Half a century ago Geddes observed: "The policy of sweeping clearance should be recognized for what I believe it is: one of the most disastrous and pernicious blunders . . . the large populations thus expelled would be . . . driven into creating worse congestion in other quarters."

Obviously, the blight of slums and class segregation can be overcome only by enabling the lower-income groups to live in decent houses in desirable locations, primarily in the expanding peripheral areas, along with the middle and upper classes. The annual cost of such a program in the United States has been estimated at $2,000,000,000 – a modest sum compared with the amounts allotted to less constructive purposes in the national budget.

The fourth major category of metropolitan land use – open land – consists in North America at present mainly of large tracts held privately for future development. With increasing leisure there is a growing need to turn some of this land to recreational uses. In this connection we should also look at the "metropolitan region," which takes in considerably more area than the metropolis itself.

Donald J. Bogue of the University of Michigan, examining 67 metropolitan centers in the United States, has shown that the sphere of influence of a large metropolis usually extends out to about 60 to 100 miles from the center. Typically, the metropolitan region includes a number of industrial satellite towns that draw on the resources of the metropolis. The metropolis, in turn, looks outward to the region for various facilities, particularly recreational resorts such as large parks, lakes, summer cottages, camps, motels, and lodges. In Sweden, C. F. Ahlberg, head of the Stockholm Regional Plan, has emphasized this role of the region around the capital city by naming it the "summer Stockholm" — the widened horizon that opens up for Stockholmers when the snows have gone. Metropolises do, of course, have their winter horizons as well, typified by the ski resorts that flourish as satellites within driving distance of many an American city.

Increasingly, the outer-fringe metropolitan region is becoming a popular retirement place for people on pensions or other modest incomes who can live inexpensively in the country without being too far from the amenities of the city. This is an intriguing reversal of the ancient pattern in which the countryside was the locus of productive work and the city was the Mecca for the enjoyment of leisure.

While we are on the subject of the metropolitan region, I should like to clarify the distinction between such a region and a "conurbation" or "megalopolis." The predominant form of the metropolis is mononuclear: it derives its identity from a single center. This is the way metropolitan areas are generally organized in the United States, and it is the only form they take in a newly settled country like Australia, where the population is concentrated mainly in five large metropolitan areas, each centered on a single city. In the older countries of Europe, on the other hand, conurbations — metropolitan regions formed by the gradual growing together of neighboring cities — are fairly common. The outstanding examples are the cities of the Ruhr in Germany and the circle of cities that form what is known as "Randstad Holland" (including Amsterdam, Haarlem, Leiden, The Hague, Rotterdam, and Utrecht). The Ruhr conurbation grew up around the coal mines. Along the French-Italian Riviera a conurbation now seems to be developing around seashore play.

There seems to be a general disposition to assume that the Boston-to-Washington axis is destined soon to become a new conurbation on a vastly larger scale than any heretofore. The available evidence does not support such a view. Each of the metropolitan areas along the seaboard remains strongly oriented to its own center. The several metropolitan regions are separated by large areas of sparse development. Conurbation can occur only when the crests of the waves of two expanding centers overlap, and except perhaps between Washington and Baltimore that is not likely to happen anywhere in North America during this century.

To get back to the problems of planning for the metropolis: How should the four main components — central business, production, residence, and open land — be organized spatially? The aims here can be expressed most clearly in the form of pairs of seemingly contradictory requirements.

First, it is desirable to minimize the need for commuting to work and at the same time maximize the ability to do so. Obviously, most people would like to live close to their place of work, but to seek such an arrangement as a general proposition would be unrealistic and too restrictive. It is estimated that half of all metropolitan households contain more than one gainfully employed person, and they are not likely to be employed in the same place. Furthermore, the preferred locations for residence and work do not necessarily match up. Freedom of choice, both of the place to live and of the place to work, will always depend on opportunity to travel from one place to the other.

A second ideal of planning is to provide quick access to the center of the city and also quick access to the open country. Most people have tried to achieve a compromise by moving to the suburbs. The resulting pattern of urban sprawl, however, has made this move self-defeating. The more people move out to the suburbs, the farther they have to move from the city and the farther the country moves away from them.

Third, the functions of the metropolis must be integrated; yet there are also strong reasons to separate them — for example, to separate residences from factories or offices. Isolation of the functions by rigid zoning, however, threatens to break up the metropolis into barren and monotonous precincts. Evidently, there is no pat answer to this problem. The optimal grain of mixture will vary with conditions.

Fourth, the social health of the metropolis requires that its people identify themselves both with their own neighborhood or group and with the metropolis as a whole. Since identification with an ingroup often leads to hostility toward outgroups, great emphasis is needed on measures that create interest and pride in the metropolis.

Fifth, the metropolis must strike a balance between continuity and receptiveness to change, between the traditions that give it identity and the flexibility necessary for growth and adaptation to new conditions.

Most of the schemes that have been proposed for shaping the future growth of the metropolis are tacitly based on these criteria, although the requirements have not generally been spelled out in precisely this form. The plans are designed to decentralize the metropolis in some way, with the dual aim of minimizing traffic congestion at the center and bringing the city closer to the countryside.

One proposal is the satellite plan that I have already mentioned. In that arrangement each of the satellite towns outside the center is largely self-sufficient and more or less like the others. Another scheme somewhat similar to this is called the "constellation" plan; it would set up several widely separated units each of which would specialize in one function, such as finance, administration, or cultural institutions. Still another plan is the "linear" metropolis, several variants of which have been proposed. It would not be oriented toward a single center but would contain a series of them strung in a line. The advocates of this plan are attracted primarily by the possibilities it offers for easy access to open land and for unlimited expansion. Decentralization was pushed to its ultimate conclusion in the "Broadacre City" plan suggested by Frank Lloyd Wright. He proposed to disperse the activities of the city more or less evenly over the whole metropolitan region. Such a plan would be practicable only if the time and cost of travel were reduced essentially to zero. They may approach but certainly will never reach that condition.

Probably the most realistic of the many proposals is the plan called the "stellar" or "finger" metropolis. It would retain the center and thrust out fingers in all directions. Each finger would be composed of a string of towns and would be comparable to a linear city. The towns in the string would be connected to one another and to the metropolitan center by a rapid-transit line. Between the fingers would be large wedges of open country, which would thus be easily accessible both to the fingers and to the main center. The metropolis would grow by extending the fingers. This outline is the basis of current plans for the future development of Copenhagen and Stockholm and of the "Year 2000" plan for Washington, D.C.

Any plan that seeks to control the growth of the metropolis rather than leaving it to the play of market forces will require the setting up of new forms of control. Because it inevitably entails transfers of value from one piece of land to another, planning of any sort is bound to come into conflict with the existing vested interests of landowners and municipalities. It is obvious, therefore, that the implementation of rational regional planning would call for: (1) the creation of an over-all metropolitan government for the metropolis, (2) public ownership of all or most of the land that is to be developed, (3) tax revenues sufficient to enable the metropolitan government to acquire the land and carry out the public works required for its development, (4) a national housing policy that would eliminate segregation by providing people at all income levels with freedom of choice in the location of their dwellings.

In terms of current American political folklore, these are radical measures. Each of them, however, has been carried out in varying forms and to a varying degree by more than one European nation within the framework of democratic capitalism.

In the long run, the development of the metropolis is likely to be influenced most powerfully by improvements in transportation and communication and by the increase in leisure time. The first may lead to an expansion of the metropolis that will embrace a whole region. The second, depending on future developments in mankind's social structure and culture, may lead to *panem et circenses* ("bread and circuses") or to *otium cum dignitate* ("leisure with dignity"). Both are possible in the metropolis.

II
METROPOLITAN AND REGIONAL PLANNING

6

Metropolitan Area Planning

The Toronto area is the first community in the Western Hemisphere that has given official political recognition to the fact that modern industrial society has created a new form of human settlement: the metropolitan area. Throughout history, men have lived either in the city or in the country. The modern metropolis is neither; it partakes to some degree of both.

The metropolitan area differs from the historical city in both function and form. In preindustrial ages the vast majority of the people lived in the country, and it was there that the world's work was done. The city was primarily the seat of the political, religious, commercial, and cultural leaders of society. This important "central" function is still being fulfilled by the modern metropolis, and it has become more important and complex than ever before. But the metropolis is also the most important seat of material production. The largest group of its population is engaged in manufacturing commodities for the nation and the world. Thus the metropolis combines the two functions — leadership and production — that were previously divided between city and country.

In its form the metropolitan area no longer shows the sharp division between the densely built town and the open country. Areas developed at varying densities are interspersed with open areas used for recreation and agriculture. There is no

ELASTICITY

Figure 1 Municipalities in Metropolitan Toronto Planning Area. *Official Plan by the Metropolitan Toronto Planning Board, September 1959.*

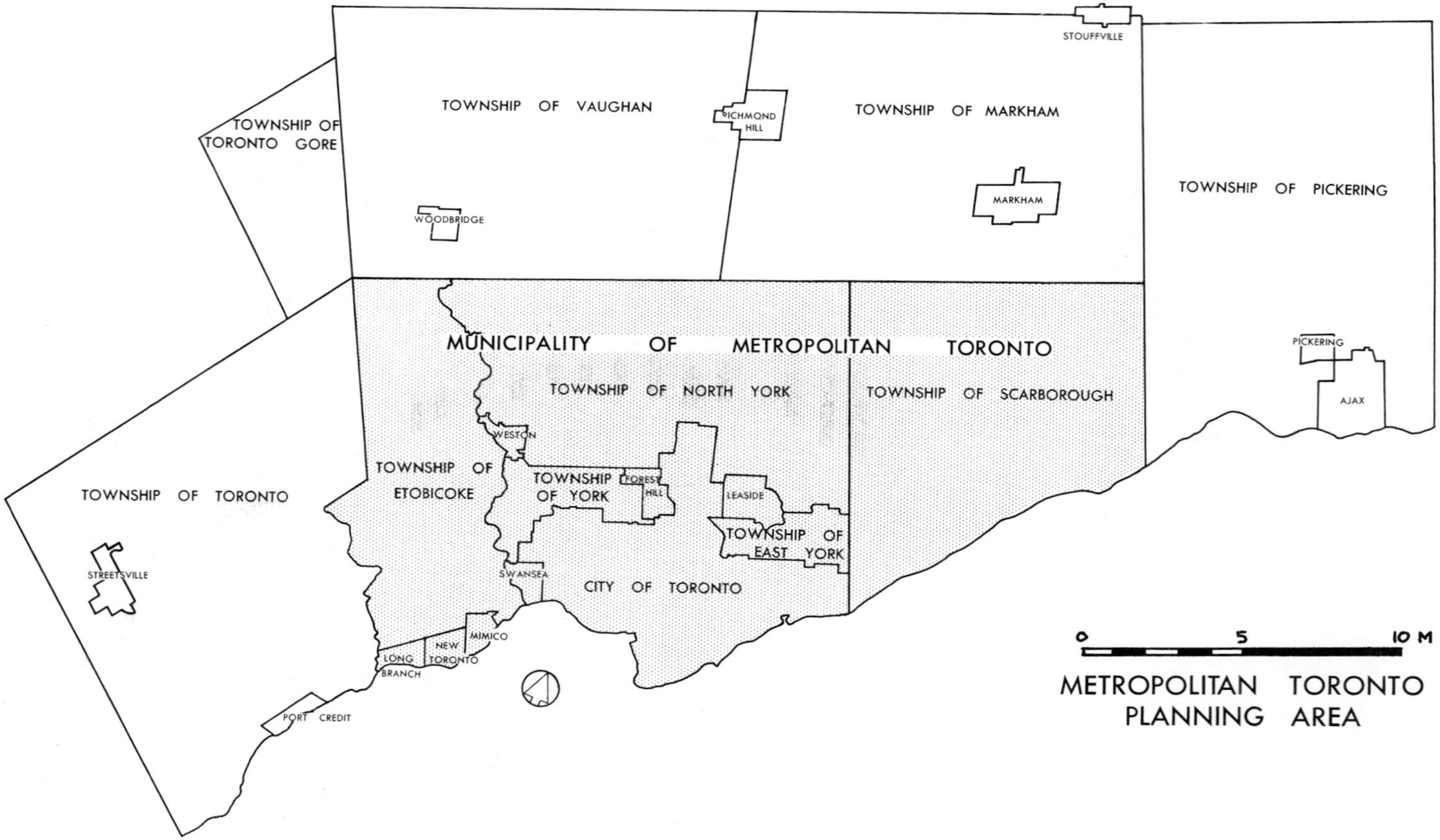

METROPOLITAN TORONTO
PLANNING AREA

fixed boundary and, apparently, no definite interior structure such as the system of streets and squares provided in the traditional city.

The problem of the form of the metropolis concerns, first, the relation between built-up and open areas and, second, the relation between the area of the "central" functions, the industrial areas, and the residential areas. The very existence of separate areas for work and for residence is, in itself, something radically new, a product of the Industrial Revolution.

We may expect that the form of the metropolis will ultimately be determined by the same factors that brought it into being: the increasing division of labor and the increasing efficiency of transportation. The only visible limit to the growth of the economy and population of a metropolitan area is the size of its "hinterland," the region that serves as its source of supplies and as the market for its goods and services. The boundary of this region—fairly elastic in a competitive economy—is determined by the means of transportation between the metropolis and the other parts of its region.

While long-distance transportation in this manner determines the size of the economy and the population of the metropolis, the size and shape of its built-up area are determined by short-distance transportation, by the means of commuting within the metropolitan area.

It is important to note that the modern means of long-distance **LARGER AREAS** transportation and communication—steamships, railroads, and telegraph—were developed about half a century earlier than those used within a metropolitan area—electric traction, the automobile, and the telephone. As a consequence, people first were concentrated in big compact cities that only later transformed themselves into still bigger and vastly more extensive metropolitan areas. We are only in the beginning of this transformation.

Because of the highly developed division and specialization of labor, all parts of the metropolitan community are strongly dependent on each other, and mutual accessibility is its primary need and also sets its limits. A metropolitan area extends as far as daily commuting is possible, and no farther.

From the need for the best possible mutual accessibility derive two apparently contradictory requirements. There should be minimum need for commuting but maximum possibility for commuting. People should be able to find a job close to their home, but they should also be able to work anywhere in the area; and, conversely, management should be able to draw on the labor force of the entire area. Therefore industries should be distributed throughout the metropolitan area so that in each of its sections there is an approximate balance between the labor force and available jobs. At the same time, the entire metropolitan area should be planned in such a way that efficient transportation between all of its points is possible.

ALL-PURPOSE AREA   If the metropolitan area were merely an industrial area, and if man's only purpose consisted in making a living, this would result in a compact development with an even distribution of industry, the whole connected by a large-scale grid of transportation lines. However, making a living is only a means for living, and the area functions not only as a complex of workshops but also as a leading center for a surrounding region.

These central functions, which serve the population and industry of the metropolitan area itself as well as the wider region, must be accessible to all. They are assembled in the central business district, the core of the city. There are at present in most central business districts some things that do not need to be there. However, the central location is essential for two groups of establishments: first, all those which are unique in the area and must be accessible from all sides, including financial, government, commercial, and cultural establishments; and second, all those which are linked to the first group, such as lawyers and printers.

Most people try to satisfy these two conflicting requirements by moving to the suburbs so that they may have the city nearby on one side and the country on the other. But as more and more people move out into ever widening rings of suburbs, they move farther and farther away from the city, and the country moves farther and farther away from them. The present pattern of suburban growth is self-defeating.

There have been a number of proposals for a radically different pattern: a "concentric" city; a "central" city with "satellites"; a "ribbon" city; or a "star-shaped" city. In practice, any such scheme will, of course, be modified greatly by geographical and historical conditions. The future shape of the

Toronto Metropolitan Area might be regarded as a variant of a "star" or "finger" scheme. However, one half of the potential fingers would be cut off by Lake Ontario. Because locations close to the lake have substantial advantages for transportation, water supply, sewage disposal, and drainage, the two fingers along the lakeshore will be longer and thicker than those to the north, and the over-all shape might approach that of a broad ribbon. The green "wedges" of the finger plan will follow the existing ravines rather than any geometrical pattern.

Metropolitan planning creates the indispensable framework for the environment in which its citizens will live. But the quality of that environment will still depend on the manner in which a multitude of public and private agents plan and build their share of it. What Napoleon once said about strategy applies, with equal force, to planning: "C'est un art simple, et tout dans l'exécution." ("It is a simple art, and all depends on the execution.")

7

Regional Planning

Regional planning is the extension of planning into a new field. Like all planning, it means exploring interaction and attempting to order all actions so that they will help rather than hinder each other.

This new field has been approached similtaneously from two directions, both of which have gradually enlarged their scope: on the one side, from local physical planning; and on the other, from segmental or departmental functional planning. It lies in the nature of planning as a discipline concerned with interrelations that it must constantly expand its field of study and of action as it discovers ever wider and more complex interrelations and attempts to influence them. But in addition to this "subjective" reason for the expansion of planning into new fields, there is an even more important "objective" one, deriving from the nature of contemporary society.

It is a commonplace that the world is getting smaller. With the development of means of transportation and communication local isolation is being broken, and what was once an unrelated event in a distant area now becomes part of the locality's own life. But it is equally true to say that the world is becoming bigger. There are three times as many people living on this globe as there were 200 years ago, and they engage in more varied activities and transform the face of the earth more markedly than any previous generation. Ever new skeins are woven into the increasingly complex tapestry of life.

Because the world is getting smaller, town planning is forced to extend beyond the boundaries of the individual community to encompass its surroundings and its relation to neighboring communities, leading to comprehensive planning primarily of metropolitan areas but, beyond that, also of larger and more loosely connected regions.

Because the world is getting bigger, populated by more people making more claims on its resources, functional planning, the planning of the activities of an industry or of a government department, is forced to take into account other activities going on in the same area, on which it is dependent and which may compete with it for land, water, or other resources. Out of the attempt to co-ordinate all functions within a given area has been born another type of regional planning, which on this continent is best represented by the planning activities of the Tennessee Valley Authority or of the Commonwealth of Puerto Rico.

Functional planning and physical planning have developed as two different disciplines; but, as far as I know, only one Western language, Russian, has developed two different terms; *planirovanye*, regarded as a branch of economics, for the former, and *planirovka*, regarded as a branch of architecture, for the latter. They answer different, though related, questions.

Functional economic planning asks what to produce, how much, at what cost, and when, and only in very general terms: "where?"

Local physical planning deals, from the economist's point of view, with one scarce resource, land. It asks primarily: "where and how?" However, it has increasingly turned to a study of the economic and social aspects of planning; by scheduling and "phasing" it attempts to answer the question "when?" and by capital budgeting the question "at what cost?"

On the other hand, functional planning, with increasing competition for land, has to deal very specifically with the question "where?" and with an increasingly complex technology, it must be able to answer the question "how?"

Thus the two types of planning converge and merge into a new discipline that we call regional planning. Our French colleagues, who use the term *urbanisme* for "town planning," have coined the term *aménagement du territoire* for this discipline.

I shall not attempt to touch that sacred cow, the definition of planning—the poor beast has been milked pretty dry, anyhow—but I cannot quite avoid talking about the definition of a region for planning.

The term "region" has long been used by geographers to denote homogeneous areas, such as the Laurentian Shield or the Wheat Belt. It seems to me that for a planning region homogeneity is not a suitable criterion. Planning is concerned with interaction, and interaction occurs between heterogeneous elements that supplement each other rather than between homogeneous ones. It is often stated—frequently in exaggerated form—that any planning unit should be relatively "self-contained." The more homogeneous an area, the more it is dependent on supplementary activities in other areas, and consequently less self-contained. Therefore, heterogeneity, rather than homogeneity, is characteristic of a planning region. I would define such a region as an area within which interaction is more intense than is its interaction with other areas.

From this concept follow two important considerations. As interaction is impeded or facilitated not only by natural but also by man-made factors, planning regions are defined not merely or exclusively by natural boundaries but equally by political or administrative boundaries—most strongly, of course, by national borders, but to some extent by any administrative division. Therefore, the act of defining an area as suitable for planning administration does, to some extent, determine a region, not merely discover one.

However, the greatest care should be used to discover where interaction is most developed and where it falls off. Thus the concept of the planning region as an area of intensive interaction leads to the concept of the "watershed." Various methods have been developed to find the boundaries separating neighboring "watersheds." The German geographer Walter Christaller in his pioneering work on "the central places in Southern Germany" used the number of long-distance telephone calls made from any given location to one or another "central place." Newspaper distribution, wholesale trade in various commodities, and many other activities can be used to find boundary lines. No two lines will ever coincide completely. There is no such thing as an ideal boundary for a planning region. Whichever is adopted will be an inadequate compromise with conflicting existing conditions; but its adoption adds a new condition that makes it more adequate.

The problems dealt with by regional planning may vary widely, but at their core will be generally the use of land and of water and development of transportation; these, in turn, largely determine the distribution of economic activities.

Two different questions arise in this connection: distribution between regions and distribution within a region. Planning for the former is undertaken mainly by large corporations or by national governments; but distribution within a planning region can be guided by provincial and various levels of municipal governments, dependent on the size of the region.

Perhaps more important than difference in size is the difference between "monocentric" and "polycentric" regions. Intensive interaction has in most cases developed from an urban center that has thereby transformed the surrounding area into its own region. In particular, in modern industrial society the metropolitan region is becoming the dominant form of human settlement.

However, there are some areas that are characterized by the existence of several centers in close proximity to each other. Probably the most important of these is the Ruhr region in Germany. But in Canada the industrial towns of the Grand River Valley and of the "Kingdom of the Saguenay" form a comparable constellation, though, of course, with a much smaller volume of population and economic activity.

In monocentric regions much of the drive for regional planning is likely to come from the central city; but in polycentric regions it will generally have to be initiated by a larger unit. In any case, regional planning requires active participation by nongovernmental agencies because so many of the crucial decisions are actually made by private enterprise. In this connection, the German "Landesplanungs-Verbaende" (Regional Planning Associations) are worthy of study. Their membership comprises provincial and municipal governments as well as representatives of the utilities, industry, agriculture, trade unions, etc.

While active participation of such nongovernmental bodies is essential, it appears that under Canadian conditions the initiative for defining regions and organizing planning bodies within them must rest with the Provinces. The time is ripe for regional planning. To assist in its development is a challenging task for the members of the planning profession.

8

Some Lessons
for Regional Planning
from the Experience of
the Metropolitan Toronto
Planning Board

At the time of the establishment of the Municipality of Metropolitan Toronto the Minister of Planning and Development designated a "Planning Area" as the area of jurisdiction of the Metropolitan Toronto Planning Board. The "Planning Area" covers a total of 26 municipalities. Of these, 13 are municipalities of Toronto, covering 240 square miles and comprising 1,800,000 people. The remaining 13 municipalities are independent, cover 420 square miles, and comprise about 200,000 people.* The 26 municipalities within the "Planning Area" retain the right to establish subsidiary planning boards, and most of them exercise this right. Zoning remains in the exclusive jurisdiction of the 26 municipalities. In this respect the setup in Toronto differs from that in Winnipeg and in Dade County, Florida.

Metropolitan Toronto is no more extensive than the territory of a European city of comparable population, and the Planning Board's relation to the Metropolitan Council is the same as that of a city's planning board to its council. However, the "Planning Area" may be regarded as a "city-centered region," albeit with narrower limits as would be required for

*These figures have been corrected to 1965 — Ed.

comprehensive regional planning. In particular, the relation of the Planning Board to the 13 "fringe" municipalities is generally similar to the relations of a regional planning board to the municipalities within its area.

An anomaly existed in that the "fringe" municipalities had no representation on the Planning Board. This was remedied, in part, by the appointment by the Minister of Municipal Affairs of four representatives for four geographical sections of the "fringe." However, several of the fringe municipalities feel that they are not adequately represented and desire direct representation. While this would be the normal procedure for a regional planning board, it would make such a board a very large and unwieldy body; it would probably necessitate the establishment of a small executive committee, and it is likely that this committee would actually become the decision-making body. This is a problem that has to be faced in establishing any regional planning agency.

Also, in contrast to the regional planning agencies of several European countries, the Planning Board does not include any representatives either of agencies on the higher levels of government or of private organizations that are important in the development of the area. However, fairly close working relationships have been established with the Department of Highways, the conservation authorities, the Canadian National Railroad, the Board of Trade, and others.

The Metropolitan Toronto Planning Board has prepared a draft Official Plan for the entire Planning Area. In conformance with existing legislation, the Official Plan determines the two basic elements of development: land use and major public works. If and when this or any other proposal is adopted by the Metropolitan Council and confirmed by the Minister of Municipal Affairs, municipal actions must conform to the Official Plan. This applies also to actions of the "fringe" municipalities, though they have no voice in adoption of the plan.

While adoption of the plan is pending, the Metropolitan Planning Board exercises fairly effective control over land use because the Minister refers to the Planning Board for its recommendations all amendments to the Official Plans of the area municipalities and all subdivision plans within the Planning Area. Moreover, the Municipal Board requests the opinion of the Planning Board concerning any proposed zoning change within the Planning Area. The Municipal Board may and sometimes does, of course, overrule the Planning Board's recommendations concerning zoning changes, Official Plan amendments, and subdivision approvals.

The situation concerning public works is more complex. Four different groups have to be dealt with:

1. *The Municipality of Metropolitan Toronto.* Adoption of an Official Plan by the Metropolitan Council implies a commitment of that council to carry out the plan that is likely to be implemented by a capital budget. The Planning Board plays an important role in preparing the ten-year capital program, which is annually adopted by the council.

2. *Municipalities and school boards within Metropolitan Toronto.* Since these municipalities through their representatives on the Metropolitan Council have a voice in adopting the Official Plan and since their debentures are underwritten by the Metropolitan Corporation, it may be assumed that they generally will be both willing and able to implement the proposed works.

3. *Municipalities outside Metropolitan Toronto.* Here the Official Plan might have the negative power of preventing public works not conforming to the plan; but it has no positive force to bring about the acquisition of parks, the construction of roads, waterworks, etc.

4. *Higher levels of government and private utilities.* The Official Plan does not bind these agencies in any way; its effectiveness depends entirely on the establishment of close working relationships between the Planning Board and these agencies.

Thus, as far as public works are concerned, the Official Plan is actually only advisory, even in the case of metropolitan works. Ultimately, its effectiveness will depend on the persuasive power of its logic. Evidently, the more all those concerned with implementing the plan have been involved in developing it from its inception, the more readily will it be accepted.

Without implementation of the public-works aspect of the plan, the land-use aspect cannot be realized. Therefore, the entire plan stands or falls with its power of persuasion. However, it is erroneous to assume that wrong decisions are made only from ignorance. Any planning decision, whether it concerns regulation by the Official Plan, zoning or subdivision approval, or investment in roads, utilities, etc., transfers value from one property owner and from one municipality to others; so does the lack of decision. Who is to settle these very real conflicts of interest? The present interests, private, corporate, and municipal, will make themselves heard. But planning is provision for the future. Who represents the industries that are not yet there, the people who will live in the areas still to be developed? Evidently, only a higher level of government can represent them; therefore strong provincial leadership is required.

Competition and conflict of interests exists not only within the Planning Area but beyond its boundaries. The Planning Boards for the Metropolitan Toronto and also for the Hamilton-Wentworth areas are attempting to prevent scattering and to channel development into continuous serviceable areas. But this prevention of premature development inevitably limits the supply of development land within the Planning Area and thereby raises its price. This provides a stimulus for developers to look for greener pastures outside the boundaries of the Planning Area. In the Metropolitan Toronto Area this is occurring, for instance, in the area of Brampton and Chinguacousy Township. The development now taking place there will have a profound and, in many ways, adverse effect on stream pollution, storm drainage, traffic, water and sewer works, and land development in the Planning Area. In theory, this could be controlled by the Community Planning Branch of the Ministry of Municipal Affairs. However, it is hardly likely that the Minister will interfere with developments strongly desired by local municipalities in the absence of a regional plan that would clearly show its interrelations with other parts of the region.

The following points summarize the experience of this plan:

1. The Metropolitan Toronto Planning Area and Board were created by the Province; they never would have come about through the initiative and voluntary agreement of the 26 local municipalities.
2. Planning is largely advisory. It requires understanding

and co-operation among all agencies participating in the development of the area. These agencies should be involved in the planning process as early and intensely as possible.

3. A planning board with representation from such a great number of agencies cannot effectively make decisions. Co-operation will, in practice, very largely depend on a small executive committee and a professional staff. A highly competent staff is therefore required for regional planning.

4. Even with the best co-operation, areas of real conflict of interests will remain. Therefore strong leadership from the Province is required.

5. The territory of a regional planning agency must encompass the entire area within which strong interaction is likely to occur during the next 25 to 30 years.

9

A Hundred-Year Plan:
The Example
of Copenhagen*

In the April issue of *Ekistics* Mr. C. A. Doxiadis proposes
that we should plan the physical shape of human settlements
for 100 years ahead and exemplifies his approach by a critical
evaluation of the recently published sketch proposals for
a plan of the Copenhagen Region ("Principskitsen til en
Egnsplan").

There can, of course, be no quarrel with Doxiadis' remark
that "we don't plan just once, but continuously." But this
does not obviate the fact that any plan which we make *now* is
a guide to decisions on making investments—public and private—*before* the plan is reviewed and changed. To the extent

Editor's note: The plan of Copenhagen discussed in this article dates back to 1947.
At that time the so-called "finger plan" was drafted. In 1959 this plan was reassessed,
and by the early 1960's a more extensive plan was produced—a plan that can be thought
of as a "sector plan" for metropolitan growth.

Dr. Constantinos Doxiadis, the noted Greek planner, wrote a critique of Copenhagen's plan in the April 1963 issue of *Ekistics*. This prompted an exchange of views
between Mr. Blumenfeld and Dr. Doxiadis. In the February 1964 issue of *Ekistics*, Mr.
Blumenfeld's thoughts were published, followed in that same issue by further comments
of Dr. Doxiadis.

Mr. Blumenfeld's article on Copenhagen is presented here alone because it represents
an application of his thinking to a given situation. The author's theses are also based on
more specific evidence and analysis than are those of Dr. Doxiadis, who speaks in broader
generalitites in a desire to urge a larger vision both on the profession and on society.
Mr. Blumenfeld's comments are no less universally directed.

Doxiadis had estimated the future population of the Copenhagen Region at 5.0 to
5.5 million; this estimate was not included in the *Ekistics* article.

that the predictions on which the plan is based and, consequently, the plan itself are wrong, the investment decisions will be wrong. Investments will be made in the wrong place and/or at the wrong time.

It follows that the plan period should not be shorter than the minimum amortization period of the investments and not longer than we can predict within acceptable limits of probability, that is, a probability substantially greater than the 50 per cent probability resulting from tossing a coin. As a minimum period we may accept the 20- to 25-year period usual for financing of investments by mortgages or bonds. Most planners share the bankers' opinion that predicting further ahead is too risky, and do not attempt to predict or plan for more than 20 to 25 or, at most, 30 to 40 years.

In view of the accelerating pace of social, economic, and technological change, it is indeed questionable whether we can predict the goals that people will pursue 50 or 100 years from now and, even more so, the means that will be at their disposal and that they will use to achieve these goals. Of course, it is true, as Doxiadis says, that "many of the projects we are creating today are going to survive for at least a century." Indeed, even if they disappear, their influence will continue to be felt. But this does not tell us which ones will and which ones will not survive or, more importantly, whether their effect 100 years from now will be a help or a hindrance to the persons then living.

Thus, the question remains: for how long can we hope to predict? The Copenhagen planners, in publishing their "finger plan" in 1947, attempted to predict for about 30 years, up to 1980. Their plan has been universally and rightly acclaimed as an outstanding achievement. Yet, after only 12 years, actual development had so far deviated from their predictions that they felt it necessary to revise them and to modify their proposals. Doxiadis believes that this failure — if it is one — would have been avoided if they had attempted to predict and plan for a much longer period, about 100 years.

It is important to note specifically the discrepancies between reality and the planners' predictions. They had correctly estimated that the old central area would remain the principal location of employment and had only slightly underestimated the total population growth. But the distribution of the resident population differed substantially, for three closely interrelated reasons:

1. Growth of automobile ownership was far more rapid than expected.
2. Land consumption per dwelling unit was twice as high as expected, 1,000 square meters (a quarter of an acre) instead of 500 square meters (an eighth of an acre).
3. Development occurred not primarily in the "fingers" but in widely scattered areas not served by public transportation and also in and around four old towns – Helsingör, Hilleröd, Frederikssund, and Röskilde – located about 30-40 kilometers (18-25 miles) from Copenhagen, which thus became "satellite towns."
4. Specifically, the substantial increases predicted in 1947 within the already urbanized area occurred exactly as predicted. In the fingers to the north-northwest, where there was already substantial development in 1947, about half of the predicted development occurred. In the fingers to the west-southwest, where there was little development in 1947, only one third of the predicted development occurred. Of the five proposed secondary centers, at distances averaging 15-20 kilometers (10-12 miles) from the center of Copenhagen, only the one to the north actually developed.

It is fairly evident in which ways development differed from prediction:

1. The level of living rose faster than expected.
2. The automobile proved relatively far more attractive than public transportation.
3. Low-density housing proved relatively more attractive than higher-density housing (Danish housing policy does not give preference to the single-family detached house).
4. Proximity to existing developments – Copenhagen, the satellite towns, the northern suburbs – proved relatively more attractive than pioneering in open country (for people seeking medium-density, medium-cost housing).

For purposes of discussion, the Danish planners offered two alternative development possibilities, one that they strongly favored and the other that they disfavored. One of the two possibilities, however, would have to be adopted as planning policy at the completion of the first ten-year stage of development. During the first ten-year stage the original finger plan would be completed; that is, development in the two southwestern corridors would be more effectively promoted.

The ten-year plan proposes to promote the development in the two southwestern corridors by providing them with accessibility by rail and road superior to the accessibility of all other areas. There are two reasons for this decision:

1. These two corridors connect Copenhagen with the rest of Denmark (via Röskilde) and with the European continent (via Köge).
2. A new commercial and industrial port is to be developed in Köge Bay.

A strong secondary center is to be developed along the Röskilde corridor, about two thirds of the way between Copenhagen and Röskilde, with one additional minor center on this corridor and two on the Köge corridor.

After the completion of the ten-year stage of development comes the development plan, which would be in operation until 1980. This is where the two alternatives, or sketches, enter in. One alternative is based on the thesis that long-distance interregional traffic should be kept separate from short-distance intraregional traffic and should not dominate the direction of settlement within the region. It proposes to attract development into satellite clusters at some distance from central Copenhagen (Fig. 8). Some of these new clusters would be in the highly scenic and attractive areas to the north and northwest. The second alternative, considering the connection toward the Continent as decisive, proposes development between the two southwestern corridors, with the main secondary center expanding into a major center serving both corridors (Fig. 7). It is also based on the proposition that the scenically attractive areas to the northwest should be left as a recreational reserve, under careful development controls. The less attractive southwestern corridor, the planners assert, could be made scenically attractive by landscape design.

It is with the latter proposal that Doxiadis deals in his discussion. Accepting the concept of the connection to the Continent as the major axis of growth and the location of a new major center along this axis between the two existing corridors, he proposes a far bolder, longer-range approach, with the axis and a series of centers, to be developed consecutively over time, expanding on a much larger scale. The new centers would absorb an increasing portion and eventually the majority of the functions now located in the historical center of Copenhagen.

Wisely and courageously, Doxiadis makes his predictions in the framework of a prediction of world population growth during the next century. His studies have produced an estimate of 24 billion by the year 2063. While I am not familiar with these studies, I presume that they are based on the assumptions that life expectancy in the "underdeveloped" countries will fairly soon rise to the level now prevalent in all "developed" countries, of about 70 years; and that the fertility rate, both in the "developed" and in the "underdeveloped" countries will not change substantially during the balance of this century and will only gradually decrease thereafter. It is this last assumption that is open to question. Doxiadis refers in passing to this possibility but apparently bases his prognosis on the assumption—which I consider the least realistic of all—that the present social-political state of the world can continue for two hundred years without leading to a catastrophe.

Seventeen years ago Albert Einstein remarked that the control of atomic energy had changed everything—except men's thinking. The vastly increased power of man over the forces of nature has led mankind to a crossroad. This power can be used for the self-destruction of mankind or for achievement of an undreamed-of high level of prosperity and culture. At present, the wealthiest and most powerful nation on earth, the United States of America, devotes more than half of its scientific brainpower and over one third of the surplus (over current consumption) of its gross national product to preparations for the first alternative; and most other nations tend to do the same to the limit of their ability. Few thinking persons doubt that if this course is continued, only pitiful remnants of mankind, if any, will survive in the twenty-first century.

Evidently, any population prediction and any planning can be based only on the second alternative, however low its probability may appear to be: that the nations of the world will find the courage to discard the illusory security of mutual deterrence and achieve security by mutual trust in a disarmed world. It is my prediction that under this alternative the transition of the "underdeveloped" areas from illiterate subsistence-peasant societies to educated urban-industrial nations will proceed far more rapidly than now appears possible. Far more equipment and knowledge from the "developed" countries will become available to them; but these, while indispensable, are of limited value without a profound change of the attitudes of the people who have to use them. The main obstacle to this change, the obsolete oppressive social-political structures and ideologies still dominating most of the "underdeveloped" countries, cannot survive the end of the cold war but will be swept away by revolutionary change.

What will be the demographic consequences of such a revolutionary change? On the surface, the correlations between prosperity and the birth rate, observed during the last century, appear utterly confusing and completely erratic. I believe that they can be understood as the result of the interaction of two trends: (1) a long-term trend of decreasing fertility correlated with the transition from a poor subsistence-peasant to a wealthy urban-industrial economy; and (2) a cyclical trend, probably operative only in "developed" economies, positively correlated with the business cycle. (In subsistence economies the death rate is, in fact, negatively correlated with changes in prosperity.) Where these two trends work in the same direction, as in postwar Japan, the decrease in the fertility rate becomes precipitous. But in a number of other countries — Germany, Austria, the Soviet Union, Italy — decreases as high as 40 per cent have also occurred within one generation. I consider it highly probable that an equally dramatic decrease in most of the presently underdeveloped countries will occur in the early years of the twenty-first century. If this hypothesis is correct, world population in 2063 would be considerably less than 24 billion, probably in the neighborhood of 16 billion.

Doxiadis also assumes that in 100 years the transition to a modern economy will be completed everywhere, with less than 10 per cent of the world's population living in rural areas and 90 per cent in metropolitan regions. He points out that this implies a more than fortyfold increase of the world metropolitan population, but evidently he does not assume a fortyfold increase of the population of the Copenhagen region to over 50 million. Regrettably, he does not indicate his thoughts about the probable distribution of the world's population. It may, however, well be worth while to speculate about the factors that may affect this distribution.

The factors that have previously determined the location of urban agglomerations, proximity to raw materials and sources of energy and easy access to transportation lines, are rapidly losing their importance. The most important determinants today are access to markets and availability of a great variety of skills and of producer and consumer services. All these are present in any large metropolitan area. But these areas themselves, apart from the very strong evidence that those which exist now will attract growth by growth, are footloose. In other words, as all other things are becoming more nearly equal all over the globe, they will develop primarily where people want to live. Therefore, world population is likely to migrate to climatically and scenically attractive areas, primarily to the shores and islands of the warm seas — to Colombo rather than to Copenhagen.

Consequently, the population of the Copenhagen region can expect to draw only on migration from its own hinterland, Denmark and Sweden. The natural population increase in these two countries is among the lowest in the world, indicating a total of perhaps 25 to 30 million in 1963, some of which may be lost by migration to warmer climes.

How many of these 30 million people are likely to live in the Copenhagen region? Evidently, this will depend on the competing attraction of surrounding large metropolitan areas. At present there are far fewer such areas within several hundred miles from Copenhagen than there are in other parts of Europe: only Stockholm to the north and Berlin and Hamburg to the south. But others might develop. Any prediction of the region's population by the year 2063 is therefore highly uncertain.

Doxiadis does not make such a prediction, but he does make a prediction of the size of the land area required (6,000 square kilometers or 2,300 square miles), which is, of course, a function of the number of people and of the average density of settlement. If the area develops primarily on the basis of automobile traffic, as Doxiadis appears to assume, the density is likely to average about 1,000 per square kilometer (2,600 per square mile) indicating a total population of around 6 million. While the population might well be as low as 4 million or as high as 12 million, 6 million is an acceptable working hypothesis.

This prediction leads to the question of primary interest to planners: where will these 6 million people live, work, and play? Doxiadis says: "geography is not going to change." This is a strange statement in the discussion of an area where geography has changed considerably. About 4 square miles in the historical center of the region, equivalent to half the area of the City of Copenhagen in 1867, are man-made, on filled land. In addition, 10 square miles have been added to the immediately adjacent island of Amager. At present, plans are under study to enlarge greatly and develop the island of Saltholm, a few miles east of Copenhagen.

But even if geography, in the narrow sense of topography, did not change, its impact on human settlement constantly changes as a result of changes in transportation. Doxiadis assumes that the potential Copenhagen region is limited to the island of Sjaelland, and he ignores the Skone peninsula on the other side of the Sund. He therefore proposes that the center of the region should shift southwestward toward the center of Sjaelland. However, this happens to be one of the few areas in the beautiful country of Denmark that is scenically totally unattractive, a drab, monotonous, treeless plain. On the other hand, the coast of Skone, terminating to the north in the marvelous Kullen peninsula, is extremely beautiful and, in addition, is dotted with a number of well-established, highly attractive towns: Malmö, Lund, Landskrona, and Hälsingborg. It is therefore a far more desirable area for the expansion of the Copenhagen area than the interior of Sjaelland—if it can be made equally accessible.

A road and railroad crossing of the Sund at its narrowest point, 25 miles north of Copenhagen, is in the engineering stage. A second crossing, directly from Copenhagen to Malmö is under study and will certainly be in operation long before the end of the century. These two crossings are likely to be followed by several others in the course of the next 100 years.

Thus, even if the present predominance of land transportation should continue, the Sund would no longer be the strong barrier that it is today. However, it is far from certain that this predominance will continue. The history of transportation shows examples of unexpected reversals. For thousands of years, since neolithic man invented the dugout canoe, water transportation was superior to land transportation, and this superiority increased until, in the beginning of the nineteenth century, canals became the superior means of transportation even in continental areas. Suddenly, and completely unpredictably, this millennial trend was totally reversed by the rapid development first of railroads and subsequently of hard-surface roads for automobiles and trucks, as well as of pipelines and power lines. However, several new developments, hydrofoil, hovercraft, and amphibious vehicles may lead to a revival of water transportation. Even more important is the growing trend of air transportation to supersede and replace the separate modes of land and water transportation. It may also again reverse the trend from public to private transportation, which has resulted from the spread of the automobile and which was another completely unexpected reversal of the consistent secular growth of public transportation.

Changed modes of transportation may decisively change not only the direction of growth in the Copenhagen region — eastward into Skone rather than exclusively westward into Sjaelland — but also its form. Doxiadis develops the theory that every settlement "in the long run tends ... towards a circle." I think that this is too sweeping a generalization. Accepting Doxiadis' premise that any unit of human settlement, which I define as a unit of frequent daily interchange, will tend to have one dominant center, I believe that its form will vary according to the prevailing mode of transportation. Whenever this mode is unchanged and of roughly uniform speed for the entire length of the trip — be it walking, bicycling, or automobile driving — the form will indeed tend toward a circle. However, if the trip is made by a combination of two modes of different speeds, a different form results. If the speeds differ greatly, at a ratio of about 1:10, and if the ratio of terminal costs to line costs (in terms of both money and time) is high, then a pattern of points along lines will develop. This was the case with the combination of travel by steam railroad, at a speed of about 30 miles per hour and of walking at a speed of 3 miles per hour, which produced the railroad suburb. If the ratio of terminal cost to line cost is close to one and the difference between the two speeds is reduced to about 3:1, the points merge into a ribbon. Such a pattern was produced by the combination of streetcar riding at 9 miles per hour with walking at 3 miles per hour.

Should air transportation by any form of vertical-takeoff craft become general for intrametropolitan trips, by a combination of air speed of about 300 miles per hour and automobile speed of 30 miles per hour, a new point pattern would develop, with "points" of a radius of 5 to 10 miles located perhaps 50 miles apart. Should the system presently under development by General Motors be successful—a somewhat frightening thought—we would see electronically operated super-super-highways with bumper-to-bumper chains of cars moving at speeds of 100 miles per hour or more and being released for manual operation at 30 miles per hour at interchanges spaced perhaps 10 miles apart. This again would create ribbons of settlement, of a width of probably 15 to 20 miles instead of the $\frac{1}{2}$ to $\frac{3}{4}$ miles of the streetcar ribbons.

The possibility that changes in transportation technology may substantially affect both the direction and the form of future development creates a series of possible alternatives. Because transportation is an unpredictable independent variable, several alternative models are possible for the dependent variable, the form of the Copenhagen metropolitan region, even if all other independent variables—total population, functional structure, and density—could be assumed as fixed. Actually, these also are predictable only within very wide error limits.

Doxiadis' prediction and plan are based on the implicit assumption of the continuing predominance of the automobile. This, in part, explains his great concern with what he sees as "the major problem of the dynamically growing city: the unnatural growth of its center."

To American planners of the 1960's, who are beset on all sides by hysterical outcries about "the dying core of the city" and by frantic efforts to save it from the threat of decentralization by all kinds of "redevelopment" schemes, at unconscionable costs in money and human suffering, it must sound rather strange that Doxiadis is concerned with the opposite danger. He states that "the center often grows much more than the city itself, because if the city's population grows by 2 per cent per year, we may well discover that the people visiting the center of the city are increasing by more than 2 per cent per year."

Here Doxiadis may be making the mistake, against which he rightly warns, of planning for conditions of the past rather than for those of the future. It may be that in the seventeenth, eighteenth, or nineteenth century, the city center grew faster than the city as a whole, though I know of no evidence to support this hypothesis. Certainly for the twentieth century the opposite can be fully documented. Even in European cities, where the center is still growing, its growth is much slower than that of the metropolitan area as a whole. In most major North American cities — New York, Chicago, Los Angeles, Philadelphia — the growth has come to a stop for some 30 years. The number of persons visiting the center of the New York region — Manhattan from the Battery to 59th Street — is the same today as it was 35 years ago. In Toronto, a smaller and younger metropolitan region, the same surprising stability has been observed for the past 12 years.

This is a very strange phenomenon indeed: everything in the world changes, but the employment in the centers of large North American metropolitan areas and the number of persons coming into them do not change! The most probable explanation is that this stable total is the product of two opposite trends that have, so far, been in balance. Employment in establishments dealing with goods — manufacturing, warehousing, and to a lesser extent, retailing which deals with persons as well as with goods — is decreasing; employment in those dealing exclusively with persons, generally in offices, keeps on increasing. In Toronto this was confirmed by a comparison of the results of employment surveys made in 1956 and 1960. It might be hypothesized that at some point the shrinking employment group would reach zero, while the expanding group would keep on growing and that, therefore, from that point on, total employment would again increase. A purely mechanical extrapolation of trends would indicate that in Toronto, for instance, this point would be reached in 1970. From that year on, the center *might* again start to grow; however, the experience of New York and other cities indicates that it more probably *will not* grow.

The reason is not hard to understand. The same process of selection that leads to an increasing specialization of the center in those functions for which it is uniquely suited, while all others move out, is also at work within the second group, the one dealing with persons. Generally speaking, two groups of functions are attracted to the center. The first are those that serve and can only be supported by the population of the entire area—in the case of today's Copenhagen, those that require a "market" of half a million or a million people. If and when the population of Copenhagen region reaches a total of 6 million, most of these people can be supplied by half a dozen or more centers of the "second highest order," while the main center can and will specialize in services of the very highest order, those which require the support of 5 or 6 million people.

The second group of functions are those which require access not primarily to all parts of the region but to each other, the "contact-oriented" activities. A third group consists of establishments serving the first two, for example eating and drinking places, or building-maintenance services. The contact-oriented establishments may also decentralize, in two ways. They may separate their contact functions from their routine functions and relocate the latter away from the center; the feasibility of this solution depends largely on the development of communication techniques. The second way consists in the development of districts for a specialized group of contact functions, such as financial institutions. Both processes have occurred and are occurring spontaneously. So far as I know, the first attempt to establish what might be called a planned office estate is now being undertaken in Hamburg, Germany. It may well be that the planning of such estates, possibly in conjunction with planned regional centers of the next-to-highest order, should form part of the plan for the Copenhagen region.

Doxiadis develops a different approach. Motivated by the fear that the historical center will be overloaded and assuming the future development of the region along a southwest axis across Sjaelland, he proposes the immediate establishment of a center about 15 miles from the present one, between the two corridors to Röskilde and Köge, to be followed by a series of centers to be consecutively established on open land along this axis, until the last one, in the center of the island, finally becomes the center of the entire region.

Doxiadis says: "This center starts without any difficulties." This is an astonishing statement. Two conditions are required for the development and growth of a center. There must be space, and there must be people and activities. The first condition, of course, creates no difficulties on open land, while it creates serious difficulties in a built-up area. However, these can be overcome in three ways: by horizontal expansion, by vertical extension, and by replacement of obsolete structures by new ones. Copenhagen has developed an excellent plan providing for a growth of its center by almost 50 per cent above the 1956 level (see City Plan Vest, Stadsingeniörens Direktorat, Köbenhavn, 1958); and further expansion is possible on the area of harbor facilities, after their relocation on Köge Bay, and over extensive railroad tracks.

Conversely, a new center of open land will have great difficulties in attracting people away from competing facilities closer to their homes. An intensive and costly effort may be able to overcome these difficulties, but it cannot well be denied that they exist.

One may object that the new center could and would start on a modest scale and would only gradually grow to its intended size. But would not the transformation of a low-intensity center for, say, 50,000 people into a major center for several millions create all of the difficulties that we are experiencing in the transformation of existing centers?

Doxiadis proposes to repeat this process several times, with one center after the other being established as the population expands along the presumed axis of growth. The phenomenon of a center shifting in response to a shift of the center of population is not unknown. It does not occur where development can proceed in all directions, as, for instance, in London, Paris, Moscow, or Vienna. In such cities the center remains in its original location, and it is well to note that such centers are the most lively and attractive ones.

The shift does sometimes, though by no means always, occur where expansion in one direction is barred by a body of water. In such a "semicircular" metropolis the center of population inevitably shifts farther and farther away from the original center on the waterfront, exerting a pull on the center to follow it. Probably the most spectacular example is New York, with the gradual and still-continuing shift of its center from the Battery to—at present—about 50th Street. This movement has left in New York, and elsewhere, a number of deserted and derelict ex-centers, which present some of the most untractable problems.

It seems to me that Doxiadis' "Dynapolis" scheme would re-create these problems on a truly grandiose scale. From this angle it appears as a scheme for planned instability.

To sum up the difference of approach in crude and over-simplified terms: Doxiadis proposes to locate the center at the point of gravity of a hypothetical region; I would locate the region around an actually existing center.

I do not claim that the form of the future Copenhagen region that I have attempted to indicate will come about, or that the various predictions that I have discussed as possibilities are more probable than those made by Doxiadis. But the number of possible alternatives, and of their combinations and permutations, is so great, that any single prediction—Doxiadis' or any other—has a probability of much less than 50 per cent. It would be a very serious mistake to base on so low a probability a plan that is to be adopted now and is to serve as a guide for investments to be made during the next ten years.

I agree with Doxiadis that we should attempt to predict whatever may be predictable. We should certainly try to *think* ahead a hundred years or more, but we should *plan* ahead no longer than we can predict with reasonable probability. The best part of our wisdom is still the Socratic "I know that I do not know."

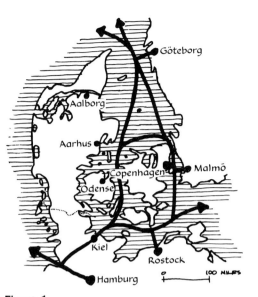

Figure 1
The Copenhagen region, with the heavy lines indicating principal sea routes.

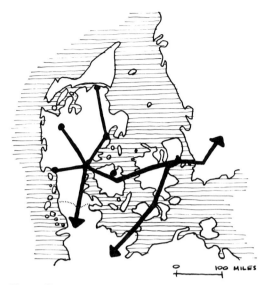

Figure 2
The Copenhagen region with the heavy lines indicating principal overland routes.

Figure 3
Copenhagen itself. Growth was radiocentric along coastal and inland spines.

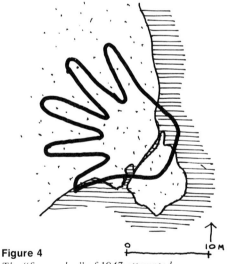

Figure 4
The "finger plan" of 1947 attempted to direct this growth along orderly corridors. This decision was supported by transportation and open space policy.

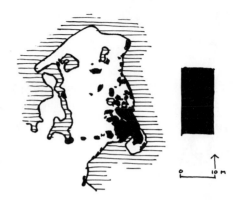

Figure 5
By 1959 it was recognized that the "finger plan" required reconsideration. Copenhagen would need an urbanized area as large as the black rectangle.

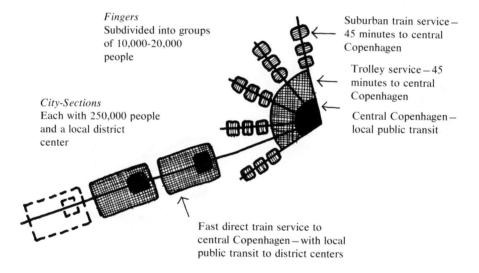

Fingers
Subdivided into groups of 10,000-20,000 people

Suburban train service— 45 minutes to central Copenhagen

Trolley service—45 minutes to central Copenhagen

City-Sections
Each with 250,000 people and a local district center

Central Copenhagen— local public transit

Fast direct train service to central Copenhagen—with local public transit to district centers

Figure 6
By the early 1960's a new plan was produced. The "finger concept" was brought up to date. It was proposed to supplement them with new "city-sections" of 250,000 people each. All decisions were based on transit operations, proper land use, open space needs, and logical directions of growth.

Figure 7

The "finger" and "city sections" are shown in plan. The sections would extend southwestward and could eventually extend further.

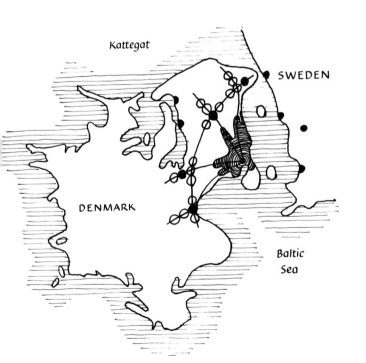

Figure 8

An alternative to the "city-section" concept. In this proposal urban growth would be directed into satellite towns.

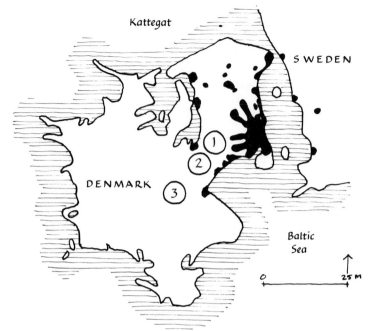

Figure 9

A proposal of Dr. Constantino Doxiadis. A new metropolitan center would be created somewhere between sites 1, 2, and 3. Site 1 would be the closest center in a present open area. Site 2 would be in the center of transportation. Site would be at "the center of gravity. Extensive urbanization would surround this new center.

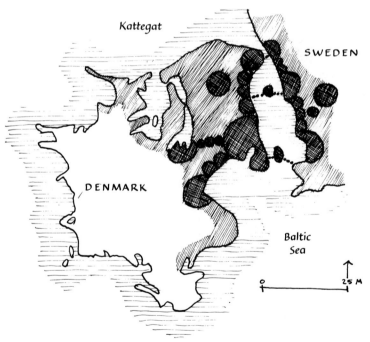

Figure 10

A proposal of the author based on current policy decisions carried forward, and on the construction of three bridges (dots) between Denmark and Sweden. Dark hatching indicates intensive urbanization; shading indicates extensive urbanization.

III

TRANSPORTATION

10

Experiments in Transportation — for What?

The program of this conference has promised you that the panel will tell you something about the coming marvels of transportation technology. I do not consider myself competent in this field. I am sure that there are many in the audience who know more about it than I do.

What I want to discuss with you are the goals of transportation and the criteria by which we may attempt to judge the value of any means of transportation, new or old. The standard introduction to most transportation reports defines the goal as "the efficient and safe movement of people and goods" — and messages, I would add.

Why do we want to move people, goods, and messages? Why can't people stay put? Why don't we all adopt the wisdom of Voltaire's Candide and just cultivate our own garden?

The answer is, I suppose, that human beings are, by definition, not wise. It is sufficient to observe the irrepressible drive of children to run — and not only to run but to race. There has apparently never been a culture in which people have not tried to beat the speed of everybody else with whatever means of transportation were at their disposal, from feet and dugout canoes to jet planes and rockets. Movement, and indeed faster and faster movement, appears to be, in and by itself, a basic human need, and we should not forget that in our planning.

But movement for movement's sake is, of course, not the purpose of most movement of people, and not at all of the movement of goods and messages. The purpose is exchange — exchange of goods, of messages, and of personal contacts and services. The more efficient the means of transportation, the larger the range of exchange. We are used to measuring efficiency of transportation and communication in terms of saving of time and money. The two are really only two different expressions of the same thing. The cost of a bus ride is the time that others have spent to build, maintain, and operate the road and the vehicle.

However, if improvements reduce the time — directly and when translated into money — of moving ten miles in the time previously required to move one mile, then goods, persons, and messages will travel ten times farther. The net result is not a reduction of time but an extension of space. Other things being equal, this extended space will contain more persons, goods, and "hubits" — Richard Meier's term for units of information — from which to choose. The net product of transportation, as well as its purpose, is the enlargement of the freedom of choice.

I said "other things being equal," but are they? Evidently, the number of persons, goods, and "hubits" contained in a given area depends not only on the extent of the area but on the population density within it. The benefits of improved transportation may be taken either as less time or as more space. Each individual locator bases his decision on a trade-off between time and space. If all decide to take 100 per cent of the benefit in terms of space, there is no gain in time and no increase in freedom of choice. In this case, the net product is not saving of time but waste of space — if it is assumed that space has a greater value to the community than it has to the sum of the individuals who constitute that community.

I shall not discuss here the difficult question of whether or not this assumption is correct. It is certain that an increase in the freedom of choice can be brought about either by decreasing time (including cost) of moving persons, goods, and messages from A to B or by decreasing the distance between A and B. Land-use planning and transportation planning are complementary. Those who assume that land is a scarce resource for the community to a greater degree than for the individual advocate a limitation of the urban periphery and a floor for densities, and they renounce the maximum use of transportation technology. Those who do not share this assumption foresee and accept the "spread city" as the urban form of the future. Some of these, extrapolating to zero the trend of decreasing time required to cover a given distance, claim that spatial relations—and hence land-use planning—are becoming irrelevant. I doubt this. It is true that messages travel at absolute speed, and therefore differences in direct time of sending messages to any point on earth are practically zero; but the difference in cost—indirect time—between calling Perth, Ontario, and calling Perth, Australia, is still quite substantial. As for the time and cost of moving people and goods, it is likely to remain very significant for the foreseeable future. At present the cost absorbs about one fifth of the total gross national product of this country.

I have included movement of messages together with that of persons and goods in this discussion because these three categories can, to a large extent, substitute for one another. When I was born, the only way to hear a prima donna sing was by movement of persons. Either you had to go to the opera house, or she had to come to your drawing room. When the phonograph was invented, one could substitute for this movement of persons the movement of a good—a disk. With the development of radio, the song can be moved from origin to destination in the form of an electronic message.

This is a somewhat esoteric example. Of far greater importance has been the invention of the telephone. We are apt to forget that within living memory all business was transacted by sending messages. To be able to talk with a person without being face to face was the most revolutionary change in the history of communication, more revolutionary than any changes that have occurred since or are presently envisaged. I have often suggested to my academic friends—so far without success—the undertaking of a study concerning the impact of the telephone on the distribution of activities in urban and metropolitan areas. Perhaps the world's wealthiest corporation, International Telephone and Telegraph, can be persuaded to make a million-dollar grant for research in this field.

What we do know, without further research, is what the telephone did *not* do. It did not eliminate the desire for doing business face to face and the concentration that serves this desire, the central business district. I am therefore somewhat skeptical about predicting the impact of new developments in communication.

Two of these developments, already available but not yet widely used, may be of importance. The first is closed-circuit television. At present, if you want to show models of your shiny new redevelopment project to the city fathers, either they have to move in person to your office, or the goods have to be moved to City Hall. Closed-circuit television might be substituted for these movements.

One could also think of television inspection of merchandise, plus a telephone order, as a substitute for shopping trips. But I doubt that many women would prefer it. Even more doubtful is the substitution of togetherness by closed television for social gatherings. Some fairly popular forms of personal contact can never be replaced by electronic messages — I hope.

The second and possibly more significant innovation is direction of automated production processes by distant computers. Since both the message from the computer and the feedback to it travel at absolute speed, a fully and reliably automated factory could be located hundreds of miles away from human habitations. More difficult, but not impossible, is the automation of mining, agriculture, forestry, or fishing. If this should come to pass, people would not have to live in dispersed and sometimes dismal places. They could and would choose to live in climatically and scenically attractive regions and, if I am right in claiming that distance will remain a factor in movement of persons, in metropolitan areas that offer them a wide range of choice in all spheres of life.

Substitution occurs, of course, not only between movement of people, goods, and messages but within each of these categories. In particular, goods can be moved in a continuous flow rather than in discrete carriers. Indeed, if we had not made this substitution during the last hundred years, our cities could hardly operate. Less than a century ago the most hotly debated question among German city planners was about the best way to move human excrement out of the city — by cartage or by pipe. How much more difficult would our traffic problems be if we still had water wagons and honey wagons on the streets instead of pipes under them. In addition, instead of moving coal and oil as sources of energy and heat by truck, we can move energy in the form of electricity by wire, heat carried by steam or hot water in pipes, and gas as a source of both heat and energy by pipe. We have never calculated the costs and benefits — including decreased air pollution — of moving energy and heat exclusively by pipe or wire within a metropolitan area.

It would also be possible to remove garbage and trash, after adequate grinding, by pipes. In long-distance transportation, an increasing number of bulk goods — coal, ores, grain — are being moved by pipeline. A more intriguing possibility for intraurban transportation is movement of piece goods in containers by pipeline. Movement of small containers through pneumatic tubes is, of course, familiar. If this could be made economical for containers of large diameter, one could envisage the establishment, in a large metropolitan area, of a system of underground tubes interconnecting perhaps a dozen terminals at which containers would be automatically transferred to and from pickup and delivery trucks.

In the category of persons' movement, the central question is the substitution of collective for individual transportation, or vice versa. In the discussions about means to revive collective transportation, or public transit, quite undue emphasis is given to the technical speed of the vehicles, generally trains. That is not the real problem. Sixty years ago the German A.E.G. (Allgemeine Elektrizitätsgesellschaft) ran an experimental line from Berlin to Zossen at 125 miles per hour, and higher speeds can be achieved easily. The problem is to make the *total* time from origin to destination competitive with that achieved by the door-to-door movement of the private automobile.

In this respect public transit is handicapped by two factors. Transit vehicles have to stop and start in order to discharge and take on passengers, and passengers have to get to and from these stops. These two handicaps are negatively correlated. Any attempt to decrease one of them increases the other. If the number of stops is decreased, their distance from the passengers' origins and destinations is increased, and vice versa.

What can be done? A partial means is convenient transfer between multistop local and few-stop express vehicles or trains. The best example of this is the New York subway system with its across-the-station transfer between local and express trains. However, traveling speed of express trains still averages only about 30 miles per hour.

It is, however, possible to improve on this method by having the express trains run through without any stops and transferring passengers between them and the local vehicles while both move side by side at the same speed. Interestingly, this was proposed almost a hundred years ago when the first elevated railroads were built in New York. I understand that a system based on this principle, on a miniature scale, was operated at the 1964 Swiss National Exhibition at Lausanne and will be used at the 1967 Montreal World's Fair.

In a large-scale application the "local" vehicles, probably buses, would be equipped with at least two large doors on their left side, identical with doors on the right side of the express vehicle, presumably a train car. They would be timed to go from a surface bus stop up or down on ramps to lanes paralleling the express tracks, hook on to the trains during transfer, and then continue up or down to another surface stop. I calculate that, with a train speed of 100 miles per hour, acceleration and deceleration at 3 miles per hour per second, and a transfer time of 20 seconds, a distance of about 8,000 feet would be required between two surface stops. People could move to and from these stops in two ways. They could drive to and from parking lots located at the stops; and the buses that serve for transfer to and from the express trains could converge from and diverge to various routes.

I have no doubt that such a system would be technically feasible. The question is: can you get enough people to and from it to make it economically justifiable? This takes us back to the second and tougher handicap of public transit, usually referred to as the feeder problem. With enough money, anyone can build an efficient rapid-transit line. The question is, how to feed it. When subways were first built in the big nineteenth-century cities, where 70 to 100 per cent of every block was covered with five- or six-story buildings, the answer was simple. People moved to and from the stations on foot, both horizontally and vertically, But present-day North Americans are willing neither to walk up five or six flights of stairs nor to live at the bottom of dark wells or canyons. They do accept working there, substituting synthetic for natural light and air, and moving up and down by elevator.

Thus, in the central business district and, to a lesser degree, in apartment areas, the feeder problem is solved by a mechanical means of vertical transportation, the elevator. Where densities are lower, passengers must be moved to and from the stations horizontally. In every case rapid transit has to be supplemented by some other means of mechanical transportation, moving either vertically or horizontally or both.

The means of horizontal transportation can be either collective or individual. Collective transportation, generally by buses, encounters our old dilemma in somewhat modified form. If bus lines are numerous and closely spaced, walking distances are acceptably short, but the service area becomes so small that the potential number of riders justifies only a few buses per hour, and waiting time becomes long. If buses are concentrated on few, widely spaced lines, service can be more frequent and waiting time shorter, but walking time becomes longer.

The inescapable conclusion is that an efficient transit feeder system can be operated only where density exceeds a certain level, probably about 12,000-15,000 persons per square mile. Without an efficient feeder system, however, rapid-transit trunk lines cannot operate.

There remains the possibility of a combined system, with rapid-transit trunk lines being fed by the private automobile. There are two difficulties in this solution.

The first is a variant of our old problem. If there are few and widely spaced stations, a very great number of cars will have to converge on them, causing congestion on the approach roads and requiring either excessively large parking lots or costly multilevel parking garages. If stations are more numerous, traveling time on the rapid-transit line becomes longer.

It may be possible to find an acceptable compromise. This will work, however, only if the residential end of the trip is in a low-density area, but the other end — primarily the place of work — is in an area of high concentration, such as the central business district. However, contrary to the general assumption, trips between peripheral residential and central work areas account for only a small and decreasing proportion of all trips in a large metropolitan area, at present about 15 per cent in Metropolitan Toronto. An increasing number of work places and other nonresidential destinations are too dispersed to be reached by walking from a station. This is the second and less tractable difficulty.

Two methods are in use for driving to and from a rapid-transit or commuter-railroad station, known as "park-and-ride" and "kiss-and-ride." Both are fine at the residential end of the trip; but what do you do at the other end? With park-and-ride you must maintain there a second car; with kiss-and-ride, a second wife.

It has also been proposed to apply the continuous-flow principle to the moving of persons, in the form of conveyor belts. Where large numbers want to travel relatively short distances, such a system may have merits. Such opportunities will rarely occur outside the central business district, and not often within it.

Similarly, attempts are being made to apply the continuous-flow principle to individual transportation, in the form of automated expressways on which cars would travel bumper-to-bumper at 100 or 150 miles per hour. The driver would approach an entrance to the expressway and punch an indication of his desired exit. Then the computer would take over, insert the car into the stream and later release it and steer it into the exit ramp, where manual operation would again take over.

This may work for long-distance travel. But inside a metropolitan area the real problem for individual as for collective transportation is not the trunk line but its feeders, not the expressways but their entrances and exits. We all know that these are the points that cause backups. The old dilemma reappears in still another form. If the interchanges are few and widely spaced, they will be overloaded. If they are numerous and closely spaced, weaving distances become too short. With the greater volumes and doubled or tripled speeds of automated expressways, difficulties will greatly increase.

I have so far discussed only land transportation. There are also water and air modes. For millennia, water transportation had been superior to movement on land, and for bulk goods it still is. In some situations it may stage a comeback in passenger transportation in the form of hydrofoil and possibly hovercraft.

Air transportation will certainly grow in importance for long-distance transportation. For movement within metropolitan areas it encounters two difficulties. First, because it operates in a moving medium, it is difficult to steer and therefore requires relatively large terminal areas, even with vertical take-off and landing. Second, anything that moves *in* the air does so *by* moving air rapidly. But rapid air movement is noise. I doubt that noiseless air vehicles are possible.

As I warned you in the beginning, I have disappointed you; I have not been able to unveil any Buck Rogers gadget that, with a magic wand, would solve "the traffic problem"—the problem that everywhere preoccupies harassed city fathers and planning officials and their harassed and harassing constituents and clients. I hope my fellow panelists will do better.

11

Transportation in the Modern Metropolis

Canadians have succeeded in building a nation against all rules in the textbooks, in defiance of the facts of geography, of history, of economics, and of ethnic and cultural differences. There is no secret about the magic wand that performed this miracle; it was transportation—first and foremost the railroads, then airlines, roads, and pipelines. Our great problem has been and is the overcoming of great distances; the problem of too few people dispersed over too much space, which forces us to devote a greater part of our gross national product to transportation and communication than does any other nation.

It may therefore seem strange that we should now be faced with an even tougher transportation problem by the opposite condition: too many people in too little space, resulting in growing congestion in our big metropolitan areas.

Before we attempt to find a solution—if any—to this problem, we may do well to try to understand the origin and the nature of this strange new phenomenon, the metropolitan area.

As did its precursor, the nineteenth-century "big city," it combines the traditional "central" ruling and organizing function of the town with the function of being the major seat of material production. However, not only are the populations of the modern metropolitan areas several times greater than those of even the largest preindustrial cities, but their daily activities are spread out over a far wider territory; and this territory includes not only "urban" but also extensive "open" areas: parks, golf courses, airfields, even farms and forests. The modern metropolis is "neither city nor country." Finally, it is characterized by separation of place of residence from place of work.

The basic *raison d'être* of the modern metropolis is the need for co-operation and communication resulting from the division of labor. Only the large metropolis offers to the highly specialized worker, in particular in the professional and managerial groups, a wide choice of employment, and to the employer a wide choice of highly specialized workers. Primarily the metropolis is a labor market, a place for making a living. This also sets its limits. It is a commuting area, extending as far as daily commuting is possible and no farther. Under present North American conditions this means a radius up to ⅝0-40 miles or an area 100 times as large as that of the nineteenth-century "big city." Within this area the land-use pattern and the transportation system should maximize mutual choice of place of employment and of persons employed by maximizing the possibility of commuting; but it should also, in order to minimize travel time and cost, minimize the need for commuting.

This makes it desirable to provide within every major section of a metropolitan area an approximate equilibrium between resident labor force and places of employment. Analysis of available data shows clearly that the percentage of residents of an area who work in different employment areas, and vice versa, decreases regularly with increasing distance between places of work and places of employment. It is therefore evident that by co-ordination of their location commuting can be minimized; it is, however, an illusion to believe that it can be eliminated, that planning can create a pattern in which "everybody walks to work." In the free choice of place of work (and of residence) many other motives are far stronger than the desire to minimize the journey to work. In Hudson County, New Jersey, for instance, an urbanized area of 44 square miles within the New York metropolitan area, there were, in 1960, 244,000 jobs and 233,000 employed residents, as close

DISTRIBUTION OF FUNCTIONS IN THE MODERN METROPOLIS

to a "balance" as one can ever hope to achieve. But over 35 per cent of those employed in Hudson County commuted "in" from other counties, and 32 per cent of the residents commuted "out." Similar patterns were evidenced by a survey made in 1954 in Metropolitan Toronto. Incidentally, this survey also found that less than 2½ per cent of all respondents walked to work.

In small towns the percentage of those walking and generally living closer to their place of work is, of course, higher. But the percentage of those who have to make very long trips, over 10 miles, is also higher. A survey made by the U.S. Bureau of Public Roads in 1951 in six midwestern and southern states found that in towns of 25,000 and over only 6 per cent had such long journeys to work, in smaller places 14 per cent, and in rural areas 29 per cent. In such small places those who cannot find satisfactory employment locally have only the choice of commuting over long distances to other places or of pulling up stakes and moving to another town. It is one of the great advantages of the metropolis that one can change one's employment without changing residence.

But the metropolis is a place not only for making a living, but also for living. Ebenezer Howard, the father of the "garden city" concept, stated that man is attracted by two "magnets," town and country. Whatever one may think of Howard's therapy, his diagnosis is certainly correct. Hence, a second pair of contradictory traffic requirements are access to the city center and access to the periphery, to "open country."

The role of the center, usually somewhat narrowly defined as the central business district, is changing. In the nineteenth century, with its limited facilities of intraurban transportation, it had been the preferred location for all activities.

Since that time there has been an increasing and still continuing shift from activities dealing with goods—manufacturing and warehousing and, to a lesser extent, retailing—to those dealing with persons, primarily the wide and growing array of business services and, to a lesser extent, of consumer services. These "tertiary" industries, typically carried on in offices, proliferating with increasing specialization, serving a wide region, and dependent on contact with each other as well as with their widely dispersed customers, are even more characteristic of the modern metropolis than is manufacturing. In view of their rapid growth it is surprising to find that in the largest metropolitan areas in the United States employment in the central business district and traffic into and out of that area has not increased during the last three decades. In Canada this leveling off occurred later. However, since 1948 the number of persons counted between 6:30 and 10 A.M. as crossing a cordon line encircling the central business district of Toronto has also remained constant.

From the central business district outward the density decreases with amazing regularity in subsequent concentric zones. Over time, there is a gradual decrease of residential population density in the inner and a fairly rapid increase in the outer zones. This regular falling off of densities toward the periphery holds true not only for residential but for all land uses. Industry and commerce also require increasing land areas per employed person, the farther from the center they locate. Employment density in new outlying industrial districts may be as much as 20 times lower than in old industrial areas near the center. This pattern of distribution of land use, population, and employment, which is the result of transportation, in turn determines the pattern of movement of goods and persons.

While the metropolitan area has inherited the bane of the big city of the nineteenth century, too many people in too little space, resulting in congestion of people, it has, paradoxically, compounded this problem by its opposite: dispersion of more and more people and establishments over too much space. The resulting distances are far too great to be overcome by walking; and densities in the outer reaches of the expanding area are too low to be served efficiently by public transportation. A rapidly increasing number of persons rely on the private automobile for their trips, and an increasing volume of goods is moved by trucks. It is this demand for space by the motor vehicle, both in movement and standing, which is popularly referred to as "the traffic problem."

The development of the internal-combustion engine and of the motor vehicle has led to a surprising and unforeseeable reversal of two closely related secular trends: (1) the trend toward replacement of individual small-scale by collective large-scale means of transportation and (2) the trend toward

LONG-DISTANCE MOVEMENTS AND TERMINALS

separation of local and long-distance transportation and the establishment of separate systems for the exclusive service of either one or the other form of traffic. The passenger car and the truck can serve both forms and thereby gain the great advantage of universal "door-to-door" service.

However, the specialized forms of long-distance transportation continue to play a vital role in the life of metropolitan areas. Transportation by water, rail, and pipes is superior to the motor vehicle in volume; aircraft excels in speed; and high-tension wires—carrying the kinetic energy stored in mineral fuels—excel in both. The location of their routes and terminals has a profound impact on development of metropolitan areas.

The impact is both positive and negative. It is positive, first, by attracting the establishments that they serve and, second, by decreasing the load on the road system. It is negative, first, because their lines and terminals interrupt the street system; second, because they may adversely affect adjacent land uses by noise, vibration, smoke, fumes, light, or unsightliness; and, third, because the traffic generated by their terminals may interfere with other traffic movements.

Ironically, it is largely the strength of the positive impact that has ultimately produced the negative effects. Most of our big metropolitan concentrations including Montreal owe their existence to water transportation. Because of the harbor, the city was built next to it. As it spread out from this original core in all directions, the core everywhere became the central business district. As activities both in the central business district and in the harbor increased, their competing claims for land conflicted inevitably. Larger ships and faster turnaround have greatly reduced the number of ships and the length of berth required to handle a given tonnage; but they have increased the need for a large area back of the berth for handling the tonnage by rail and road. Thus a relocation of the port on new land becomes necessary. Port cities of Europe, such as Rotterdam, Marseilles, and Hamburg, have been more forward-looking in this respect than most of those in North America. New York is only now beginning to eliminate its downtown piers on the East River.

Each new means of long-distance transportation has repeated this pattern. With enthusiastic citizen support, ter-

minals of railroads, over-the-road trucks and buses, and airlines have been located as close as possible to the center. As
both the cities and the volumes handled by each means of
transportation grew, conflict arose. At great expense railroads
had to relocate their yards and grade-separate their lines; and
the process is far from complete. Truck terminals are only
beginning to relocate on the outskirts and to break up systematically the large loads of long-distance trailer trucks for distribution by local pickup-and-delivery wagons. Airports pose
by far the greatest problem: because of their size; because,
unlike railroad yards, they cannot be crossed by viaducts; and
because their flight paths extend beyond their boundaries. But
we appear to be bent on bringing them as close to the center
as a level field can be found, thus repeating on a gigantic scale
the erection of barriers to future urban growth that we have
experienced with railroad facilities — and the creation of obstacles to future extension of airports, more confining than those
which the railroads experienced when they were faced with
the need for expansion.

Only pipelines and wires, being always grade-separated,
generally avoid this mutual interference of land use and means
of transportation. We have never systematically investigated
their role in the transportation of goods — and of messages — in
the metropolis. Yet it is not so long ago that water and sewage
were carted through our streets, instead of being carried in
pipes, and that messages were delivered by boys on foot or on
bicycle, instead of being transmitted over a telephone wire.
Technically it is entirely possible to replace all fuel and refuse
trucks by supplying energy by wire and heat by pipes carrying
oil, gas, steam, or hot water, and by grinding garbage and trash
into particles that can be carried off in sewage pipes. We do
not know how the costs of such a substitution compare with
the benefits of relieving street congestion.

However, vital as the problems of goods transportation are,
they are overshadowed in the modern metropolis by the problem of moving people.

MOVEMENT OF
PERSONS WITHIN A
METROPOLITAN AREA

Traffic surveys made during the past few years in Metropolitan Toronto indicate that the inhabitants of that area made
an average of 1.6 trips per capita on an average workday, with
an average trip length of close to 4½ miles, or about 7 miles

per person, within the boundaries of the Metropolitan Municipality. Thus the 1½ million inhabitants of that area traveled, by mechanical means, a total of about 10 million miles daily, an average of over 4,000 miles per square mile. By far the most (60.3 per cent) and also the longest, of these trips, were made to or from work. Somewhat less than one sixth (15.5 per cent) were made for social or recreational purposes, only 10 per cent were shopping trips, 5 per cent were made for business, and the remaining 10 per cent for other purposes, primarily education. The great majority of these trips were made from or to the home, but about 16 per cent were made between two points other than home. Almost 40 per cent of these were for the purpose of "work," indicating the great number of persons — presumably businessmen, salesmen, repairmen — who had to travel in performance of their work. Actually there was one of these "second or subsequent" work trips for every six trips from home to work; and their total number exceeded the commonly overrated number of trips from home to shopping. Surveys in the United States reveal generally similar patterns.

PRIVATE AND PUBLIC TRANSPORTATION

All these trips are made either by public transit or by private car, and their optimal distribution between these two modes of transporation is the most vexing problem of the modern metropolis.

The spread of the private automobile has made the operation of public transit more difficult in three ways. First, by depriving it of a substantial portion of its passengers, it has decreased its vehicle load, necessitating either higher fares or curtailment of service or both, leading to further decrease in passengers. Second, by congesting the street surface that it shares with transit vehicles, it has slowed down transit movement, thereby increasing its cost of operation and decreasing its attractiveness. Third — most fundamental and least understood — the private car has created a pattern of low-density development that can no longer be served by public transportation because it becomes impossible to assemble a sufficient payload on any one line.

Under the impact of these three factors public transit has lost ground since the end of the war. As the service offered can be curtailed only very slightly, this implies a continuing drop in the number of passengers per vehicle mile, the most important factor in economy of operation. This ratio has dropped in Canada from 7.4 passengers per vehicle mile in 1946 to 5.3 in 1960. The vicious circle of decreased riding, higher cost per rider, decreasing service, and increased fares, and resulting further decrease in riding, has clearly started. In many smaller communities in the United States and in some in Canada, this vicious circle has run its full course and led to exclusive reliance on the private automobile.

It is hardly necessary to dwell here on the many reasons that have led to the rapid and continuing growth in car ownership. However, the fact that the number of registered passenger cars in many metropolitan areas equals or surpasses the number of households does not mean that every family owns a car; moreover, different members of a household have to make different trips, and relatively few households own more than one car.

The Chicago Area Transportation Study estimates that in 1980 still 13 per cent of all "spending units" in their area, as well as in the United States, will have no car, while the proportion of families with two or more cars may increase from 10 per cent to 23 per cent. Car ownership in Canada is not likely to exceed these figures during the next 20 years. It is evident that there is continuing public interest in providing transportation for a large group of citizens who have no private car at their disposal. But, in addition, growing street congestion and shortage of parking space make it evident that any attempt to solve the urban traffic problem by the private car alone is likely to be self-defeating. To the costs of streets and parking spaces and to the time losses of public transit vehicles, pedestrians, and the private cars themselves as a result of congestion there have to be added the costs of accidents, of air pollution, and of nervous wear and tear. Finally, the private car is not an all-weather means of transportation. In heavy snow or dense fog only rail transportation on its own right-of-way, particularly in a subway, can move on schedule.

For all these reasons there has been in recent years a growing willingness to maintain and improve public transit by public action. There is, however, less clarity about the role that private and public transportation, respectively, are best suited to play.

It is not too difficult to define the role that various means of transportation are best suited to play. The decisive factor is the density in the zones of origin and of destination of the trips.

The private automobile must serve all movements within low-density areas, including travel to work in outlying factories and travel to rapid-transit and railroad stations. In addition, it must serve movements in medium-density areas in unusual directions and/or at unusual times. Finally, those people who use their cars to move about during business hours have to bring them to the downtown concentration during the day.

Public surface transportation serves most movements in medium-density areas, including feeder movements to rapid-transit and suburban railroad stations, short- and medium-length movements from medium-density areas to the high-density downtown area, and very short movements within the downtown area.

Rapid transit serves long- and some medium-distance movements within medium-density areas, most movements from medium-density areas and some from low-density areas to the downtown area, and very short movements within the downtown area.

Suburban railroad lines serve mostly the movement from the more distant low-density areas to the downtown area. These may travel directly to the downtown area or by transfer to rapid-transit lines.

If, where, and when major outlying concentrations are developed, these may also be connected with the downtown area by rapid transit or suburban railroads.

The distinction made here between "rapid transit" and "suburban railroad lines" does not necessarily refer to the operating agencies, but rather to the type of service. The former operates on headways from 90 seconds to 5 minutes, the latter generally on headways from 10 minutes to one hour.

"Medium" densities are here defined as those with residential densities between 10,000 and 25,000 persons per square mile.

Public transportation requires concentration of trips not only in space but also in time. If 1,000 persons want to travel from point A to point B during the same 5-minute period, it is obviously more rational to carry them in one train than in 700 cars, each carrying one or two persons. If the same 1,000 persons made their trips between the same two points during 200 different such periods, they would have to use their cars.

The main concentrations in time occur, of course, during the morning and evening rush hours, as a result of the journey to and from work. It is therefore not surprising to find that transit loads are increasingly concentrated at these hours while the private car has become more and more predominant for trips at other hours and on weekends. While generally not more than 20 per cent of all person-miles in private cars are made during the two morning and two evening rush hours of the five weekly workdays, about 50-60 per cent of all transit rides are concentrated during these periods. This means that structures (very expensive in case of rapid transit), vehicles, and personnel are fully used only during 20 out of the 168 weekly hours during which they have to be maintained.

In Metropolitan Toronto in 1959 about two thirds of all trips were made by private car and one third by transit. However, while only one out of five trips for social and recreational purposes was made by transit, two out of five of the trips from home to work were transit trips. Of the trips most highly concentrated in space and time, the rush-hour trips to and from the central business district transit still accounted for over 70 per cent, the same percentage as in 1929.

It is evident that private and public transportation fulfill different purposes. Movement into and out of the center is best served by transit and within the center by walking. However, private cars cannot be completely barred from the center, because many of the people working there need them for their work. Probably the only feasible way to limit their number is rationing by price, by raising fees for parking, in particular all-day parking, in the central business district well above the price for parking at outlying stations of rapid transit and suburban railroad lines. The remaining road traffic should interfere as little as possible with pedestrian movement. This can be achieved to some extent by creating "pedestrian islands" as has been done on a temporary basis in Ottawa and in a number of small American towns, and permanently in some European cities, notably Rotterdam and Coventry. Complete elimination of the conflict between vehicular and pedestrian traffic by creation of a second, upper level has been proposed for Fort Worth, Texas, but has so far not been implemented. However, in a small part of the center such a scheme has been successfully carried out in Stockholm and another one is planned in Philadelphia.

Decisive for the potential of public transit to attract riders is, in addition to speed (including headways), comfort, and price, the connection between the stations or stops and the points of ultimate origin and destination of its passengers. The great attraction of the private car is its ability to provide door-to-door service. Public transportation must always rely on some second means to assemble and distribute its riders. These means are walking, driving a private car to and from a parking facility at a station, and riding other transit vehicles and transferring. In the central business districts of big cities large numbers of passengers, sufficient to support rapid-transit trains at frequent headways, can be assembled and distributed by a combination of walking and the use of elevators, a means of public transportation that is usually not considered as such. In areas of medium densities a sufficient number of passengers can be assembled by walking to support surface transportation by streetcar or bus, and by combination of transfer from surface lines and walking, rapid-transit stations can be fed. However, this necessitates relatively close spacing of transit stations, resulting in a relatively low traveling speed. It is therefore hardly feasible to extend rapid-transit lines of this type far out into the peripheral low-density areas, because total traveling time would become too long to be competitive with private automobiles. Also, the loads that can be assembled in these outer areas are too small to justify use of the long and frequent trains that are required on the inner sections of a rapid-transit system. These outer areas can be better served by a different system with widely spaced stations, relying for the assembling of its passengers largely on the private automobile, the "park-and-ride" or "kiss-and-ride" method.

As stated, traffic to and from the center has leveled off, and traffic within the inner ring of medium density is also not increasing. As places of employment disperse, a greater proportion of work trips from these areas is bound to go to dispersed destinations. All future growth of residential population will necessarily occur in the outer rings. If it continues to take place, as it has during the past 10 years, at densities averaging about four to five households per acre of residential neighborhood, it will be impossible to provide it with public transportation even in the main direction toward the center. However, this type of development is by no means entirely the result of consumer preference but largely of public policy. The Central Mortgage and Housing Corporation in Canada and the Federal Housing Authority in the United States have encouraged home ownership of detached houses on large lots; municipalities have excluded more intensive development by zoning. As the effects of these policies are becoming evident, they are beginning to change, and some increase of residential densities in the outer zones may be expected. Even so, it is inevitable that the proportion of all trips that are made by private automobile will continue to increase because of the increasing dispersal of destinations for employment, shopping, and recreation. Peripheral, "ring," or "bypass" expressways are required to handle the increasing number of trips to these destinations. While these movements originate and terminate in a multitude of thin streams, they collect for a major part of their way in a mighty flow.

It is more questionable whether radial expressways are desirable, because they tend to pour more cars into the overloaded streets and parking facilities of the center. On the other hand, they serve a very useful purpose for trucks, for the considerable number of cars that are needed for use during the working day by persons employed in the central business district and for trips outside of rush hours. However, they should terminate not in the central business district but in an inner ring that also serves to bypass the center, and this ring should be fairly large to permit the location of a sufficient number of interchanges spaced widely enough apart to allow for weaving, acceleration, and deceleration.

COST AND BENEFITS OF PUBLIC AND PRIVATE TRANSPORTATION

Both private and public transportation require substantial investments and large operating cost, and these have to be weighed in assessing their respective roles.

According to the Gordon Commission of Canada, the total cost of a passenger car mile averaged 10.5 cents. If a transit fare of 15 cents is assumed, this indicates that driving a car without passengers is cheaper for distances up to 1½ mile;

with 1, 2, or 3 passengers, up to 3, 4½, and 6 miles, respectively. It is therefore evident that in a considerable number of cases it is cheaper for the individual to drive than to ride, even if he figured the total cost. However, about three fourths of the cost of operating an automobile consists of more or less fixed costs; and, in practice the driver counts only the "out of pocket" cost of operation which averages 2.8 cents per mile. So, except when he has to pay for parking, from the point of view of the individual car owner it is always cheaper to drive.

On the other hand, one bus lane carries during a peak hour 5 times, one streetcar track 10 times, and one rapid-transit track up to 50 times as many persons as an ordinary street lane. About 12 expressway lanes would be required to carry the volume of passengers now carried during peak hours by the Toronto subway. Transit vehicles travel 2½ to 5 times more miles annually than passenger cars. While a private automobile performs about 15,000 person-miles annually, a bus (excluding interurban) averages over 500,000, a streetcar over 800,000, and a subway car about one and a half million person-miles annually. Thus, despite its underuse during all but the 20 peak hours of the week, one subway car performs as many person-miles as 100 passenger cars—and requires no parking space.

A considerable distortion of the comparative cost of private and public transportation results from the fact that frequently the driver does not have to pay the full cost of parking. This occurs not only if he can park on the street or if public off-street parking is provided at less than full cost (including taxes), but also where a firm provides free employee parking. For the firm the cost of such parking, which may range from ten cents to two dollars per employee workday, is a tax-deductible business expense. For the employee, it is actually a payment in kind, which, however, is not considered part of his income, as a reimbursement of his transit fare by his employer would be. It may be worth considering a change in the federal income tax law that would disallow employee parking as a deductible business expense. This would force employers to make employee parking self-supporting and thereby face the employee with a rational choice between the cost of using public transportation and the full cost of using his private car. One desirable result of such a change certainly would be increased car pooling.

It is evident that today the market does not allocate resources in the most rational way to private and public transportation, respectively. As indicated, the greater part of the cost of operating an automobile consists of fixed costs. If public transportation is to compete with the private car, a substantial portion of its cost will also have to be transformed into fixed costs. The only practical way of doing this is by covering them out of general tax revenues. It might be objected that it is unfair to ask the auto driver to pay for a service that he does not use. However, he benefits from the fact that the transit rider, by leaving his car at home, frees the street for the driver.

Support of public transit out of tax revenues underwrites a deficit (obviously an undesirable procedure), or it assumes responsibilities for all or part of the capital cost (in particular of rapid-transit lines), while the operating agency must cover the operating cost out of user charges. This militates against a rational weighing of capital versus operating costs and may lead to a curtailment of surface feeder lines that frequently can only be run at an operating loss and to subsequent under-utilization of the rapid-transit lines and of the capital invested in them. The only sound procedure is for the municipality to pay in accordance with the service performed, that is, per passenger-mile or per seat-mile. This method has now been adopted by the state of New Jersey for subsidizing suburban railroad service.

A strong case could be made for operating public transit as a public service free of charge. This would permit considerably faster loading of buses, resulting in greater speed and consequent economies of operation. There is a precedent for this in vertical public transportation. The entire cost of elevator service in office and apartment buildings is always assessed as a "fixed cost" as part of the rent, regardless of the amount of use of the service by the various tenants.

NEW TECHNOLOGY

It is not likely that some technological breakthrough will reverse the trend from public to private transportation or will make private transportation more adaptable to use in areas of concentrated activity. A moderate increase in street capacity can be achieved by an electronically operated system of traffic lights, such as is now being tested in Toronto. A system of electronic controls of car driving, presently under development by General Motors, could greatly increase the capacity of expressways but, by doing so, would only increase the pressure on urban streets, as soon as these cars leave the expressway and return to manual operation. Similarly, hovercraft may become useful for long-distance travel, but will hardly have the flexibility required for movement in city traffic. Possibly, waterways might regain a role for the movement of persons within metropolitan areas by the use of hovercraft or of hydrofoil. Helicopters may perform some service in medium-distance travel, but both the space that they require and the noise they produce militate against their use for urban mass transportation.

The widely discussed monorail does not differ substantially from traditional two-track rapid transit. The suspended version permits a slight reduction in weight of a supporting elevated structure, in the vertical distance between sidewalk and platform, and in the radius of curves. But these minor advantages are more than offset by two major flaws: first, commitment to a costly elevated structure everywhere, even where the situation makes it possible to locate the rails in a cut, on an embankment, or at grade; second, extreme difficulty of switching operations. Both flaws are particularly objectionable in yards. Except for the switching problem, it makes little difference whether a car is supported on one or on two rails. The much advertised differences in construction cost refer to the differences between a subway and an elevated structure. The objections to elevated structures in residential or commercial areas are well known. They are acceptable only if they are at least 100 feet away from windows. This implies a distance of about 250 feet between building lines, which is rarely to be found. However, where such width is available, it is possible, and of course preferable, to locate a rapid-transit line in an open cut. Therefore elevated rapid-transit structures, whether for monorail or for two-rail, are likely to be built only on those sections of a line which traverse industrial or warehouse areas.

Technical improvements in transit facilities, important as they are, cannot entirely overcome the severe handicap of competition with the speed of the private automobile because of the need to stop fairly frequently to load and unload passengers. This could be overcome only by providing auxiliary "pickup and delivery" vehicles that could hook on to a moving train and interchange passengers with it while moving. Interestingly, such a proposal was developed almost 100 years ago for the New York elevated system. I have suggested to the Washington National Capital Transportation Agency a study of the possibility of transferring passengers between moving buses and trains of the suburban railroad type of rapid-transit system that they are contemplating. It would, however, still be necessary to have some outlying stations for transfer between private cars and trains, as well as stations in the central area.

So far in this discussion we have dealt with traffic as a function of land use, assuming the distribution of land uses as given. Studies undertaken during the past 15 years, primarily the origin and destination studies initiated by the U.S. Bureau of Public Roads, have shown that it is indeed possible to predict within acceptable error limits, the distribution of trips between places of residence, employment, shopping, etc. Several fairly sophisticated traffic studies, using electronic computers to simulate future traffic flows, are presently under way.

INTERRELATION OF TRAFFIC AND LAND USE

In these studies an assumed future distribution of land use has been treated as an independent variable, and traffic as the dependent variable. However, while it is true that traffic is a function of land use, it is equally true that land use is a function of traffic. Any change in traffic facilities changes the relative accessibility and hence the relative attraction for various land uses of every piece of land in a given area. Therefore, it is equally valid to treat traffic facilities as an independent variable and land uses as a dependent variable. The great difficulty facing any attempt to construct on this basis land-use models that would simulate the behavior of people, locating their residences and business establishments, lies in the fact that such behavior is determined by many other independent variables in addition to accessibility.

The role of the transportation system in determining the specific shape of a metropolitan area depends primarily on the difference in speed between various modes of transportation used by its population. Where the difference is very great, as between 30 miles per hour for traveling on a suburban railroad and 3 miles per hour for walking to and from the station, a pattern of isolated dots develops. With streetcars, where the speed is less and stations are closer together, the dots merge into ribbons. But whenever a means of individual transportation predominates, whether it be walking, bicycling, or car driving, and consequently trips proceed from door to door in any direction at fairly uniform speeds, dots and ribbons merge into a "sprawling" mass, differentiated only by the gradual decrease of densities from the center to the periphery.

It is therefore not realistic to believe that under today's conditions in Canada transportation planning can "prevent sprawl," as some planners hope. If we want to bring about a pattern of land uses that will decrease the need for ever more and ever longer trips and relieve the resultant congestion, a combination of other planning measures will have to be used: limitation of private development by zoning and subdivision controls, and its stimulation by public works, notably water and sewer facilities, but possibly also publicly sponsored residential, industrial, and commercial development. Consistently applied, such measures may result in a better balance between the resident labor force and jobs, in densities sufficient to support bus services, and in well-developed outlying centers — secondary downtowns, as I have called them — within reasonable distance of any part of the metropolitan area. This could alleviate the traffic problem, but it will not "solve" it. There will still be plenty of work to do for our traffic engineers.

12

Transportation in San Francisco

At the time of the Gold Rush, when the enterprising citizens of this community succeeded in establishing San Francisco on the wrong side of the Bay, separated from its natural hinterland and expansion area, they created for their successors the most exciting and beautiful city on the North American continent — and its most monumental traffic problem. The two are not unrelated. Because San Francisco is contained on three sides by the waters of the Pacific and on the fourth by the hilly neck of a narrow peninsula, it grew up in the concentrated form and at the relatively high density that has given it the strongly urban and urbane flavor that is generally only found in the great historic capitals, such as Paris or London.

All other American cities that have grown up as contemporaries of San Francisco have used the ease of movement provided by modern means of transportation to spread out farther and more thinly. This is indicative of the effect of transportation on the distribution of population, employment, and land use. We think of improvements of transportation as a means of saving time, and we measure their benefits in those terms. But, actually, everyone who makes a decision on location of residence or of business is engaged in a trade-off between minimizing time or maximizing space, and so is every community in deciding on a transportation policy. If the benefit is taken out entirely in more space, it will be no easier to get around after the improvement has been made than it was before. Only if this is not the case, will increased speed mean increased mutual accessibility and thereby widen the freedom of choice, which is the basic reason why people congregate in cities in the first place—freedom of choice between the place where one lives and the places where one goes for work, business, shopping, education, recreation, culture, and social contacts. There is considerable evidence that the time spent by people on their trips to work and for other purposes remains fairly constant, on the average, but that the range of opportunities of which they can and do avail themselves increases with increasing travel speed. The ultimate benefit and criterion of a good transportation system is not saving of time but enrichment of choice, not how fast you get there but what you can find at the end of a trip of a given length. Transportation planning and city planning are not two different things but two sides of the same coin.

When we talk of the length of a trip in terms of time, as well as of its cost in terms of money or inconvenience, it is important to remember that what matters is the entire length of the trip from door to door. Most trips in urban areas use a combination of means: individual transportation by walking or driving, collective transportation by riding transit vehicles or elevators.

In every big metropolis a battle royal is raging between the advocates of a rapid-transit system and the partisans of a freeway system, and great emphasis is put on the speed and the capacity of rapid-transit lines and of freeways. But neither rapid-transit lines nor freeways constitute a system. Neither can carry persons or goods from door to door. Given the money, anyone can build a rapid-transit line or a freeway and hire competent engineers to build it well. The problem is: how do you get to it from where you are, and from it to where you want to go? A transit system is no better than the feeder system that brings people to and from the stations, and a road system is no better than the interchanges, streets, parking and loading spaces to which the cars and trucks must get from the freeway. There is no point in increasing the speed and capacity of the trunk lines beyond the capacity of the other elements of the system.

If one thinks in terms of a transit system and a road system, it is not difficult to define the role that each can play best. If you go back to your home in one suburb from a party in another suburb at two in the morning, you cannot expect a bus or train but have to drive your car. But when a thousand people want to go from point A to point B in the same five minutes, it is obviously more sensible to carry them in one train than to have a thousand cars compete for street and parking space. High density requires transit, and transit makes high density possible. Low density requires individual car driving, and universal use of the car requires low density.

The greatest concentration in space and time occurs, of course, in travel to and from the central business district during the morning and evening peak hours. Therefore a rapid-transit system logically consists of radial lines from the center to the periphery. Freeways should basically constitute a large-scale grid to carry movements in all directions between all other less intensely developed parts of the metropolitan area. The volume of these movements is rapidly growing, as not only residences but all other activities multiply in the peripheral areas, while the number of people working in and coming to the central business district remains fairly constant, in San Francisco as in all other big cities in North America. This does not mean that these centers are dying, but that they are specializing increasingly in those functions for which they are best suited: those dealing with people and requiring contact between people. Those dealing with goods, manufacturing and warehousing, and also some types of retailing, move out. Because contact is the lifeblood of the city center, concentration and ease of pedestrian movement are its most essential requirements.

It is certainly true that good access for vehicles is also essential for the center. But it does not follow that all vehicles that go there are essential. The space required for parking a car is at least equal to the amount of space occupied by a person working. If all those employed in the central city would insist on going to work in their own cars, half of the floor space would be required for parking garages, not counting those required for the really essential short-term parking for business, shopping, etc. The essential concentration would be diluted, pedestrian movement impeded and delayed, the streets and the expressway exits and entrances completely congested. The number of these interchanges is necessarily limited by the weaving distances; and the more the freeways are improved in terms of speed and number of lanes, the greater are the weaving distances required.

It is quite unrealistic to attempt to dimension freeways on the basis of potential peak hour travel demand in the central city. A computer simulation made in Montreal on this basis showed that in 1980 every freeway link within six miles from the center would have to have from 14 to 22 lanes. Urban freeways, unlike interurban freeways, should be designed for off-peak loads. As they always will be filled to capacity during most hours of the day, they might as well be designed for the speed that maximizes their capacity, 35-40 miles per hour.

The problem consists in reserving central city freeways for the essential traffic — trucks, buses, taxis, and cars used for business and shopping — and to induce the all-day worker to use public transportation. When demand greatly exceeds supply, it must be rationed in some way. We now ration it by congestion — first come, first served. It would be far better to ration it by price: by making all-day parking downtown very expensive, while providing short-term parking at reasonable cost.

This is only one side of the equation. The other one is to make transit sufficiently attractive to compete with the door-to-door service of the private automobile. In this competition rapid transit normally faces two serious handicaps: most people have to make a detour to get to the rapid-transit line and find they can reach their destination faster by more direct routes, even if they move slower; and, in order to shorten the approach to the station, stations must be spaced so closely that the advantage of rapid-transit speed cannot be fully utilized.

In San Francisco's particular situation, these two handicaps do not exist for approaches to downtown from the east and from the north. There is no choice of more direct routes across the Bay or the Golden Gate; everyone has to detour to reach the bridges, which inevitably will be congested and slow at peak hours. On the other hand, rapid-transit lines can take full advantage of their speed on sections several miles long without intervening stops. You have therefore very wisely given first priority to a rapid-transit crossing of the Bay.

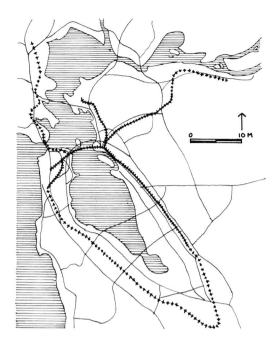

*The highway net-
work and the rail
rapid-transit system,
authorized and pro-
posed.*

Figure 1
The San Francisco
Bay Area.

Demand from the north, from Marin County, is much smaller
than from the east, but basically the situation is the same:
rapid transit can provide much faster access to central San
Francisco than can be provided by any feasible road system.
In addition, it could carry three times as many persons as an
eight-lane freeway and would not disrupt the most intensely
developed part of your beautiful city. There is no doubt in my
mind that a rapid-transit crossing of the Golden Gate should
have priority over a second road crossing.

I am aware, of course, that it had to be deferred because of
its high cost. The cost of a second road crossing, however,
would be at least twice as high; and such a crossing could be
deferred for a very long time, perhaps forever, if a rapid-transit
crossing would relieve the Golden Gate Bridge of the burden
of the peak-hour load.

It is sometimes objected that a bridge would pay for itself,
while a rapid-transit line would not. The calculation is faulty
on both sides. The real cost of a ride downtown is the cost of
the entire trip, which is by no means fully paid for by the
driver's bridge toll, gasoline tax, and parking fee. William
Vickrey of Columbia University, a leader in the field of public-

utility economics, has calculated that a capital investment of $25,000 is required to enable one additional commuter car to come to downtown Washington, D.C. It is not likely to be less in San Francisco.

On the other hand, the benefit of a transit system accrues not only to the rider. The tests of various transportation systems that we have made by computer simulation in Metropolitan Toronto showed that improved transit saved about as much time to the car drivers as to the transit riders. Public transit is a public service and should be financed as such. Actually, the best cost-benefit ratio would be achieved if transit service were free to the user. This principle is, at present, not acceptable to the public when applied to horizontal collective transportation, although everybody accepts it as a matter of course when applied to vertical collective transportation by elevators.

The rapid-transit system that you are building here is different from those operating or under construction in Toronto and Montreal and most other cities. These are city subways, serving medium-density areas. They are characterized by large volumes of riders, riding for relatively short distances. They assemble these, mainly by surface transit, at stations spaced generally about half a mile apart, resulting in a travel speed of no more than 20 miles per hour. This speed is too slow to compete with the private automobile in long journeys from the expanding outer suburbs. Here a different system, really an efficient modern suburban railroad, is required — with lower volumes, higher speed, greater comfort, and more widely spaced stations, relying on feeding primarily by private automobile. We are now studying in Toronto the feasibility of such a second system. You are building this second system first, rightly, under your specific local conditions.

Ideally, the two systems should have a combined right of way with two local and two express tracks, the latter extending much farther out than the former. You are approaching this on the Market Street section of the BARTD* system. There remains the task of developing within the city an efficient feeder service to the two lines planned by BARTD and of improved transit service for the parts of the city not served by these two lines. After all, over 70 per cent of all downtown

*Bay Area Rapid Transit District

workers live in San Francisco. It is too easily forgotten that short trips constitute the overwhelming majority of all trips.

This is as true of those made by automobiles, and also by trucks, as those made by transit. I know from my own experience in designing freeway networks that there is an irresistible temptation to draw lines connecting major gateways; and it is most natural to think of a freeway connection between the Bay and Golden Gate Bridges. But actually less than 2 per cent of the vehicles crossing the Bay Bridge cross the Golden Gate. It is hardly justified to build a freeway to carry less than 2,000 vehicles a day.

The real need is to carry vehicles from the Golden Gate Bridge and the northwestern parts of the city to the central area. I am not entirely convinced that this need can only be served by an eight-lane freeway. I have had the opportunity to study the highly competent and imaginative proposals contained in the reports on the Golden Gate and Panhandle freeways. They wrestle with the interrelated two Hobson's choices that one has to face in the design of any urban freeway, but that are particularly difficult in a city as beautiful and as intensely urban as San Francisco: the choice between destroying a residential area or destroying a park, and the choice between ruining the view of the freeway or ruining the view from the freeway. I have also noted with great interest that some proposals use an approach that is far too rarely considered, that of choosing different locations for the two directions. These are, in fact, two one-way streets, and there is no compelling reason to combine them. Separating them can improve the view both of the freeway and from the freeway and greatly simplifies the problem of connection with the surface street system, which is really the most critical one in the design of urban freeways.

Our attempts to deal rationally with the transportation problem are, in this area as elsewhere, bedeviled by institutional arrangements that were devised to answer needs entirely different from those of the present and future. Decision-making is splintered not only horizontally between a multitude of municipalities but also vertically between separate agencies dealing with separate functions of transportation, such as bridges, freeways, streets, parking, rapid transit, and local transit. Particularly serious is the complete distortion of any rational weighing of costs versus benefits by the fact that financial contributions from the higher levels of government are available for some elements of the total transportation system but not for others.

You are now well on your way to gaining a comprehensive view of the Bay Area's transportation problem through BATS.* However, BATS will not be able to deal with the many and intimate interrelationships between redevelopment planning and transportation within the city of San Francisco. It seems to me that you need a high-level body that can base its decision on weighing the benefits of increased freedom of choice between destinations, provided by transportation improvement, against the benefits of preserving and enhancing the attractiveness of the destinations from which your citizens and visitors can choose.

My students at the University of Toronto, when they become confused by all the difficulties of learning to be planners, sometimes ask me to tell them the most important thing for a planner to know. I reply that the most important thing is to know when to jump from the frying pan of inconclusive research into the fire of arbitrary decision. I, coming here from the outside, cannot offer you a specific recipe, but I thank you nevertheless for listening to me today.

*Bay Area Transportation Study

13

Montreal's Subway

The Montreal subway, now under construction and scheduled for completion in 1966, takes in many ways an original approach which may be illustrated by a comparison with Canada's only existing subway. Toronto now operates the world's biggest subway cars, 10 feet two inches wide, 74 feet 6 inches long, and seating 84 passengers. Montreal uses unusually small cars, only 8 feet 3 inches wide, 52 feet long, and seating 40 persons. Toronto trains are six cars long, Montreal trains consist of three groups of three cars each, the middle one of each being a "trailer" so that the length of the train is about the same. However, a Toronto train provides 504 seats, against 360 in Montreal, and slightly more standing room, so that it can carry, without excessive crowding, at 3 square feet per standee, about 1,300 passengers, compared to about 1,115 in Montreal. However, Toronto trains, running on steel wheels and requiring longer braking distance, cannot be safely run at headways of less than two minutes (though London's steel-wheeled subway operates at tighter headways). Montreal's rubber-wheeled trains, with their shorter braking distance, can safely operate at 90-second headways. They could thus carry 44,600 passengers per hour compared to Toronto's 39,000.

It should be noted, however, that the shorter the headway, the more difficult is exact observance of schedules and the greater the danger of cumulative overloading of some trains.

The ability to bring a train to a dead stop over a shorter distance was an even more important consideration for the adoption of rubber wheels than the obvious one of reduction of noise. Other operating advantages are the ability of rubber-wheeled vehicles to climb steeper grades (up to 6 per cent) and the ability of short cars to make curves of short radius. These two factors permit greater flexibility of alignment, both horizontally and vertically, which has made it possible to locate the tunnels in rock for most of their length. The narrow cross section of the cars has made it possible to locate both tracks in a tunnel only 23 feet wide and 16 feet 3 inches high at the center. By applying tunneling techniques developed in mining, it has been possible to reduce the cost of the tunnels to one half of those in Toronto, where, in the predominant soft soils, a wide concrete box, built in open cut, has been generally employed, or, in a few cases, two parallel tunnels.

Partly offsetting this substantial saving in construction cost are higher capital and maintenance costs of rolling stock, as well as slightly higher operating costs, because 35 Montreal trains are required to carry the 39,000 passengers per hour that can be carried by 30 Toronto trains (assuming comfortable standing room in both cases). A Toronto car has 8 wheels, a Montreal car 24. The Montreal car has, first, a set of steel wheels, because steel rails are required for safety in case of a blowout and for guidance, especially on switches in yards; second, 8 rubber-tired wheels, on which the train normally runs; and finally, 8 small horizontal rubber-tired wheels, running against vertical guides. It is probable because of their unorthodox type that Montreal cars cost $122,000, while the larger Toronto cars cost only $110,000. Thus, a Montreal train costs $1,098,000, compared to $660,000 for a Toronto train, and trains required to carry 39,000 passengers per hour cost $38,430,000 in Montreal and $19,800,000 in Toronto. Also 16.7 per cent more motors, 74 per cent more doors, and three and a half times as many wheels have to be maintained in Montreal as in Toronto.

However, in Montreal, where construction costs can be reduced by taking advantage of the rock, which is close to the surface in most parts of the island, the choice of this particular system is certainly well justified.

The technical characteristics of the system form the basis of the station design. The cross section of a station is conditioned by two factors, location of tracks and method of construction. The resulting basic types are presented in Figures 1 through 8. These are schematic; no existing station conforms exactly to any of them. Either the tracks are in the center (Figs. 1-4) and are served by two side platforms, or they are on the sides and are served by one center platform (Figs. 5-8). The station can be built either by tunneling (Figs. 2, 4, 6, 8) or by construction in an open cut (Figs. 1, 3, 5, 7). Side platforms require a mezzanine in order to provide access to both side platforms. Mezzanines are generally also located over center platforms in order to provide access close to the middle of the platform. Mezzanines have to be located at an intermediate level between street level and track level; and as it is desirable to minimize the vertical distance between street and platform, they are usually as low as possible.

The resulting spatial arrangements are generally rather confusing and visually unsatisfactory (see Figs. 3-6). The connections between the street or vestibule at street level, the mezzanine, and the station tunnel are not clear, and low ceilings and narrow halls produce a cramped feeling.

In most subway systems these basic spatial arrangements have been decided by various technical considerations, and architects have been called in only after these have been made. Montreal decided to make each station a distinct and different work of architecture and involved the architect of each station in its basic design from the start. The only precedent for this approach was in Moscow. Both cities also avoided, as a matter of principle, the unsatisfactory location of entrances and exits on crowded sidewalks by providing vestibules at street level, either in separate pavilions or, preferably, on the ground floors of larger buildings.

However, different conditions have led to quite different approaches in these two cities. For a number of reasons, Moscow had decided to locate its subway in tubes deep underground; with large cars and very poor soil conditions, this led to two parallel tubes and center platforms. A center platform

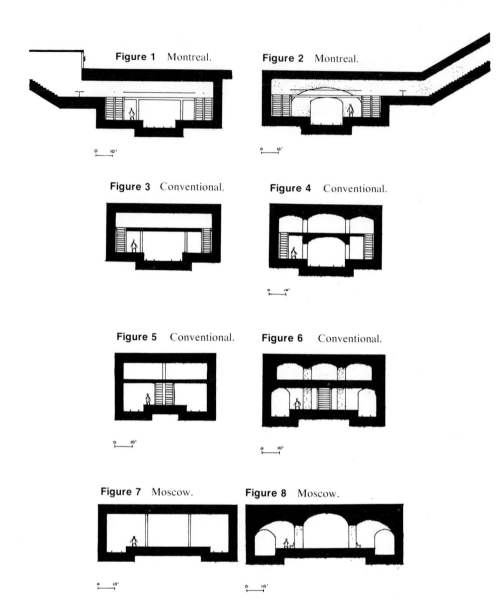

Figure 1 Montreal.

Figure 2 Montreal.

Figure 3 Conventional.

Figure 4 Conventional.

Figure 5 Conventional.

Figure 6 Conventional.

Figure 7 Moscow.

Figure 8 Moscow.

has the great advantage of relegating the tracks to the sides and providing a wide unified space for people at the center. In the conventional arrangement (Figs. 5 and 6) this advantage is not developed, because the center space is cluttered up with columns and, worse, with stairs leading to the mezzanine. The Moscow architects made the most of their opportunity. By locating stairs and escalators only at the end of the platform,

150　TRANSPORTATION

they created an uncluttered central nave, over 500 feet long and up to 25 feet wide and 20 feet high. With the regular rhythm of arches or columns, this results always in a magnificent space, however overornate or gaudy the details may be (Fig. 8). The same basic form, only lighter and more open, was also used in the few cases where stations were built in open cut (Fig. 7). Once one accepts the slight inconvenience of a long distance between the end cars and the foot of the escalator, as the Moscow builders did, one can dispense entirely with a mezzanine, wherever the subway is located off-street and the vestibule can be located directly over the line; the narrow inclined space of the escalators is then a direct and clear mediating link between the two large halls, the vestibule and the central nave.

In Montreal most stations are also in tunnels. However, the location of both tracks in a single tunnel precluded a center platform. Normally, side platforms are connected by a mezzanine, resulting in a low ceiling over the platforms. The Montreal builders found a basic solution to this difficulty, applied in various ways in most stations, by replacing the closed and isolated mezzanine by an open *passerelle*, or bridge, located, where possible, midway between the two ends of the station. Over this bridge the ceiling is raised by a barrel vault, which intersects with the long lower barrel vault at a right angle. From one end of the bridge the escalators and stairs lead to the vestibule, which had to be located to one side because the tracks always have been located under a street (Fig. 2).

Where stations have been built in an open cut, closed mezzanines have also been replaced by open bridges wherever possible. Ideally, the entire excavated space is left open, from the tracks to the ceiling supporting the pavement, and it is widened to accommodate the stairs leading from the platforms to the bridge (Fig. 1).

This basic theme allows for many variations in the way the flow from the vestibule to the platforms, with its changes of direction, is articulated. It is worth noting that in one important aspect the Montreal approach is opposite to the one adopted in Moscow. While both achieve clearly articulated spaces, Moscow created "underground palaces" in which the tracks and trains are almost hidden from view. In Montreal the "view from the bridge" makes these basic functional elements even more visible than they are in the conventional subway station.

THE SUBWAY IN THE CITY The variations on the theme are derived largely from the specific requirements of each individual station. Differences result from different depths below street level, from accommodation to existing buildings and underground utilities, but primarily from different relations to points of access for pedestrians and for transfer to and from buses or other subway lines.

In the general alignment Montreal also differs from the conventional method of locating subway lines under main arteries. The conventional method has the great disadvantage of interrupting traffic on these main arteries during construction, with adverse effects on the adjacent uses, which in some cases, such as South Broad Street in Philadelphia, have lasted for many years. Therefore, Toronto has chosen locations parallel to the arteries, generally in mid-block, about 200 feet behind the main frontages.

Montreal has taken advantage of its characteristic long and narrow blocks—a heritage from the strip fields of the original settlers—to locate the main north-south section of its most important line (Line No. 2) under secondary streets (Berry and de la Jeunesse) midway between two important arteries, St. Denis and St. Hubert, thus providing easy access to both of them. This also provides, as in Toronto, opportunity to locate sheltered bus-loading platforms at the stations, away from the main stream of traffic.

The east-west line (Line No. 1) has also been located not under St. Catherine's Street, as originally planned, but one block farther north, under Ontario and Burnside Streets. Since Burnside Street is being rebuilt, this location permits extensive redevelopment related to the subway stations. It also provides direct access to the rear of the big department stores, all of which are located on the north side of St. Catherine's Street. Finally, it provides better access from the stations to Sherbrooke Street, to the north, than would have been available from St. Catherine's Street.

A similar approach has been taken in the alignment of the southern section of Line No. 2, which makes a right-angle turn to the west toward Victoria and Dominion Squares. Originally it had been intended to locate this section directly

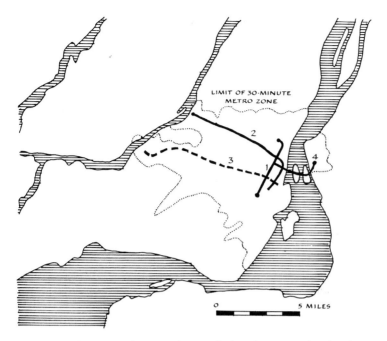

Figure 9 *The Montreal Metro, showing the lines being completed and Line 3, a future extension.*

under St. James Street. Now it will run 800 feet to the north and in a valley 50 feet below the level of the James Street, under Vitré Street, which also is being reconstructed and redeveloped. Stations are to be connected to St. James Street by galleries that will cross the valley, including Craig Street, on columns, and St. James Street as an underground passage. Thus, these galleries will also serve as grade-separated and weather-protected pedestrian crossings of heavily traveled Craig and St. James Streets. Location on Vitré Street also brings the stations within easy walking distance of the important artery of Dorchester Street.

Location of stations away from great arteries and, in two important sections, on streets scheduled for reconstruction has made it possible to acquire sizable areas around most stations and to devise plans for their redevelopment for the more intensive use that a subway station tends to attract. Thus the Montreal subway, both in its stations and in the projects stimulated by them, presents significant challenges to Canadian architecture.

Table 1.   Comparison between the Montreal and Toronto Subways

	Montreal	Toronto
Car Size		
Length	52' 0"	74' 6"
Width	8' 3"	10' 2"
Train Length		
No. of Cars	9	6
Length	468'	447
Passengers Sitting		
Per Car	40	84
Per Train	360	504
Passengers Standing		
Per Car	84	133
Per Train	755	796
Total Passengers per Train		
Standing	360	504
Sitting	755	796
Total	1,115	1,300
Headway between Trains	1½ Minutes	2 Minutes
Trains per Hour	40	30
Passengers per Hour	44,600	39,000
Cost		
Per Car	$122,000.00	$110,000.00
Per Train	$1,098,000.00	$660,000.00
Cost of Trains to Carry 39,000 People per Hour	$38,430,000.00	$19,800,000.00
Other Factors		
Number of Motors	16.7% more	....
Number of Doors	74% more	....
Number of Wheels	3½ times as many	....

14

Monorail for Toronto?

The main reason for the present interest in monorails is the desire to find a cheaper substitute for subways. Construction costs of subways are much higher than those of elevated structures for rapid transit. All presently proposed monorail installations are on elevated structures.

SUBWAY VERSUS ELEVATED

Elevated railroads preceded subways on the North American continent. The old cumbersome and rattling steel structures of the New York and Chicago "els" have discredited this type of structure. It is, however, perfectly possible with modern techniques to minimize both the unsightliness and the noise of elevated railroads. These techniques are equally applicable to conventional two-rail and monorail installations. In the further extension of the Toronto rapid-transit system serious consideration should be given to the use of elevated structures in suitable locations.

However, it should not be overlooked that subways and elevated structures are not the only alternatives for the location of rapid-transit lines. It is possible to achieve lower construction costs by location at grade, on fill, or in cut. This method has been successfully employed on sections of the Yonge Street line and is proposed for the entire length of the Spadina line north of Dupont Street. However, the cost estimates for this line have shown that the savings in comparison to subway construction are not as great as expected. This is due to the fact that a very substantial part of the construction cost is represented by items that are not affected by location:

rails, power supply, signaling system, station equipment, storage yards, and maintenance facilities.

Nevertheless, it remains highly desirable to reduce capital cost of rapid transit by finding locations other than subways. The question arises: under what conditions are elevated railroads preferable to construction either in subways or in open cut?

Even with modern construction methods, elevated structures, whether for monorail or conventional two rails, obstruct vision and light on the street, especially at stations, and also produce some noise. They will not be generally acceptable at distances of less than 80 or 90 feet from windows of residential, office, or retail premises and will therefore be acceptable only on streets with a width of about 200 feet or more between the building lines. On such wide streets, or boulevards, it is equally feasible to locate a cut in the center of the street. A width of 80 feet would be sufficient for both tracks and stations and would leave 60 feet for two one-way streets on either side of the cut, sufficient for up to four lanes and an ample sidewalk. Building in a cut would be considerably cheaper than any elevated structure, monorail or other, and would completely eliminate the sight and practically eliminate the noise of the trains.

Location on an elevated structure would be acceptable on narrower streets, or on off-street rights of way, where these are flanked by industrial buildings or warehouses. However, since such areas generate relatively few passengers, they are not generally suitable for the location of rapid-transit facilities.

It must be concluded that elevated structures for rapid transit are advisable only in exceptional cases for relatively short sections of any lines. No such section has been found on any of the alignments studied to date for the Toronto rapid-transit system.

SUSPENDED VERSUS SUPPORTED   While all presently proposed monorails are elevated railroads, they fall into two radically different categories, suspended and supported.

In the suspended type the rails are located above the cars, which hang from the wheels. Most present proposals employ "split rails," that is, two rails located close together rather than a true monorail.

The advantages of suspended over supported railroads are:

1. Sharper curves or, conversely, higher speeds in curves of the same radius.
2. Smaller vertical distance between sidewalk and train platform.
3. Greater vertical distance of rails, the main source of noise, from street level.
4. Somewhat lighter supporting beams because of lower lateral stresses.

The disadvantages are:

1. Commitment to costly elevated structures everywhere, including service yards where circumstances would permit more economical location at grade, in cut, or on fill.
2. Higher and therefore costlier supporting columns.
3. Where the location is underground, higher and therefore costlier tunnels.
4. Extremely complicated, costly, and time-consuming operations for switching.
5. Difficulty of access to tracks for inspection and maintenance.

In the supported type the rails are under the cars, as in conventional railroads. In genuine supported monorails the wheels are arranged in tandem, as in a bicycle; therefore, the cars must be held in position by some special device; either a gyroscope or horizontal guide wheels running on vertical guide boards (actually additional rails).

Presently proposed types are not genuine monorails, but they employ two wheels spaced closely together. Many of them are of the "saddle" type, with the car floor lower than the top of the wheels. This arrangement somewhat increases stability by lowering the center of gravity in relation to the rails and also slightly decreases the vertical distance between the sidewalk and station platforms, but it leads to a very awkward and uneconomic car design, the center being obstructed by the boxes shielding the wheels. The latest designs (in Seattle) have, therefore, relinquished the "saddle" type and locate the body of the car above the wheels. The only inherent difference between this type of monorail and a standard-gauge elevated railroad is the smaller lateral distance between the wheels, which results in a narrower but higher and bulkier shape of the beam that supports the rail.

RUBBER VERSUS STEEL WHEELS   Practically all present proposals for monorail are designed for rubber wheels, while most standard-gauge rapid-transit lines employ steel wheels. There is no inherent correlation whatsoever between these two aspects. The only existing monorail system, at Wuppertal, Germany, employs steel wheels on steel rails, while the Paris subway system uses rubber wheels on concrete "rails." The question therefore boils down to the advantages and disadvantages of rubber versus steel wheels.

Figure 1   The Wuppertal, Germany, monorail.

The following advantages are claimed for rubber wheels:

1. Less noise.
2. Greater adhesion making steeper grades possible.
3. The smoother ride makes it possible to employ lighter and cheaper cars, which, in turn, makes lighter structures possible.

The disadvantages are:

1. In wet weather, and in particular with snow and ice, traction is poor, and trains may be slowed down or completely stalled.
2. Blowout of tires may lead to interruption of service and to accidents. Because the rails are simply flat surfaces, horizontal guide wheels, guided by vertical boards or "rails" are required.
3. Consequently, switching is slow, difficult, and cumbersome.

4. The structure becomes bigger with consequently greater obstruction of light and air.

5. More moving parts have to be kept in working order, increasing both costs of maintenance and risks of failure.

Concerning the question of noise, it should be noted that the movement of steel wheels on steel rails is by no means the only source of transit noise, though it may be the most noticeable one. Also, considerable reduction of noise can be achieved with steel wheels, by systematic improvement of rails and of wheels and by the installing of sound absorbers both along the right of way and on the cars.

Concerning the weight of the cars, other factors such as durability and safety and smoothness of ride are cited as reasons for heavier cars.

Monorail is not a new invention. A suspended monorail, horse-drawn and used for freight transportation, was in operation in England as early as 1821. In the 145 years since that time, numerous monorail lines, both of the suspended and of the supported type, have been built and, in most cases, abandoned; and many millions of dollars and vast amounts of engineering and promotional talent have been devoted to the development of monorail. However, only one mass-transit line was ever built, the Wuppertal line, which has been in operation since 1901. Unique local conditions made a suspended elevated line the most appropriate solution in this area.

All other lines presently in operation are either purely experimental or adjuncts to fairs. Supported lines of the ALWEG type have been built near Cologne, Germany, in Houston, Texas, and at Disneyland in California. In Japan

A SHORT HISTORY OF MONORAIL

Figure 2 The ALWEG monorail in Disneyland, California.

there are three short single-car monorail lines for pleasure rides. A monorail line is under construction from the center of Tokyo to the airport, but no action has been taken on proposals for a monorail system of a special type for Caracas, Venezuela. Recently the Los Angeles Metropolitan Transit Authority rejected the proposals for monorail, and consultants for the San Francisco Bay Area Rapid Transit District concluded that monorail was not suitable for its operation.

THE AMF-SAFEGE SYSTEM   The SAFEGE suspended monorail at Châteauneuf-sur-Loire, France, is a serious and interesting experimental installation, developed jointly by two French engineering firms and the administrations of the French National Railways and the Paris Metro System.

It is not a monorail but a "split" rail, with the supporting concrete rails forming the body of a hollow beam. Because the rails and wheels are protected by this beam, rubber-wheel traction is independent of the weather. Nevertheless, steel rails and wheels are also provided so that the train can continue to run on steel if a tire should blow out. In addition, two horizontal rubber guide wheels, operating on the inner walls of the beam, are provided. Switching is accomplished by lowering and lifting different sections of the beam; it is claimed that this can be done in ten seconds.

Because of the smooth ride on rubber wheels, light cars are employed. Because of this reduction in weight and because of

Figure 3 The test section of the SAFEGE monorail near Orléans, France.

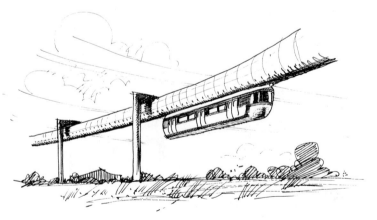

the decrease of lateral stress resulting from the low point of gravity of the suspended cars, the strength and weight of the beam are reduced substantially.

Because of the location of the wheels and motors inside a hollow beam and high up, noise both in the cars and on the street below is reduced to a minimum. It is also claimed that the high location of the beams is visually less objectionable. However, the beam is 6 feet 2 inches wide and 6 feet 7 inches high.

If, when, and where conditions indicate the advisability of a suspended monorail, this is the best system available.

THE ALWEG SYSTEM

The ALWEG supported monorail at Seattle, Washington, is a short line, slightly over one mile long, connecting the city center with the site of the 1962 World's Fair. There are no intermediate stations. Only two short trains, each of four sections, are in operation, shuttling back and forth on each of the two tracks. There are no storage or repair yards, and consequently no switches. Because only one train runs on each track, no signaling system is required.

It is reported that the trains do not reach the speed of 70 miles per hour originally anticipated, that they slow down considerably when the rails are wet, that deceleration is slow, and that the ride is bumpy over the expansion joints.

As the cars are lightweight and run on rubber tires, there is little noise. However, despite the low capacity and consequent low weight of the trains, the supporting beams are quite heavy and unsightly, being five feet high and over three feet wide.

The Seattle installation is not a mass-transit system and has not demonstrated the feasibility of the ALWEG type for such a system; it has developed several "bugs" not found in conventional rapid transit.

RUBBER-TIRED SUBWAYS

The Paris Metro System has experimented for a number of years with rubber wheels on the rapid-transit cars of one of its lines. Recently this system has been extended to a second route. Rubber wheels have been added to the steel wheels. The rubber wheels run on concrete strips or "rails." If the rubber wheels are fully inflated, the steel wheels do not touch

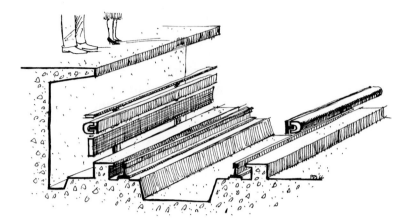

Figure 4   Cross-sectional view of the roadbed of the rubber-tired rapid-transit system at a station in Paris.

the rails. Additional horizontal rubber guide wheels, running along a low vertical concrete wall or "vertical guide rail," keep the cars from leaving the concrete "rails." The steel rails serve a dual purpose of carrying the cars in case of a blowout and of guiding the trains through switches and in the yards, where the vertical guide rails would seriously impede movement.

The system has worked satisfactorily. It is planned to extend it gradually to the entire Paris Metro System. The city of Montreal has also adopted the rubber-tired system for its two new subway lines.

The Montreal system differs from the Toronto Subway also in the size of the cars, which are to be only 8 feet 3 inches wide compared with 10 feet 5 inches in Toronto.

The following advantages are claimed for the Montreal system:

1. Less noise.
2. A smoother ride with less vibration.
3. Lighter and cheaper cars, because of smaller size and smoother ride.
4. Narrower and less expensive tunnels.
5. Ability to manage steeper grades.

Against this the following disadvantages are cited:

1. Narrower cars are less convenient.

2. Fewer passengers can be seated in rush hours (in nonrush hours additional folding seats are used).

3. Lighter cars will require more maintenance and more frequent replacement.

4. Stations will have to be longer, resulting in higher construction costs and poorer distribution of the passenger loads.

5. Six sets of rails and wheels are used in place of two sets of rails and wheels and, hence, will require more maintenance.

6. Where the line runs under the open sky (at grade, in cut, on fill, or on elevated structure), traction will be a problem in wet weather.

I raised this last point with the Paris engineers who are acting as consultants on the Montreal project. They claimed that the concrete rails could be kept permanently dry by heating them electrically, at small cost. (ALWEG makes this same claim, apparently based on experience in Western Europe and Japan.) This claim cannot be accepted without extensive testing under Canadian weather conditions. Certainly the Montreal experience will warrant close study.

CONCLUSIONS

1. There is no such thing as "monorail." The systems presently advertised under that name all employ *four* or *six* rails and wheels, where "conventional" rapid transit employs two.

2. The one common element of these "monorail" systems is the employment of a beam in place of the platform used by conventional elevated railroads to carry the rails. However, it would be perfectly possible to support the rails of a "conventional" elevated railroad on two parallel beams that could be made smaller than the beams of all current "monorail" proposals.

3. The claim of lower construction costs is not borne out. Other things being equal, the cost of the monorail is equal or higher than that of a "conventional" elevated railroad. A very thorough study made by Parsons, Brickerhoff, Hall and Mac-Donald in 1953 for the San Francisco Regional System found that the construction costs of a suspended monorail system would be 11.7 per cent higher than those of a conventional elevated railroad (exclusive of development costs, fees, and contingencies).

The ALWEG Company claims lower construction costs in comparison with "conventional" elevated railroads. No comparison is given for construction cost at grade, in cut, on fill, or on masonry structure. In these cases the cost relation is likely to be reversed; it certainly is reversed in a tunnel.

4. The most promising conditions for monorails are lines between two terminal points, without intermediate stops, such as from the city center to an airport, or to a major recreational facility. The few existing or seriously contemplated installations of the ALWEG System are all of this type.

The possibility of a monorail connection between Union Station and Malton Airport, in Toronto, over existing railroad tracks, has been investigated previously and rejected for the following reasons:

1. The numerous grade-separated street crossings would require extremely costly three-level structures.

2. Buses, since the completion of the Gardiner Expressway and of the access road from Highway 27 to the new airport terminal, travel at 50 to 60 miles per hour from end to end;* a monorail could not provide faster service.

3. A majority of air travelers use private cars, rented cars, or taxis. The low usage (and consequent infrequency) of the present fairly fast and convenient bus service indicates that the probable usage and revenue of the monorail would not warrant the required very substantial capital investment.

A monorail line to the Toronto Islands also has been suggested. Such a line would require the construction of either a high bridge or a deep tunnel. As substantial volumes of traffic to the Islands are restricted to about twenty days of the year, the required investment cannot be justified. The same reason would weigh against a monorail to the Canadian National Exhibition.

No other suitable location for monorail exists in the Metropolitan Toronto area.

In Toronto, efforts should be directed primarily to the following points:

* Actual bus time averages 24 minutes for a distance of 19 miles.

1. To find locations for rapid-transit lines other than in subway tunnels.

2. To reduce the cost of signaling and fare-collecting systems.

3. To reduce noise.

4. To develop a means of transit of a capacity intermediate between the 40,000 passengers per hour of the subway and the 4,000 passengers per hour of the bus. In this respect, the experience of improved high-capacity tramways overseas, notably in Germany, should be studied.

5. To speed up the feeder bus system, both by traffic regulations favoring buses over private vehicles and by introducing less time-consuming loading and fare-collection systems.

6. To explore the possibility of developing a "jitney" feeder service in low-density areas.

15

Why Pay To Ride?

There is nothing revolutionary about providing "free" transportation. It is done by every elevator in any office building or apartment. The cost of the service is collected as part of the rent from all tenants, whether they use it 100 times a day or not at all. Why do we collect fares for aircraft flights and not for elevator rides? Why shouldn't bus and subway services be financed like elevator services instead of airline services?

If air travel were "free," junkets to Florida would absorb a lot of labor and capital that could be put to better use. But few people ride on buses or the subway in rush hours just for fun. At other times it costs no more to have all seats filled, rather than half of them.

The person who benefits from a service pays for it. This was a valid reason for charging fares when the alternative to transit riding was walking. It would have been grossly unfair to ask the man who walked to pay so that his neighbor could ride in the streetcar or subway train.

But today the alternative is generally not walking. You can drive your own car. The driver benefits when his neighbor leaves his car at home and takes the subway or bus. But if everyone who comes downtown each day by public transport drove a car, there would be an enormous traffic jam. It is true, of course, that not everyone wants to drive downtown. But, then, not everyone uses a park or playground, yet all pay for it.

From the point of view of fairness, there can be no serious objection to financing municipal transit by taxes, rather than by a pay-as-you-ride system.

What are the disadvantages of charging fares? Nobody collects fares on elevators for the simple reason that it would cost more than it was worth. The collecting, checking, and bookkeeping of fares adds to the operating costs of big-city transit operations.

If fares were abolished:

1. Passengers could board streetcars and buses at two or more doors. This would reduce running time by as much as 10 per cent. Faster rides would attract more passengers.

2. Some 30 per cent to 40 per cent more passengers would be carried. Half the increased number of passengers would be those who otherwise would drive their cars. This would keep one of every ten cars off the streets, thus reducing traffic congestion.

3. Less traffic would mean reduced expenditure on roads and streets (particularly widening), on parking facilities, and on street maintenance.

It now costs Metropolitan Torontonians $40 million a year in fares to maintain the public transit system. If fares were abolished, the cost of running the system with general tax monies would not be any higher—and Torontonians could get 400 million rides a year, instead of fewer than the 300 million they get today. Looking at it from the other side, one can see that the cost per ride would drop from 15 cents to around 10 cents.

IV
RESIDENTIAL AREAS

16

Residential Densities

All planning is an amalgam of prediction and prescription. Planners, as they always emphasize, merely give advice to those who actually develop land: individuals, corporations, or governments. They also advise governments to make prescriptions concerning developments by private enterprise. But it should be evident that people, acting as a community, will not accept prescriptions that do not conform to what they do, acting as individuals.

Prescriptions can work only in the framework of prediction. They can see to it that what is going to happen anyway will happen smoothly and efficiently. Thus the primary concern of planners is and should be the correct *prediction* of residential densities on which all planning of facilities depends. It is not impossible to make reasonable predictions, if such factors as topography, past density trend, transportation facilities, and relation to places of employment and to the city center are correctly evaluated. The behavior of men in the mass shows measurable regularities on which predictions can be based. A recent analysis of the outward movement of zones of constant densities in the "inner suburban belt," 3 to 8 miles from the city center, showed a ratio to the rate of population growth of 0.83 in the Philadelphia area, and of 0.85 in the Toronto area. More research along these lines is needed.

However, the present discussion is concerned primarily not with prediction but with prescription, with the means for bringing about the "right" residential density in urban areas.

Does anybody know what the "right" density is? I do. It is 12,000 to 60,000 persons per square mile of residential area (20 to 100 persons per acre).

In other words, acceptable conditions can be created within a wide range of densities; and the location, family type, and consumer's preferences determine which one is appropriate in any particular case. But there are upper and lower limits beyond which serious disadvantages appear.

With poorly developed means of transportation and the resultant excessive concentration of population, too high densities have been—and still are—the main danger that planners have tried to prevent by prescription, mainly by zoning regulations requiring minimum lot sizes, setbacks and yards, and maximum coverage and height or floor area ratio (the proportion between lot area and a building's total floor area). These prescriptions are fairly effective in setting an upper limit. As economic pressure has tended to cause full utilization of the zoning "envelope," they are also reasonably close indicators for prediction.

With the development of the private automobile and of high-speed roads, a very different situation has developed in the peripheral areas of our large cities and in the surrounding suburbs. If such areas are within the city limits, zoning sometimes permits relatively high densities, and in such situations it is found that development occurs at considerably lower densities than zoning would permit. Suburban municipalities almost universally enforce low densities by zoning and subdivision controls. Planners have enthusiastically supported these "high standards" in the name of "public health and welfare," and the courts have approved this interpretation.

It is hardly a secret that municipal governments are prompted by quite different considerations to adopt these "high standards." These standards effectively keep out people with low incomes who can only pay low taxes and generally require more municipal services for education, health, and welfare than their more fortunate neighbors. The "high standards" are an effective means of protecting the pocketbook of the taxpaying "ins" against any "outs" who cannot pay an equal or, preferably, higher share of taxes.

The result, which has duly been viewed with alarm by an increasing number of observers of the urban scene, is an increasing class division between the suburbs and the central city, in which the lower-income groups are being concentrated. This concentration has alarmed city taxpayers, their elected representatives, and the banks holding city bonds and mortgages. So they are now trying to "reverse the trend," to beat the suburbs at their own game of attracting the higher- and excluding the lower-income groups. Under fancy names such as "urban redevelopment" and "urban renewal," low-income housing is being destroyed and replaced by housing for the middle- or higher-income groups.

Where does this leave those whom "God must love," according to Abraham Lincoln, "because he made so many of them"? As Hugh Pomeroy remarked, "the poor are being zoned out into the Atlantic Ocean." Both the suburbs and the central cities are enlisting the planners as mercenaries in this merciless class war of the "haves" against the "have-nots."

Redevelopment has been something less than a success. But neither are the low-density suburbs happy. Like other modern weapons, enforced low density burdens and endangers the bearer as much as the "enemy."

The disadvantages of excessively low density development, of 4.5 houses or less per acre of residential area, can be summarized under three headings: (1) overextension of urbanized area; (2) isolation of daily life; and (3) difficulty in finding labor for industry and commerce.

1. Urbanization of a very extensive area has the following inconveniences:

   a. Very large investments for roads and utilities to serve this extensive area.
   b. Very long travel distances from the inner areas to open areas.
   c. Very long travel distances from the outer areas to the commercial, civic, and cultural facilities in the center.
   d. An increase of daily vehicle-miles roughly equal to the square of population increase.

2. Even more serious may be the effect on the daily lives of the residents in the newly developed residential areas. Most residents of such areas who work in the city center and practically all who work in other areas travel by car. With growing

dispersal of places of work, the percentage of those traveling to work by car will tend to increase.

It must be assumed that the great majority of residents will, in the future, as at present, consist of one-car families. It is therefore important that transit stops and neighborhood facilities such as local shopping and community centers, schools, churches, etc., should be within walking distance of the homes.

Walking distance may be defined as one quarter of a mile as the maximum, or a circular area of less than one fifth of a square mile, which, at a density of 4.5 families per acre, contains not more than 500 to 600 families. This has the following consequences:

a. Bus service at adequate headways of 10 minutes or less can be maintained only during rush hours in the direction to and from the central city. At other hours and in other directions, service can be maintained only at headways of 30 minutes or more. Even such a limited service can be maintained only if heavily subsidized by the taxpayers.

b. A population of 500 to 600 families can just barely maintain a public elementary school of eight classes (or six classes with a three-level system) and kindergarten, if 80 to 90 per cent of all children in this age group attended the public elementary school. If higher percentages of children go to separate schools, public schools have to be more widely spaced. Separate schools as well as junior and senior high schools are beyond the normal walking distance for most of the students.

c. A local shopping center requires a market area of at least 1,000 to 1,200 families. Consequently, at least half of the families in such areas live beyond the normal walking distance from a local shopping center.

d. The same holds true for churches, clubs, and other community facilities. Observations in large communities that have been developed at such low densities confirm that housewives lead isolated lives, restricted to contact only with their immediate neighbors, resulting in lack of participation in civic, school, church, social, and cultural affairs and ultimately in a sense of frustration.

3. Most municipalities designate extensive areas for industry and commerce and want to encourage their develop-

ment. Practically all industrial and commercial enterprises require a certain percentage of low-wage earners. Many of these workers, notably female labor, do not have cars at their disposal. On the other hand, few workers of this type will be found in detached houses on relatively large lots. The consequences are:

a. At best, many workers have to travel long ways, with adverse effects on morale and productivity; at worst, employers are unable to recruit a full staff.

b. In the long run, the neighboring communities cannot be expected to supply the lower-paid segment of workers but will adopt similar restrictive zoning policies. Carried to its ultimate consequence, this would undermine the economic base of the entire area from which the people occupying the more expensive homes derive their income.

Thus the policy of picking the raisins out of the cake and throwing the crumbs to one's neighbors finally defeats itself. We cannot go on developing all new areas at the densities of 4.5 houses or less per acre of residential area such as those now prevailing in new subdivisions. There must be a floor as well as a ceiling for densities.

That is easier said than done. Under our system of private land ownership and land development, the function of municipal planning is largely negative. We can and do say "no" to the developer. We can, within limits, tell a fellow: "Thou shalt not live here." We cannot—thank God—prescribe: "Thou shalt live where I think it is good for you." The "enlightened" absolutists of the eighteenth century *did* prescribe that on a certain street everybody must build three stories high over his entire frontage. I do not suggest that we follow their example.

Nor do I suggest that we tailor our residential zones so tightly to the anticipated demand that the resulting land monopoly raises land prices to a point where people are *forced* to build at higher density than they want to.

We can and should do two things: first, advise and encourage people to build, in suitable locations, apartments, row houses, and other types of group housing less wasteful of land than the detached house on its 60- or 80-foot lot; and second, remove the zoning and subdivision restrictions that now prevent this type of development.

17

Comments on the Neighborhood Concept

"Mencius says in his dialogue with Dunn Wan Kung that if a neighborhood of eight families is formed, the inhabitants will work together, will keep each other company while resting in the evening, will guard their property against trespassers from outside, will look after the sick and help the weak, and attend to their private matters after the communal work is done."[1]

I cannot think of any better formulation of the concept of neighborliness than these words spoken by a Chinese sage 2,000 years ago. Planners advocating "the development of neighborhood consciousness and pride [as] fundamental to achieving sound urban social relationships"[2] vaguely hope to recapture in the modern metropolis some of these values, typical of a folk society.

Such hopes imply several tacit assumptions that should be spelled out, questioned, and answered:

1. Is it desirable that citizens of a city identify themselves strongly with any one relatively small group?

2. If yes, is territorial proximity the best basis for such group?

[1] C. Z. Chen. "Some Ancient Chinese Concepts of Town and Country," *The Town Planning Review*, Vol. 19, pp. 160–163 (Liverpool, 1947).

[2] *Greater Winnipeg*, 1947, p. 41, and any number of other planning reports.

3. If yes, can such identification be brought about by physical features such as boundaries and central location of services?

4. What is the size of a group that permits a "human scale" of relations that is *qualitatively* different from those existing in such large groups as a city or a nation?

I shall try to discuss these questions in inverse order.

It is hardly an accident that Mencius speaks of a group of eight families (which are supposed to work in common a ninth field, devoted to public purpose). A modern English planner[3] observes that "the basic and most important social intercourse is that between immediate neighbors, two or three families on both sides of the dwelling... mutual visiting... more important, mutual aid in every aspect of domestic life, in sickness and in the care of children." It is indeed groups of *about six to twelve families* who "keep each other company while resting in the evening" and "will look after the sick and help the weak" in each other's houses. Such groups are, as Chapman rightly remarks, "too small or too intangible to enter into his [the planner's] calculations." It may be added that they are to be found fairly generally, without benefit of planning, even in the large city.

However, there is no doubt that in some larger groups, such as a farm village of *50 to 100 families,* there is also a very close relationship between all the people, each of whom knows everyone else as a person, by his face, his voice, and his name. How large is the group normally that any one individual knows in this way? Strangely enough, I have come across no answer to this elementary question in sociological literature, but from my own chance observations I would say that it begins to fade out in villages with much more than 500 or 600 population. I am, therefore, inclined to agree with Chapman, who mentions 40 to 100 families as the "next level" characterized by "face to face contact" and by its ability "to throw up natural leaders." He adds a third level of "*400 to 500 families* who can support ... a local shopping center... a day nursery school, nursery school, infant school [for five- to seven-year-olds], social

[3] "Social Aspects of Town Planning," lecture delivered by Dennis Chapman before the Town and Country Planning Association of Covent Garden Summer School in Cambridge on August 27, 1948, and excerpted in *The Architects Journal,* Vol. 108, p. 316 (London. September 30, 1948).

club...branch library...restaurant." It is interesting to note that the Russians, after a rich and varied experience of many years, have arrived at a similar size for their unit in planning residential areas, the "living complex" organized around institutions for children from one to seven years and a social club, and that most public housing managers seem to consider this the most desirable size for a project. While in such a group of 1,500 to 2,000 people there is no longer a universal mutual "face to face" acquaintanceship, such relation is still possible among the housewives and among the children and adolescents of each age group.

Apparently, this number represents about the maximum size of a group of "human scale." Once that limit is passed, it is doubtful if there is any *qualitative* difference between a group of 10,000 and one of 10,000,000. The population group of 5,000 to 10,000 persons required, under current educational standards, to support an elementary school is probably much too large to form social relations that would give content to the title of "neighborhood" that planners have so confidently bestowed on it. It will, however, frequently correspond to the size of an island, or "superblock," bounded by major traffic arteries, thus enabling the children to encounter fewer traffic hazards on their way to school. That is all to the good and an aspect worth considering in designing a system of major traffic arteries—but it is hardly an adequate means to save the city, the nation, and the world from impending disaster, as the prophets of the "neighborhood concept" would like to make us believe.

Except for meeting at the parent-teachers' council, there is not much that these 5,000 to 10,000 people have in common. Each family will do its shopping at the nearest center—at different points on the periphery of the superblock. These families will not fill the first specification of Mencius, to "work together." Working together still establishes stronger bonds between people than does passive residing together. It is the very essence of city life that every person has bonds with different groups on the basis of work, residence, religion, politics, sports, and a host of other interests. Are we so sure we want to change this pattern and subordinate all ties to a single dominant group loyalty? And if so, should and would the dominant interest not be work rather than residence?

Of all the neighborhood activities mentioned by Mencius only one is being practiced by our "neighborhoods"; they do "guard their property against trespassers from outside." I do not share Mr. Isaacs' opinion[4] that the "neighborhood concept" is responsible for this attitude; that seems to me an over-estimate of the influence exercised by the planners' gobble-dygook on the mores of America. But I do agree that "neigh-borhood identification" is not necessarily a civic virtue.

Now it has been justly pointed out that the term "neighbor-hood" frequently is used not to denote any functioning social unit but simply to mean a "service area." We are told:[5] "A 'neighborhood unit' is that portion of a larger community or city which is specifically developed for the safety, health, comfort, convenience, and welfare of the residents of that area...." If nothing more is implied, I would suggest the neutral term "residential area." I would further suggest that each service unit of each service function—education, health, shopping, recreation, etc.—be analyzed separately as to opti-mum size and service radius and distributed accordingly. If some such units can be grouped together for convenience, it should be done. But if it works out so that a fellow living in "neighborhood" A sends his children to school in B, has his teeth pulled in C, takes his wife to the movies in D, and has his beer in E, then I would not consider him a bad citizen or the city a bad city. Such planning requires more detailed study, and the results will not look as neat on paper as the simple method of slicing the city up into neat packages of 5,000 to 10,000 people and plunking down a "community center" plus a "shopping center" in the middle of each. However, it may function better, and it seems to me that in practice most planners have had good sense enough to work that way rather than to be satisfied with the pat "neighborhood" solu-tion they advocate in theory.

But—to return to my old Chinese sage—"but," Mencius concludes, "the success of this system still depends on how you carry it out."

[4] Reginald R. Isaacs, "Are Urban Neighborhoods Possible?" *Journal of Housing,* Vol. V, No. 7 (July 1948), pp. 177-180; "The Neighborhood Unit Is an Instrument for Segregation," *Journal of Housing,* Vol. V, No. 8 (Aug. 1948), pp. 215-218.

[5] Harold S. Buttenheim and Robert C. Weinberg, *Planning the Community for Family Living,* paper prepared for the National Conference on the Family, Washington, D. C., May 6-8, 1948.

18

"The Good Neighborhood"*

"This book is an attack on current city planning and rebuilding," says the opening sentence of *The Death and Life of Great American Cities*. It is an angry book. Like other reformers and prophets, the author combines a great wealth of sharp observations and sensitive understanding with sweeping generalizations and dangerously oversimplified recipes. The strange title — putting death before life — indicates the lopsided approach to the problems of the city. Mrs. Jacobs, an active citizen of Greenwich Village, is concerned exclusively with the inner areas of great cities because, as she correctly states, they have been "evaded in planning theory." What concerns her is that they have not been evaded in practice but are being ruthlessly destroyed in the name of "slum clearance" and "urban redevelopment." Having opposed the concept of "urban redevelopment" since 1939, as it developed in the United States and is now spreading to Canada, I am naturally biased in favor of a book that opposes it far more effectively than I have been able to do.

Rather strangely, Jane Jacobs never clearly spells out the basic fallacy of "slum clearance." Slums are bad, not because they look unpleasant or because they prevent land from being put to its so-called "highest and best use," but because people are forced to live in them under conditions impairing their

* Review of Jane Jacobs, *The Death and Life of Great American Cities* (New York: Random House, 1961).

health and happiness. They live there because they cannot afford better housing. In order to enable them to afford it, either their income must be raised or rents (or prices) for decent housing must be lowered. Tearing down slums does neither. To the contrary, it takes a slice out of their money income—and often an enormous slice out of their "psychic income"—by forcing them to move; and, by decreasing the supply of low-rent housing, it raises its price (or rent). If clearance proceeds wholesale, it invariably also destroys a sizable number of acceptable houses. We need more old houses, not fewer (in addition to many more new houses). "Slum clearance," as Mrs. Jacobs rightly remarks, does not abolish slums; it shifts and spreads them.

What holds true of dwellings holds equally true of industrial, commercial, and service establishments. Here Mrs. Jacobs brilliantly analyzes the need of a great variety of such establishments for cheap premises that they can find only in old buildings. In particular, she protests, with full justification, against the ruthless destruction of small neighborhood stores run by individuals who are deprived, without compensation, of their capital invested in building up "goodwill," and who usually cannot re-establish themselves elsewhere. She overlooks tenants, whether of dwellings or of stores, who are daily evicted without compensation by private landlords. Public slum clearance accepts at least some responsibility for the fate of its displaced persons.

Her wrath is turned not only against this destruction but even more strongly against the new construction that usually takes its place: housing "projects." Public housing projects in the United States have not turned out to be the cure-all for "crime and delinquency" that their early advocates had promised; in many cases these are worse here than in the "slums." Mrs. Jacobs is therefore against any public housing. Here she takes a strangely provincial view, ignoring completely the generally favorable experience of public and semipublic housing in Britain and Europe, and ignoring also the history of housing in the United States.

In European countries since World War I, governments have assumed responsibility for housing the urban population by a great variety of policies. The basic housing policy of the United States and of Canada has always been and still is to rely on the "filtering-down" of dwellings vacated by the more affluent to house those of lower income. During the depression the U.S. Congress agreed that some make-work projects be directed toward producing housing—hence the designation "projects." However, in order to make sure that these projects would not disturb the market for acceptable housing, the legislation prescribed, first, that only slum dwellers were eligible and, second, that they were eligible only if and as long as their incomes were so low that they could not possibly afford any kind of decent housing. Thus, public housing has been from the start burdened with a dual negative tenant selection: those who value good housing so highly that they skimp on everything else to pay for it out of a low income cannot get in; those who are able and willing to work hard to increase their income also cannot get in or, worse, are thrown out if and when they succeed.

Those least able to find decent housing are, of course, families with many children, in particular those without a male breadwinner. Quite rightly, they have the highest priority in getting into public housing. But the result is a complete and thoroughly unsound unbalance between the numbers of adults and of children. Children should play under the eyes of adults, preferably in their own backyard. But when public housing is tied to "slum clearance," it must pay the price of the capitalized profits from slum dwellings, which are notoriously high, to clear the land on which it has to be built. The resultant high land value forces high density, which can be achieved only by building multistory elevator buildings, totally unsuited for children.

Any neighborhood with such handicaps must produce many problems. In order to cope with them and to maintain at least a minimum of external order under the watchful eyes of its many enemies, public housing has resorted to increasing regimentation. This regimentation, together with the lopsided composition of the "project" population, makes many eligible families unwilling to move into public housing. In the United States the problem is further compounded by racial prejudice. Thus a vicious circle is started, often resulting in what Mrs. Jacobs calls an "immured slum."

The reasons for this sad issue of a noble experiment are clearly the handicaps built into the authorizing legislation by those who did not like it in the first place. The failure is not due to the fact that it was carried out in "projects," meaning large-scale housing developments, nor even to their design, despite its great deficiencies, which Mrs. Jacobs justly criticizes.

However, since the basic reason for people living in slums is the gap between their income and the price of decent housing, it has been suggested that the best way to close it would be to supply those in need with "rent certificates," to be honored by the public treasury. The proponents of this solution overlook that just this has been and is being done by welfare agencies. The main result has been a further subsidy to slum landlords. This points up another aspect of the "housing problem." The market has not been effective in housing — as it has been in the field of most consumer's goods — in calling forth the best product possible at the existing level of technology. This is not the place to discuss the reasons, but world-wide experience over a hundred years has clearly shown that housing built for the purpose of use — whether by governments, cooperatives, trade unions, philanthropists, or even by employers — has been far superior to most housing built for the market.

Our mistake consists in confusing the two aspects of the housing problem. Mrs. Jacobs, while she is generally aware of this, has not entirely freed herself from this confusion. She says: "We need subsidies for a portion of city families." And we also need to promote housing projects, big and small, built by whoever is willing and able to build and manage them at decent standards. They should be built, in the main, where they can be built at the lowest cost, on open land. This does not enter into the purview of Mrs. Jacobs. For all her boldness in discarding conventional thinking, she still thinks in the terms of "city" and "suburbs" as separate worlds, instead of as closely interdependent parts of the same metropolitan unit. She even rejects metropolitan government on grounds valid only against absorption by one overcentralized big-city government, though she very ably explains, in considerable detail, the need for and the possibility of establishing district governments within the larger unit.

Better housing can and must, however, also be created in the older areas of the city, by improvement of the existing housing and environment, with gradual replacement of obsolete structures by new facilities. It is often claimed that this cannot be done. It is one of the great merits of Mrs. Jacobs' book that she shows that it has been done; and it has been done without help from government or financial institutions.

As mentioned earlier, the gap between income and the cost of decent housing can be closed also by raising incomes. Such a rise in real incomes has actually taken place in the United States and Canada during and after the last war. Moreover, wartime restrictions made many consumer goods unavailable so that more savings accumulated in the hands of ordinary people than ever before. They were thus able to improve their housing conditions. Normally, they would have had the choice between two ways of doing this: (1) rehabilitating and improving the houses (or stores) that they occupied; or (2) buying a house in the suburbs and a car. But during the war and for a number of years afterward both cars and suburban houses were in short supply, and so many of them took the first option. Today, since per capita real income in the United States and Canada is rising only 1 or 2 per cent annually, most people have debts rather than savings, and cars and suburban houses are flooding the market. It is therefore risky to base generalizations as to the permanent attractiveness of such areas on the experience of the period from 1940 to 1960, as Mrs. Jacobs does. Actually, many of the younger families are right now moving to the suburbs from Boston's "North End" and from the Chicago "Back-of-the-Yards" area, the only two of her examples of areas that are inhabited exclusively by "ordinary people."

Despite this caution, the fact that "unslumming"—as she calls it—has occurred in a number of areas deserves the greatest attention and raises the question as to the conditions that have made it possible. Jane Jacobs attempts to answer this question. She believes that the basic cause of slums is "the Great Blight of Dullness" and that the cure is "Diversity." In particular, she considers "lively sidewalks" with many people both on them and watching them from doors and windows as the *sine qua non* of good city life.

The book opens with a long chapter on safety, and throughout the book the author returns again and again to this theme. She feels that any place can be safe from crime only if it is constantly watched by many pairs of eyes; every street should be solidly lined with buildings so that there are no hiding places. It is an appalling comment on American urban civilization that safety should be considered the overriding goal of city planning. Aristotle remarked that people first come together for security, then stay for the good life. It seems we have come full circle.

In Canadian cities safety from crime is hardly a major concern. Moreover, it is obviously quite impossible to have many people around everywhere all the time. Mrs. Jacobs herself speaks at length about crime in the elevators and hallways of apartment houses. It also occurs in the stairwells of walk-up tenements. Only single-family houses with locked doors might be safe; but in a street lined with such houses the sidewalks would be empty, and crime would come in by the window.

The problem of crime cannot be solved by physical city planning; Mrs. Jacobs' discussions of this point are irrelevant. Fortunately, she has better reasons for lively sidewalks. One is the casual supervision of children; another reason is the opportunity for casual contacts and the emergence of "public figures," primarily small shopkeepers. Mrs. Jacobs believes that only in such conditions can effective political action on the district level be developed. This is hardly borne out by experience; nor is the action of such local groups always beneficial.

Probably her best reason for lively sidewalks is the simple one that they are fun. "People are attracted by people," she says, and rightly adds that most planners have ignored this and have thought only of the attraction of "nature," of trees and grass, the sun and the sky. Actually, of course, most people want both liveliness and quiet, both company and solitude, at various times and in various proportions, and different people attach different values to each. It is the great merit of Mrs. Jacobs' book that she explains the values and attractions of liveliness. She has much that is pertinent to say about the destruction of diversity by what I have called "isolationist planning": the tendency to divide the city up into neat packages of "neighborhoods" of separate and over-simplified "land-use areas," of "single-family" and "apartment" areas. She shows convincingly that continuity, inter-action of various functions, and "cross-use," to use her term, are the very essence of the city.

The core of the book is its prescription for the production of "lively city districts." Mrs. Jacobs considers that four conditions are indispensable:

1. High density of people present in a district as residents, workers, shoppers, or for any other purpose.
2. A mixture of "primary" uses, that is, not only residence but also industry, private and public offices, and places of entertainment serving all or large parts of the city beyond the district.
3. Short blocks.
4. A mixture of old and new buildings.

This is indeed "an attack on current city planning" on all four counts. To take the last point first: Mrs. Jacobs states quite rightly that a district needs not only "high-yield" stores and services but also marginal "low-yield" establishments, and that the latter can afford only old buildings; also that a mixture of old and new houses will lead to a natural and close-grained mixture of people of varying incomes. But how is it to be brought about?

By definition it is impossible to do this in new districts, and every district must start as a new one. Mrs. Jacobs says that many districts remain slums because they could not overcome the "obvious misfortune of being built all at once." She does not say how else you can build. Once a district is built and at the high density and with the continuous frontage that Mrs. Jacobs demands, new buildings can be built only by buying and demolishing old ones. This is economically possible only if the district is extremely attractive. Thus, a symptom and result of "success" is stipulated as its cause and condition. Mrs. Jacobs' whole argument might be dismissed as circular reasoning; however, it is worthwhile to consider briefly her other three points.

While it is true that densities can be too low as well as too high and that high densities have advantages as well as faults, the reasons for open space around buildings are too numerous and weighty to be disregarded. Distance between buildings is needed for light, air, and sunshine, for cooling breezes, for privacy from sight, sound, and smells. Open space at ground level is needed to grow trees, for children to play, for adults to sit, and for parking cars. Mrs. Jacobs is right in demanding that people move in the city by transit rather than by private car (though she completely fails to understand the policies that are required to eliminate unnecessary cars and retain necessary traffic). But this does not eliminate the universal desire to own a car for travel on week ends, during holidays, and for visits outside the inner city area. Aside from the few people who manage to find a curb space for overnight parking, only two kinds of people can live in Greenwich Village: those so poor or otherwise handicapped that they cannot own cars, and those so rich that they can pay $40 a month for a space in a commercial garage.

Mrs. Jacobs demands densities of 100-200 dwelling units per net acre. She gives the density of Le Corbusier's "Radiant City" (which she rejects, rightly) as 1,200 dwelling units per net acre; actually, it is about 120. She gives the density of the Boston "North End" as 275. A minute's calculation would have shown her that this would require an average height of six stories; and few, if any, buildings there have more than five. The Boston City Planning Commission, from whom she obtained the figure over the telephone, has long ago discovered the error; in reality, the density is only little more than half as high. It is strange indeed that somebody who writes scores of pages on densities — and is the wife of an architect — should be so completely unable to visualize densities in terms of three-dimensional reality.

The density of the Boston "North End" is still, of course, unusually high. It is achieved only by a ground coverage that even Mrs. Jacobs considers excessive; and it is made tolerable because it is surrounded on three sides by the open space of the Atlantic Ocean and of abandoned piers along its shores — but not tolerable enough to hold the one fifth of its population that has left it during the last ten years.

The North End, like Greenwich Village, enjoys the attraction of a concentration of interesting little stores and restaurants. In both cases this is possible because the areas are close enough to the center to be easily accessible from all parts of the city; and in both cases this concentration developed historically because they were the original location and have remained the center of two special groups now spread all over the city and beyond: artists and writers in the "Village" and Italians in the North End.

The peculiar richness and variety of their stores and restaurants can therefore not be duplicated in the vast "gray areas" that spread at considerable distances from the center and represent the bulk of the "blighted areas." These districts can contain only the establishments that can be supported by their own purchasing power—or what is left of it after the department stores, the supermarkets, and the car dealers have taken the lion's share. These will be mostly run-of-the-mill and inevitably rather thinly spread, even with high densities.

It is therefore surprising that Mrs. Jacobs wants to spread them even thinner by adding to the length of street fronts. In order to obtain "short blocks," she proposes to punch streets through the middle of long ones. This is supposed to encourage "cross-use" of streets and thereby promote vitality.

The most unorthodox of Mrs. Jacobs' four points is her advocacy of a mixture of industry and residence. Zoning has been obsessed with the notion that only sameness can "protect property values." This protection was and is the reason for zoning. Zoning is not planning; but in trying to use this available but basically unsuitable tool for planning purposes, planners have far too long adopted its obsession against mixing uses or types of buildings. Mrs. Jacobs is right in stating that certain industries, if they are not too big or too numerous, can be an asset rather than a detriment to a residential area. But industry is dynamic, and only continuous control can prevent the asset from becoming a nuisance. The "size zoning" that she proposes is quite inadequate.

The inadequacy of the four points put forward by the author does not, however, invalidate her basic thesis that old city areas are not "cancerous blight" but valuable and irreplaceable assets; that they should not be "cleared" but improved by adding to them what is lacking. She refuses to recognize that one of the elements lacking is open space, not only within the blocks, but also in schoolyards and small parks and playgrounds. But she is right in advocating the addition of places of work, offices, selected factories or workshops, and places of entertainment, as well as the insertion of civic and cultural buildings in focal points in "ordinary city" environment, instead of their isolation in lifeless "civic centers" and "cultural centers." This will involve a good deal of demolition; and the improvement of the area will require rehabilitation of most of the dwellings. If this is not to result in the displacement of most of the present inhabitants, rents will have to be kept low by public subsidies. This will be costly, but far less so than the present policy of "clearance and redevelopment."

Mrs. Jacobs is right in emphasizing that the transformation must be gradual to preserve the continuity of the social fabric, the complexity of which she has brilliantly analyzed. In a perceptive chapter on "the self-destruction of diversity," she describes the destructive impact of "cataclysmic money." It is therefore strange that she puts her main reliance on extension of credit facilities to property owners. Necessary as these aids are, they may do as much harm as good if not guided by a plan for the step-by-step transformation of the area. Implementation of such a plan will hardly be possible without public ownership. I have for many years advocated that redevelopment powers be used for this purpose. That is a vastly more difficult task than clearing an area from all existing life and planning something else on a *tabula rasa*. It will require continuing painstakingly detailed work, unending patience, and most of all that sensitive understanding of the life of human beings that Mrs. Jacobs shows in her discoveries of aspects of city life that planners and sociologists have overlooked.

This impassioned commitment is the great strength of this strange and remarkable book. It is also its weakness because it has carried away its author into many misstatements that may mislead the uninformed and may cause the informed to refuse to take the book as seriously as it deserves. It is a profoundly thought-provoking book that should be read and pondered by everyone concerned with the future of our cities.

19

Urban Renewal

"Urban renewal" has become a slogan. In the United States it has long received official recognition in legislation and by the establishment of a well-financed federal agency. As usual, we in Canada are bent on following the example of our neighbors to the south—including their mistakes.

Although the term "urban renewal" was coined only about ten years ago by an American housing economist, Miles Colean, the thing is as old as cities themselves. While life changes, buildings stand still; and being more solid and resistant than brick and mortar are, street lines and property lines that have been established remain, sometimes for hundreds and even thousands of years. As Professor Anthony P. Adamson wisely remarked, "Cities are always out of date and always out of order."

Just like automobiles and refrigerators, cities and parts of cities become obsolete from the moment they are produced—and sometimes before. Obsolescence is the reverse of progress; the faster progress develops, the more obsolescence occurs. Only in a stagnant society is there no need for renewal. In Canada, as our cities are rapidly growing and maturing, the patterns and structures that had been developed to serve the urban life of yesterday are no longer suited to serve the life of today and tomorrow.

Strangely, we have chosen to describe this natural and inevitable process of urban obsolescence by such emotionally loaded terms as "the cancer of blight," and we try to cure it by "a major surgical operation." The place of the surgeon's knife is taken by the bulldozer. In most big cities of the United States large areas, comprising scores and sometimes hundreds of acres, have been expropriated at tremendous cost to the taxpayers. Thousands of families and scores of small businesses have been uprooted. Then, on a man-made desert, apartments have been built, most of them at high rents.

All this is done in the name of "slum clearance." In fact, it means slum shifting. Half a century ago the father of the modern city planning movement, Patrick Geddes, wrote: "The policy of sweeping clearance should be recognized for what I believe it is: one of the most disastrous and pernicious blunders in the chequered history of sanitation . . . the large population thus expelled would . . . be driven into creating worse congestion in other quarters, to the advantage of the rack-renting interests." The director of the Roman Catholic Archdiocesan Conservation Council of Chicago summed up the results of this type of "urban renewal" in fewer words: "planned social anarchy."

In Canada we have so far avoided this kind of "urban renewal." But we are all set to repeat the mistakes of our neighbors, having copied their legislation. Huge sums of federal money are being offered to Canadian cities by the federal government for destroying houses — but hardly a penny for building and renovating them.

Our experience certainly raises doubt as to the wisdom of this policy. Actually, there are no extensive "slums" in Toronto. There are many overcrowded dwellings and many where crowding has led to sharing of bathrooms and to running down of the structure. But overcrowding can be cured not by tearing down houses but by building new ones and by conserving and improving those that we have.

Of course, this is actually going on all the time. A great amount of "urban renewal" is being carried out by private enterprise. A great deal of renewal can be done within existing buildings, by structural repairs and changes as well as by replacing obsolete equipment with new. A great deal of adequate housing could be supplied if public support, financial and technical, were given to this activity.

In many other cases the entire structure has become obsolete, but it can and is being replaced by a new one on the same lot, within the existing pattern of property and street lines.

But to a large extent this pattern itself has become obsolete as a result of technical progress, in particular of the automobile and the elevator.

A tall building, whether it is an apartment house or an office building, must have a fairly large floor area to pay for the cost of elevators. Other modern commercial and industrial buildings also need large areas to function efficiently. All buildings need parking space. These needs cannot be satisfied on the traditional small and narrow lots, which were designed for an entirely different kind of building. The private developer can assemble an area of a size sufficient for a modern building only at great difficulty; frequently a single "holdout" can frustrate a large, worthwhile scheme. It is here that government aid is required. By using their power of expropriation, municipal governments can and should assemble tracts of land of a size and shape suitable for modern development.

Frequently, however, it is not only the division into properties within the block that is obsolete but the entire pattern of blocks and streets. Our street system was designed for a modest volume of slow-moving traffic, with each street serving both for access to the adjoining properties and for through traffic. The automobile age requires separation of these two functions: traffic arteries with a minimum of access and access streets with a minimum of through traffic.

This could only be achieved by urban renewal on a very large scale. Evidently, it can be achieved only gradually over a long period. It is generally recognized that "urban renewal" by the all-too-familiar bulldozer approach faces two big obstacles: the high cost of acquisition and the difficulty of finding accommodations for the displaced families and business enterprises. It is not always recognized that both of these difficulties reflect the simple fact that we still need the old buildings that are being destroyed. Every normally functioning city consists of a mixture of old and new buildings. Those households and those commercial and industrial enterprises — in particular, new ones struggling to establish themselves — which can only afford old buildings are just as essential to the functioning of the community as are its more affluent families and enterprises that can afford to buy or rent new buildings.

"Urban renewal" must be freed from any connection with the disastrous and pernicious idea of "slum clearance." This negative and destructive approach must be replaced by a positive and constructive one. It should start from the demand for new uses and then seek the most suitable location for them. If the new use is really "higher and better," it will generally also be able to absorb the cost of displacing the old one.

In those extensive areas where this is not the case, the transformation from the old one to the new can only be a gradual one: demolishing a house here, building a new one there; closing a street here, widening another there. But all must be fitted into a plan for the gradual transformation of the entire area. Such genuine urban renewal requires thoughtful study and design rather than bulldozers—brain instead of brawn. Probably it can be carried out only by a public agency. Existing renewal legislation should be used to assist this process.

There is another untapped area for the use of renewal powers and of renewal funds that is receiving increasing attention from American experts. Obsolete street and lot patterns are to be found not only in densely built-up areas but also in many areas where development has not yet started or is just beginning. Here assembly and resubdivision of land by use of the powers conferred to municipalities under renewal legislation, including the power of expropriation, could achieve enormous improvement at little cost. An ounce of prevention is still better than a pound of cure.

20

Problems
of Urban Renewal

The comparatively rapid development and the continuing transitions in the Riverside area of New York City indicate that a thorough investigation here will yield results that can be applied to other congested areas, both in New York City and in centrally located residential areas in other large cities. Before drawing conclusions and venturing proposals for the future, it may be well to summarize the findings briefly and to make some suggestions as to their implications.

A GENERAL REVIEW   This study deals with the changing residential characteristics of the area, as caused by the accumulation and replacement of structures and by successive changes in their use that have been brought about by economic forces acting over the 40-year period from 1910 to 1950. All of this area was built up almost solidly by 1900, with only a few sites left vacant, except in the northwest quarter, where entire blocks were still empty. There were a good many fine houses and high-rent apartments in the best locations, but most of the original construction consisted of old-law tenements and row houses put up by speculative builders. There have been successive waves of demolition and rebuilding in many locations ever since, but especially along Riverside Drive, West End Avenue, Central

Park West, and the wider cross streets. The newer buildings are all elevator apartments, many of them very large.

Total construction and population growth have kept pace with each other all the while, so that the average amount of gross floor area per capita has remained constant; but local contrasts have become more intensified, with buildings from several boom periods standing close together in many locations. Conversion of single-family houses to apartments, sometimes quite make-shift and accompanied by changing population characteristics and overcrowding, has further intensified the contrasts. Much of the area was originally overbuilt with one-family houses, so that change to meet the actual demand took place almost from the first. Community facilities, schools, playgrounds, churches, etc., have not kept pace with the growth of population. Local retail and service establishments, however, have adjusted automatically to changes in population. Thus each locality is well provided with food stores, restaurants, and repair shops that are well adapted to the local population groups.

The Riverside location has many advantages. It provides fine sites on high ground, close to grand parks and only a few miles from the great assets of mid-Manhattan: shopping and cultural centers, and a great labor market for all classes of workers. These advantages, together with the peculiar assortment in the stock of housing, have brought about an unusual mixture of population: a high proportion of elderly people and a low proportion of children; high-income groups able to pay for the best apartments and low-income groups crowding into the older houses. Middle-income families with children are generally inclined to leave this area for the suburbs.

Riverside has become an area containing *two* distinct types of housing and *two* different population groups. There are upper- and middle-class tenants, generally engaged in white-collar work in midtown, predominantly small families. Many are single persons and childless couples. On the other hand, there are many lower-income families, engaged in service industries or manufacturing, also generally in midtown. Many, though by no means all, have children.

The first housing type consists of old- or new-law tenements in almost all of two subareas, and of converted single-family row houses and some old apartment houses occupying nearly all of the east-west streets in the other four subareas. Most of them were built before the turn of the century. During the past 50 years, houses of these types have been replaced on most of the frontage on the main arteries and in spots elsewhere by elevator apartments, which now contain the majority of all dwelling units.

These newer buildings are almost exclusively occupied by the upper- and middle-class tenants, although many members of this group, especially single persons, also live in the older buildings. The low-income group occupies the bulk of the older structures.

What should be done with this area? What can be done? What will happen if the current trends noted in this study are allowed to run their course, without planned modifications other than scattered redevelopment projects, whether public housing or privately financed?

BASIC ALTERNATIVES   The entire Riverside area might be redeveloped so as to restore a "normal" population, requiring numerous additional schools and playgrounds and a reduction of present density and population by almost one half. A large fraction of the adult population, now living in the area chiefly because of its unique location, would have to move to less convenient places. It is doubtful that such a proposition applied to so large an area could be justified politically or financially. On the other hand, if the trends in population and in building that have been consistently at work in Riverside over the last half century were carried to their ultimate conclusion, the area might be developed for an exclusively adult population in fifteen-story elevator apartments. With the present fairly adequate average of 400 square feet of gross floor area per person, 300,000 adults would require 120 million square feet. This would mean that the apartment houses would cover 8 million square feet, roughly 185 acres, or less than one fifth of the present gross residential area. The remaining four fifths would be available for streets, parking, recreation, and cultural and commercial facilities.

It would not be difficult to design attractive redevelopment schemes that would accomplish either of these alternatives. The old buildings on the ordinary east-west streets would be demolished, and most of these streets would be closed, creating sizable superblocks. New construction within each of these housing groups would be designed so as to supplement the remaining buildings and create balanced residential communities, with open planning and landscaping.

A development planned for a population having normal age and income characteristics would require a very high subsidy. But under the second alternative (virtually all-adult population) there is little doubt that there would be sufficient effective demand among the 15 million people of the New York area. No other section, except the already fully developed eastern and southern rims of Central Park, enjoys so fortunate a location adjacent to large parks and near the business center. While such a scheme would require the exercise of eminent domain for land assembly, the write-down in land cost might be moderate. It might also be outweighed by the increase in taxable value of the existing elevator apartments as a result of the physical and social improvement of their surroundings.

Whatever the policy decision may be, many questions arise: **QUESTIONS RAISED**

1. Is it really desirable to segregate our population by age and to establish a whole area of 300,000 people without children? Moreover, if the Riverside area with its two big parks cannot be made suitable for children, which part of Manhattan can? Or should all of Manhattan become a childless island of two million people?

2. Even if it were accepted as desirable to develop the Riverside area for an exclusively adult population, is it possible? Children have a way of coming into the world as a result of certain deeply ingrained parental habits. As long as children are small, it will not be hard to find play space for them by establishing tot lots near the new apartments, or by taking them to the park. Once they pass that age, will their parents be willing to leave an area in which they have established many ties? Obviously, many will not, which means that some schools will have to remain. But if there are only a few school children scattered over the area, it will be even more difficult for them to get to school across heavily traveled streets.

3. Suppose these problems can be solved. Then what is to become of the more than 100,000 people who live in the old houses that would have to be demolished? Many of the middle-

class single persons who now live there in fairly spacious, if somewhat seamy, apartments will be neither able nor willing to exchange these for much more expensive new smaller apartments, however bright and shiny.

4. Are we going to establish an area segregated not only by age but also by class? If not, we shall have to build a substantial amount of public housing in the Riverside area. And if we want to stick to the purpose of developing the area for people who have good reason to be close to the central city, we shall have to reserve these apartments for working adults. Are we prepared to create such a new and unusual type of public housing? Would we be justified in diverting public housing funds, while the needs of large families and of old people remain unsatisfied?

5. What about the low-income families with children who now live in the area? We may agree that they would be better off in housing in areas of lower density farther out. But where is such housing available? Can it be made available in any foreseeable future? Most new public housing is required to rehouse tenants displaced by slum clearance, because there are no other acceptable low-rent vacancies.

6. If we agree — as reason compels us — that slum clearance must be deferred until more low-rent vacancies are available, how can we expect to clear the Riverside area, while many worse slums remain in the city?

7. If clearance of the area has to be deferred for a long time, a whole new set of problems arises. What can we do to make the best out of the existing old houses?

8. How much can be done by better policing? The gridiron street pattern, whatever its faults, is easy to police. Why can't it be done? Why can't garbage and trash be collected more frequently in areas where high densities inevitably produce large quantities of waste products? To what extent is the problem of Riverside a problem of poor public management?

9. To what extent is it a problem of poor private management? Structurally most of the buildings are sound. They are overcrowded, poorly maintained, poorly serviced — and frequently highly profitable. The same structure, rented at reasonable rents at decent occupancy standards, reasonably well maintained and serviced, would be a less profitable, hence a less valuable, building. Could not the federal redevelopment

subsidy be used to write down the value of the building to the level that it would retain after restrictions on rent, occupancy, and higher standards of maintenance and services have been imposed on it? And could not the power of eminent domain be used to assemble such buildings and sell or lease them under such restrictions?

21

The Cité Ouvrière
of Mulhouse, France

ANCIENT HISTORY? Public housing is regarded as a new twentieth-century venture both by its friends and by its enemies. However, it has its antecedents, and the problems faced by "housers" in the early days of the Industrial Revolution are strangely similar to those discussed in our day.

Then, as now, the specter of communism haunted established society. The Chartist movement stirred England, and revolution was rife on the Continent. In February 1848 the storm broke in Paris; in March and April it swept all over Europe. On May 18, 1848, Prince Albert made a sensational speech stressing the need for improved housing for the laboring classes, and he followed up these words by the erection of model homes at the London World's Fair.

"The subject now submitted to the consideration of the Royal Institute of British Architects is one to which their special attention has not been previously invited." With these oddly familiar words, Mr. Henry Roberts, architect of the model houses, introduced his paper to the venerable institute on January 21, 1850. The ensuing publication[1] was at once translated into French and widely circulated on the recommendation of Louis Napoleon, then President of the Second Republic. In September 1851, Mr. Jean Zuber, a young manufacturer of Mulhouse in Alsace, read a paper on English housing before the Industrial Society of his home town. In

[1] Henry Roberts, *The Model Houses for Families Erected by Prince Albert* (London, 1851). See also Henry Roberts, *The Dwellings of the Laboring Classes* (London, 1853).

Mulhouse the seed found the ground well prepared. Often walking as long as four hours a day, the workers in the city's rapidly expanding textile mills came from the surrounding villages. In order to overcome the resulting inefficiency, several manufacturers had erected rental dwellings for their workers. Now the Industrial Society decided to try to promote home ownership. They went about it in a well-considered manner. First, the city's leading industrialist, Mr. Jean Dollfus, commissioned an architect, Mr. Emile Muller, to design four houses. At the end of the year the tenants of these houses were consulted. In addition, a commission studied all available French and foreign models. It was recognized that the English models could not be copied because of the difference in living habits, while the tenement type prevalent in Paris was rejected as undesirable. Finally it was decided to try out three different types. In 1853 a limited-dividend company was organized, a site plan drawn, and a hundred houses built. The number was soon raised to 900, and by 1870 a total of 3,000 houses had been built, housing almost one third of the city's population.[2] In addition, the competition of these houses had resulted in marked improvements of the other dwellings throughout the city.

Following the annexation of Alsace to Germany, the migration of the textile industry to France interrupted the growth. Nevertheless, in 1920, about 15,000 persons were living in the "Workers' City," as it had come to be known. Several nearby cities—Guebwiller, Colmar, and Beaucourt—followed the example of Mulhouse. In their time, these Alsatian "Cités Ouvrières" attracted visitors from all European countries and also from America.

Housing almost one third of a city's population is indeed a feat that compares rather favorably with our achievements to date in rehousing "one third of a nation." How was it done?

At the outset the housing company issued 60 shares at 5,000 francs each, which were taken up by the leading members of the Industrial Society of Mulhouse. These original shareholders elected the administration that served for a lifetime and without pay. The dividends were limited to 4 per cent, about 1 per cent less than the current interest rate for first

STRUCTURE AND POLICY OF THE COMPANY

[2] A. Penot, *Les Cités Ouvrières de Mulhouse* (Mulhouse-Paris, 1867).

mortgages. To the 300,000 francs thus raised was added a government grant of 150,000 francs that was used exclusively for streets and utilities. A second grant of 150,000 francs was given to complement the investment of the next 300,000 francs, which, however, were only partially raised by the issue of new shares, the balance being covered by mortgages. Here again the Mulhouse project was remarkably modern. The French interest rate being high, they obtained mortgages in Basle, Switzerland, at 4.5 to 5 per cent. This was probably the first venture of international capital in low-cost housing. Further extensions were financed entirely by private capital without state subsidies, resulting in somewhat higher prices for the houses.

The houses were sold in installments over a period of up to 15 years, the annual payments amounting to about 8 per cent of the value. Normally a down payment of about 10 per cent was required, but in some cases this could also be paid off in installments over the first year. At first, the workers were hesitant because of uncertainty of employment. As a matter of fact, during the cotton crisis caused by the American Civil War several workers were unable to keep up their payments and lost their titles. However, the rules of the company had made a remarkably liberal provision for this case. The dweller was regarded as having lived as a tenant, and all money paid in excess of the normal shelter rent was refunded — down payment as well as annuities.

Because the costs of maintenance, administration, and insurance were low and utilities were not included, rents were considerably lower than installment payments. For a 3,000-franc house, for instance, the monthly rent was 18 francs, the monthly installment 25 francs. After 13 or 14 years, the owner had acquired free title, having paid a total of 4,327 francs, or the equivalent of 20 years' rent. This was a good bargain, considering that the houses were well built and are still in use today after more than a hundred years.

The company was careful to keep out speculators and to protect the character of the development. Without the consent of the company, nobody could sell his house before he had fully paid up and in no case before ten years. No alterations, exterior or interior, were allowed without consent. Houses, gardens, and fences had to be kept in order. Subletting was prohibited. However, the company was inclined to close an eye or two on this point if the owner used his increased income to make speedier payments.

Premiums were paid for good maintenance of house and garden. Regular school attendance of the children was also a consideration in the distribution of these premiums. This is characteristic of a certain paternalism that pervaded the whole enterprise. The company sold to the inhabitants various articles of prime necessity — potatoes, coal, iron stoves and ranges, even overcoats. A family home was established for working girls. However, as our author notes with regret, "few girls consent to submit to the sweet and salutary discipline which is imposed on them."

Perhaps it is due to this paternalistic attitude that the development was planned from the very start as a complete community by the architect, who designed the dwellings as well as all other buildings. The site was well chosen, between the old city and the factory district that had sprung up near the freight yards. Later an extension was built on the left bank of the Ill Canal, close to the industrial suburb of Dornach (Fig. 1).

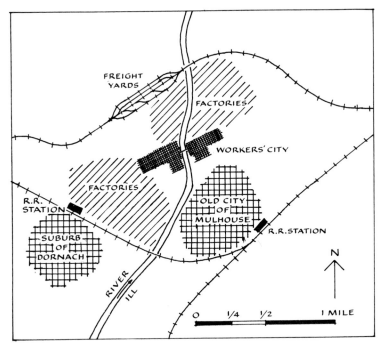

Figure 1
Mulhouse in 1920.

THE CITÉ OUVRIÈRE OF MULHOUSE, FRANCE   203

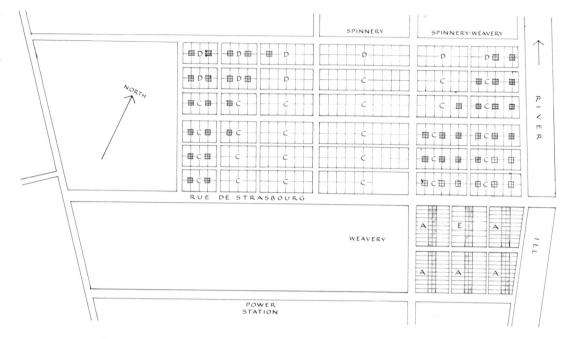

Figure 2 *The portion to the right (east) of the River Ill was built first. The portion to the left (west) of the river was an extension.*

While the immediate vicinity of factories may not conform to modern standards, proximity to work was justly considered of prime importance in an age lacking the means of mechanical transportation. Although the erection of the first houses immediately stimulated building on neighboring sites, the company was still able to acquire sufficient land for extension at the moderate price of 0.70 to 1.00 franc per square meter.

The original site was developed along a main street, 36 feet wide (Fig. 2), which was later extended across the canal, and along two parallel streets 26 feet wide. The extension on the west bank of the canal made a remarkable step forward by differentiating traffic streets from service lanes. Only every third street is a thoroughfare, 26 feet wide, while the other houses are served by 13-foot lanes. A central plaza was faced by three-story houses and flanked by buildings containing a laundry and baths and a bakery and restaurant, respectively. In the second section of the development the company erected a second bath and laundry and even an indoor swimming pool. Two kindergartens took care of 250 children each. A physi-

A. Two-story row houses, back to back.
B. Two-story row houses, with front and rear yards.
B.' Same as B, larger type for foremen.
C. Two-story houses in groups of four.
D. One-story houses in groups of four.
E. Furnished rooms for single men.
F. Three-story houses.
1. Baths and laundry.
2. Bakery and restaurant.

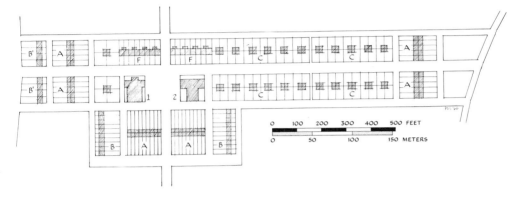

cian and a nurse were encouraged to settle in the development
by receiving houses free of rent. A home with furnished rooms
and a community hall took care of single men. A library served
the cultural needs of the community. All streets were lined
with linden trees. The need for public parks and playgrounds
was not yet felt, partly because of the proximity of open
country.

THE HOUSES In the main, the need for outdoor life was satisfied by a
garden 1,300 square feet in size next to each house. Carefully
cultivated according to age-old Alsatian tradition, these plots
produced vegetables of a value about equal to two months'
rent.

The first houses built were back-to-back row houses with
flues in the party walls for cross ventilation. This type was
soon abandoned because of lack of light in the deep rooms and
because the ventilation flues did not work. A very pleasant
five-room row house was the next step (Fig. 3). However,
aside from the disadvantage of cutting up the open space into
a front garden and a rear yard, this type proved too costly
(3,380 francs as against 2,900 for the first type) and was built
mainly for foremen.

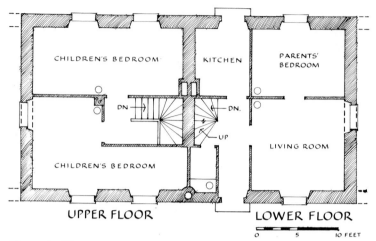

UPPER FLOOR   **LOWER FLOOR**

Figure 3   *This two-story house was usually built in rows of ten. Foremen's houses were in rows of four. Stoves were in each room. The house had a basement.*

Its place was taken by an interesting group of four two-story houses, costing 3,100 francs each. Cross ventilation was replaced by corner ventilation. Entry was through the kitchen instead of through a separate entrance hall (Fig. 4). Toilets were relegated to the outside but provided with ventilation flues carried up to the roof. The quadruplex arrangement resulted in a very desirable shape for the garden plot. While in the foremen's houses a small bedroom was provided on the

Figure 4   *This two-story house was built in groups of four, all back to back. The house had a basement.*

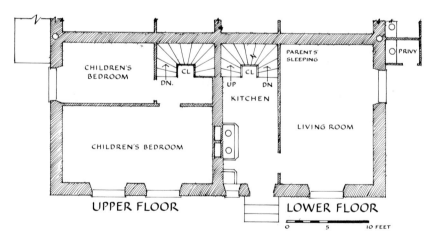

UPPER FLOOR   **LOWER FLOOR**

first floor, in the workers' houses the parents slept in the living room, and the large bedrooms upstairs were destined for their offspring of both sexes. French families were large in the good old days, 7.5 persons per house being the average in the Mulhouse development in 1865.

For smaller families, one-story quadruplexes were built, costing only 2,555 francs. While in the two-story houses the attic was kept low in order to prevent its use for living purposes, in the one-story house provision was made for addition of a fourth room in the attic with a window in the gable. Even this smallest type, like all the others, had a basement, 6 feet 3 inches high (Fig. 5).

In Guebwiller the builders who also started with deep back-to-back row houses approached the problem in two different ways. One was a group of six two-story four-room houses, each 27 feet 6 inches wide and only 15 feet 6 inches deep. All rooms received plenty of light, and four out of six dwellings had corner ventilation. The second type was a one-story row house, with provision for a fourth room in the attic and for a workshop in the cellar. In these houses the kitchen stove was placed in such a way that the mother could watch her children playing in the living room while handling her pots and pans.

In all of the houses, both in Mulhouse and in Guebwiller, there is double flooring over the cellar. The brick walls are 16 to 18 inches thick, and the roofs are covered with tiles.

Figure 5
This one-story house was built in groups of four, all back to back. It had an attic and a basement.

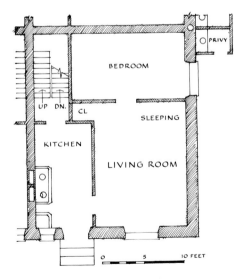

With the kitchen as the only heated room — except in the foremen's houses — double-glazed windows were a necessity. In Guebwiller they are 7 inches apart, allowing room for flowers. The architectural expression of the houses is simple and straightforward; well-studied proportions and carefully worked out detail give them a certain dignity.

LESSONS FROM THE PAST

All told, the Mulhouse Cité Ouvrière not only was a remarkable achievement in its own day but developed many useful approaches that are even today far from being generally accepted. These are:

1. Co-operation of private enterprise and government aid.
2. Limitation of the dividend to a rate slightly below the current interest rate on first mortgages.
3. Financing unrestricted by the limits of a national money market.
4. Consultation of the prospective inhabitants prior to drawing up plans.
5. Creation of a complete community with all facilities.
6. Design of the site, the dwellings, and all other buildings by the same architect as parts of a comprehensive plan.
7. Differentiation of traffic streets and service lanes.
8. Combination of the advantages of tenancy and of home ownership.

In this last respect, the Mulhouse plan has remained unique. Here the family could enjoy the pride of home ownership and take care of maintenance of the house, thereby achieving substantial savings without risking the loss of its investment in case of unemployment or other adversity. At the same time the company was freed of maintenance troubles in case the inhabitants returned to tenant status and their excess payments had to be refunded. The company still retained the profit or interest accrued in the meantime and was therefore in a better position than with a pure and simple rental project though, of course, burdened with greater responsibilities than is the speculative builder. As the bitter experience of millions of small homeowners has shown, it is precisely the risk of economic adversity that must be put on the shoulders of a stronger agency, public or private, while the home occupant can and should carry the burden of main-

Figure 6 Mulhouse, the Cité Ouvrière, in 1965.

tenance. The Mulhouse plan distributed the responsibilities in just this way and therefore deserves the most serious study. Some such plan may prove the only possible way of attack on the rural nonfarm slum, that bleak no-man's land untouched by any agency in the government.

EPILOGUE – 1965   The foregoing was written in 1940, but the war made it impossible to bring the story up to date. A letter mailed some years after the war to the administration of the Cité Ouvriène remained unanswered, and only a quarter century after the original writing in 1965 was I able to visit the development.

It became clear immediately why my letter had not been answered. There was no longer any "administration." In conformance with the original intention, all the houses had become the property of their occupants. The development was no longer a "project." It had become a normal part of the city, inhabited by normal working people living normal lives.

After more than a hundred years it was obviously still a desirable residential area. There were no signs of "blight." The houses and gardens were well maintained and lovingly cared for, with a profusion of roses in bloom. The street pattern, the row houses, and the quatrefoils were still there. But there was none of the monotony that must have characterized this, like almost any large-scale development, at its inception. Practically every homeowner had made some changes, added a wing or a porch or a garage, or a room in the attic, and had painted his house according to his taste. Some owners advertised small businesses carried on in their homes, including a few cafés and beer gardens, and on the wider streets a few stores had been established.

The big Dollfus textile factory was still within a few minutes' walk from the development. At the other sides the city had grown around it in a fashion so similar that it was hard to identify the boundary. At the corners were two schools and a children's playground. The narrow lanes were not barred to traffic, but the occasional car moving slowly along them did not interfere with the playing children. It remains to be seen whether in the future the shortage of space for moving and parking cars will become disruptive. Even if that should happen with increasing car ownership, the Cité Ouvrière will have served its inhabitants well for more than a century.

V
URBAN DESIGN

22

Universal Dilettante

Having observed the merry-go-round of planning fads for over half a century, I cannot but agree with the remarks in the editorial in the January *Newsletter** about planned obsolescence. But what can be done about it? Evidently, once the pendulum has swung wildly in one direction, it will swing back in the opposite one. It swings so wildly because, at a given time, planners have looked only at one side of their task and forgotten the others. The only cure is—to use Patrick Geddes' term—synopsis. In part this means looking at the picture from all sides: from the angle of the architect, the landscaper, the engineer, the traffic engineer, the economist, the lawyer, etc. But there are specialists in all of these professions who claim, and rightly so, to have their say in planning. The planner deals never—never!—with any field in which there is not some professional who knows more about it than he does. In every single one of these fields, he is a dilettante—the universal dilettante. His only specialty consists in having none, and therefore he is able to look at every one of them from the outside; and, strange as it may seem, I have found that the professionals value this outsider's look quite highly.

A dilettante is a man who takes delight in his work. This may be sinful in the puritan's book. In mine, there is no more honorable vocation. Even, and in particular, if one is a "planning official," as I have been for many years of my life, one has to remain a universal dilettante, or one ceases to be a planner.

*Newsletter of the American Society of Planning Officials, Vol. 30, No. 1 (January 1964).

The editorial objects to planners "returning to civic beauty" and says that "civic design played an insignificant part in creating these effects." This statement is demonstrably false. This is obvious in the case of all civic design in the Renaissance tradition. They all have exactly the effect they were designed to have.

Of course, there are things built by human hands that owe their beauty not to conscious design but to adaption to nature, function, and custom. Many villages are of this type. Many observers believe that the urban beauty of medieval cities is of this "natural" character. I thought so too. In 1952, when I enjoyed every morning the magnificent view of the Church of San Domenico in Siena, it never occurred to me that "civic design" had anything to do with it. Actually, when the church was built in the fourteenth century, this view did not exist. It was deliberately created in the following century by a decision of the city council to buy and demolish some houses in order to open up that view.

Let me give you a contemporary example from my home town of Hamburg, Germany. I cannot here relate the long and fascinating story of how the deliberate actions of several centuries transformed the swamps surrounding a little creek, the Alster, into three water basins, different in size and character. Every visitor to this city recalls at least two "effects" of this design: the clearly delineated rectangular shape of the "Inner Alster" in the very heart of the city, and the view of the tall spires of the old town from the Alster basins. Both were gravely endangered during the postwar years.

Not long after their liberation from Nazi tyranny, advertising agencies loudly claimed the inalienable right of free enterprise to huckster their wares by means of colored neon signs displayed in the most visible locations, on the walls and roofs of the buildings surrounding the "Inner Alster." It is only because the head of the City Planning Department put up a magnificent fight for several years that the citizens of Hamburg can still see every night the shape of their watery central piazza clearly outlined by rows of white lights reflected in the dark water.

Several years later, when the West German boom hit its stride, a number of big corporations asked for exemption from the height limit that had been established by zoning in the old city core. There was no doubt that these firms — and the city's economy — needed big corporate office buildings and that they could not expand horizontally. But the proposed office towers would have destroyed the beautiful silhouette of the old town. The City Planning Department solved this dilemma by proposing the creation of a "second central business district," five miles from the old one but equally accessible by both private and public transportation and fully equipped with retail and service establishments; in lengthy negotiations the department obtained the agreement of all the authorities and corporations concerned. The second central business district is now in being, and the citizens of Hamburg can still enjoy the view of their beloved spires rising over the mass of lower buildings and broad expanse of water.

If you ask them, most Hamburg citizens will say that they really do not have much to show you in the way of civic design but that theirs is still a pretty city because all that water and those old spires just happened to be there. But it did not just happen. It was not "serendipity"; it was "civic design."

I have told this tale of my home town because it destroys the triple alibi by which American planners excuse the ugliness of their cities: (1) The civic beauty that Americans admire abroad was created by kings, popes, or dictators; it cannot be done in a democracy. (2) The Old World cities have grown slowly; we do not have the time. (3) What is beautiful in those cities was inherited from the distant past and is now embellished by our sentimental nostalgia.

Hamburg's conditions did not differ from those in many of our cities; the alibi does not hold. What, then, is the reason for the difference? Is it because Americans do not care for civic beauty? Maybe, but I doubt it. I think they do care, but they have been conditioned to believe that they cannot do anything about it. It is the duty of city planners to show them that they can.

23

Scale in Civic Design

We hear much about the human scale in city planning these days. The term is used in a dual sense — referring to the social content and to the visual form. Sometimes the two are linked as in the following statement by Sir William Holford on the neighborhood idea: "Without it architecture would either go out of scale altogether, or lose itself in the byways of style and decoration." As I understand this statement, it means that the designer has only the choice of attempting to master the metropolis by blowing up all elements of design to gigantic scale or renouncing any attempt to master it as a whole and being satisfied with decorative embellishments of this or that part. The "neighborhood," on the scale of the traditional town, can be dealt with by traditional means — though the question of the design relations between neighborhoods remains unanswered.

But what exactly is this human scale? How can it be defined? In terms of social content, I would define it as a group, in which every person knows every other person by face, by voice, and by name. The size of this group generally does not exceed a few hundred people — far less than the 5,000 to 10,000 of the so-called neighborhood.

In terms of visual form — which is our present concern — we should go back to the same basic concept: that the human person must be visible. This concept limits the distance from the object; and from this distance can be derived the over-all size of the object as well as the size of the smallest part, which serves as the module on which it is designed.

It is rather amazing, in view of the many judgments on scale that have been and are being made everywhere, that apparently only one serious attempt at scientific definition has been made. In 1877 a German architect by the name of Maertens published a book entitled *The Optical Scale in the Plastic Arts*.[1] Maertens refers to a statement by Aristotle, who said that the size of the composite beautiful object is by no means arbitrary; if it is too small, the details become confused; if it is too large, its unity and wholeness disappear. Maertens starts from the fact that the part of our field of vision occupied by any object is defined by the angle formed by the rays from our eye to the outline of the object. It is known from physiological optics that the smallest discernible difference is one minute; this means that one cannot discern any object at a distance more than 3,450 times its size. This determines the distance at which a person can be recognized as such, which averages about 70 to 80 feet. Maertens relates this distance to the width of the nasal bone, as the smallest of the parts of the human body indispensable for perception of the person, and postulates it as a module for the smallest architectural profile of a building of "human" scale. The distance of about 70 feet determines not only the module of the building but also its over-all size. We desire, as Aristotle put it, to perceive its unity and wholeness, which means that the whole object should be visible at a glance. Maertens states, and experience confirms, that the maximum angle at which an object can be perceived clearly and easily is about 27 degrees, corresponding to a ratio of 1:2 between the size of the object and its distance from the beholder. This limitation is more noticeable and important in the vertical than in the horizontal direction, and here it undergoes the further modification that about two thirds of the normal field of vision is above the eye, one third below. From this might be derived dogmatically a number of maximum dimensions for a building of "human scale": horizontally about 36 feet, vertically 24 feet above the eye or 29 to 30 feet above the ground. These figures are derived from a distance of 72 feet — which would also determine the maximum street width. Both

[1] H. Maertens, *Der optische Masstab in den bildenden Kuensten,* 2nd edition (Berlin: Wasmuth, 1884).

this width and the height—three stories—seem to coincide fairly well with pragmatic concepts of "normal" size.

Now, as Maertens also recognizes, the distance of 70 to 80 feet and the angle of 27 degrees, while they are the basis of what we might call the "normal human" scale, are not the only significant measures. Indeed, if we seek the visual correlation of a human community of people known to each other, we must adopt a distance from which a human person can be recognized, as Maertens puts it, as a "portrait"; that is, we must be able to perceive easily his individual facial expression. This allows a distance—and street width—of not more than about 48 feet, maximum horizontal dimensions of 24 feet, and a maximum height of 16 feet above the eye, 21 feet above ground, or two stories. We might call this the "intimate human" scale. We tend to feel that there is a qualitative difference between this intimate character of one- and two-story buildings and the character of higher ones. In this feeling other factors certainly also play a role: trees are visible above the roofs of one- and two-story buildings, giving a feeling that space is continuous beyond the buildings, while higher buildings rigidly limit space.

There may also be some significance to the distance at which we may still perceive the presence of a human being, which seems generally to be not much more than 4,000 feet. It is interesting to note that the distance from the Washington obelisk to the Lincoln Memorial, which appears perfectly "in scale," is 4,200 feet, while the distance to the Capitol, which seems a bit "too far," is 7,300 feet. The view of the Capitol remains impressive only thanks to the supporting elevation of the hill. The same holds true of the vistas of the Art Museum in Philadelphia and of the Arc de Triomphe in Paris, both of which also extend for about one and a half miles. The axis of Peking—probably the greatest of all achievements of civic design—from the gate of the Tatar City to the top of Coal Hill measures over 8,300 feet, but this vista is time and again broken by buildings, so that it actually consists of a sequence of courts of varying size and proportion; in addition, elements of the landscape strongly enter the picture (Fig. 1). I know of no uninterrupted urban vista extending beyond one and a half miles that does not become empty and fatiguing. None of the great vistas of baroque Rome exceeds a mile. Here may be

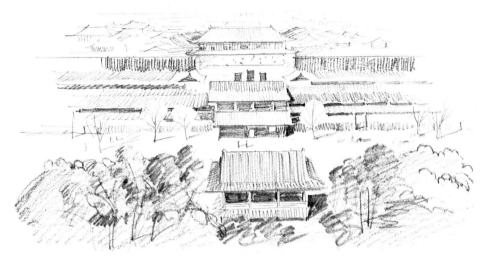

The magnificent axis of the Imperial City does not become tiring despite its length of over 8,000 feet, because it is experienced as a sequence of courts of varying size and shape.

Figure 1
Peking,
view of the Forbidden City
from Mei Shan.

the limits and elements of what we might call the "public human" scale.

But even more important than absolute distances are the angles of perception. At an angle of 27 degrees (height-distance ratio 1 : 2) the object appears, as Maertens puts it, "as a little world in itself," with the surroundings only dimly perceived as a background; at an angle of 18 degrees (1 : 3) it still dominates the picture, but now its relation to its surroundings becomes equally important. At angles of 12 degrees (1 : 4) or less, the object becomes part of its surroundings and speaks mainly through its silhouette. This may have some bearing on the frequently mentioned rule of thumb that the ratio between the two dimensions of a plaza should not exceed 1 : 3.

If the angle increases beyond 27 degrees, some image of the whole may still remain up to a distance of 1 : 1 (45 degrees); Maertens thinks this is the best distance from which to study the details in their relation to the whole. More important is the fact that the impressions received from the periphery of the field of vision are essential to the perception of space, as those at intermediate angles convey plastic perceptions, while at small angles we perceive objects mainly as silhouettes.

It is important to study proportions not merely as they can be measured on a system of horizontal and vertical planes but as they appear on our perisphere of vision, to be measured by the angle of vision from the eye of the beholder. A contemporary Greek architect, Doxiadis,[2] has studied ancient Greek urban compositions, analyzing the angles under which various objects are seen by the beholder standing at a significant point, such as the Propylaea of the Athenian Acropolis, and has found that harmonious proportions obtain between these angles, regardless of the absolute size and distance of the objects.

As the reader may recall, Viollet-le-Duc said that the Greeks had a "module," but not a "scale," while the Middle Ages had a scale, given by the size of man. The scale of the classical orders is indeed relative to the entire order, each part growing or shrinking as the whole grows or shrinks while it is absolute in regard to man. In the Middle Ages, on the other hand, each characteristic part has a fairly constant size related to man and is therefore absolute in regard to the size of the building as a whole. In the classical building the number of elements (columns, doors, profiles) remains constant, while

[2]Constantinos A. Doxiadis, *Raumordnung im Griechischen Staedtebau* (Heidelberg and Berlin: Kurt Vowinckel, 1937).

Figure 2
Door of the Erechtheion, Athens.

In classical design the size of any element such as a door, and of every one of its moldings, is determined by its relation to the whole order. The number of these elements is constant, and their dimensions may increase with the size of the building.

their size varies; in the medieval building their size remains constant, while their number varies.

A comparison of the façade of Bourges Cathedral, with its five pairs of small doors and the multiplication of small columns and archivolts surrounding each pair, with the one big door of the Erechtheion clearly illustrates this different concept of scale (Figs. 2 and 3).

While it is important to realize that these are two different approaches to the problem of scale, it should not be over-

In medieval design the size of any element, such as a door, and of every one of its parts, is determined by its relation to the human person. Their size is roughly constant, but the number of doors, and of columns and archivolts surrounding each door, may increase with the size of the building.

Figure 3
Bourges Cathedral.

looked that the most perfect, truly "classical" creations of each of the two groups do not ignore the concept of scale generally characteristic of the other. Maertens points out that in Paris, Rheims, and Amiens the figures of the kings and the structural members have a module clearly discernible to the beholder at a distance equal to the height of the nave—that is, the front can be seen as a whole with clearly articulated parts. Even more significant is the relation of scale of the temples of classical Greece to the human being, a relation that in the art of Asia Minor, Rome, and its derivatives is often sacrificed to the desire for the colossal. Richard Dinsmore has pointed out that the flutes of the Doric column have the dimensions of a human arm or a clear multiple of that basic dimension. Maertens emphasizes that no temple in classical Greece exceeded the height of 65 feet; it was visible at one glance, at an angle of 45 degrees, from the "normal human" distance, and with the module related to normal human size.

Clear visual perception is, of course, our main instrument for experiencing spatial relations, but it is not isolated. In bright daylight vision we receive at the focal point a clear image that, however, rapidly becomes blurred toward the periphery. In dim light, at night, we cannot get any object into clear focus but receive equally blurred impressions from a wide field of vision. Goethe expressed this in a beautiful verse in the "Trilogy of Passion":

> *Des Menschen Leben scheint ein herrlich Los*
> *Der Tag, wie lieblich, so die Nacht, wie gross* [3]

The day is lovely, full of color and distinct form; the night swallows all this loveliness, but she gives something else: grandeur. Some may have perceived how much stronger are spatial experiences at night, both of spaces in nature—a valley, a forest clearing—and of man-made streets and plazas. Perhaps many have never perceived it; not only do we seem bent on expelling the grandeur of night from our cities—except when the revival of barbarism blacks them out—but our glaring headlights chase her even from the open country. Sometimes I wonder whether the general atrophy of spatial feeling has

[3] "The life of man appears a glorious fate
  The day how lovely, and the night, how great."

not something to do with this disappearance of night vision Probably, however, it is primarily related to a more basic orientation of our culture: the categorical imperative to "keep your eye on the ball," to narrow your focus on the isolated fact, on the immediate goal. Just as this attitude hampers the development of general theory in the field of science, so does it blight the unfolding of comprehensive vision in the field of art.

If we take our eye off the ball and open our senses to the richness of the world, we shall receive spatial sensations through all of them. In entering Chartres Cathedral, the reverberations of our steps, and even more so of music, convey to us its vastness. The radiation from our body to the coolness of its walls and vaults conveys their mass; we do not have the same experience in an imitation lath-and-plaster vault. Most important are our vasomotor sensations. In turning our eyeballs and our heads upward, we experience its soaring height; in walking toward the choir, we experience the length of the nave. All of these sensations contribute to our experience of the scale of our environment.

In the cathedral this scale can hardly be called "human." Indeed, the field of the "normal human" and especially of the "intimate human" scale has been the field of the home builder rather than that of the architect. Civic design has been directed primarily to exalt the human beyond his normal scale; almost all its works are on this exalted scale, the grand scale, the monumental scale! We may call it the superhuman scale and define it as a scale that goes beyond the normal human but is definitely related to it, so as to develop the feeling of grandeur out of its contrast to what is found or expected as normal.

We have touched on the problem of this superhuman scale in talking of the "public human" scale as going beyond the normal human. We have come closer to the concept in discussing the impression of a Greek temple and of a medieval cathedral when seen at less than an angle of 45 degrees. A building that at the "normal" distance rises to fill the entire field of vision rises beyond the normal human scale to convey a feeling of grandeur.

The content and intent of this superhuman scale has been perfectly expressed by Corneille — the grand poet of France's Grand Century — in the verse:

Et nous fait présumer, à ses superbes toits
Que tous ses habitants sont des dieux ou des rois[4]

A scale of gods or kings, not of men. A scale different from the human, indeed opposed to the intimate human. When talking about scale, when attempting to design in scale, we should know clearly which scale we are seeking: the intimate, the domestic, conveying the feeling of being at home, being at ease; or the grand, the monumental, the surprising, the thing "out of this world," which conveys feelings of exaltation or of awe.

Buildings and spaces designed on these two scales may reinforce each other by their contrast, as long as they remain commensurable, that is, as long as the superhuman can be related to the human scale; otherwise, it becomes gigantic, colossal, inhuman.

It has been said that there are two opposite kinds of the monumental: the one that exalts the human being because he identifies himself with its strength and grandeur, the other that overawes him as an alien and threatening force. There may be some truth in this; certainly the monumental may range from the boundary of the dignified human to the boundary of the colossal.

What we propose to call the superhuman scale is not entirely identical with the grand or monumental scale. It is any design that makes objects or spaces appear as large or larger than they are. As Leon Battista Alberti observed, curved streets will make a city appear larger, because you do not see it all at once; there is the element of surprise and discovery.

The cities of the Islamic Orient owe their charm very largely to this element of surprise and discovery. On the outskirts of Samarkand there is a group of mausoleums of the Timurides, lined up along a path that leads to a sanctuary known as Shah Zindé, "the Living King," which has given its name to the entire group. It is actually quite small: from the entrance gate to the center of the sanctuary only 650 feet, the length of a Manhattan city block. Yet it seems an entire world; after spending hours walking around, you feel there are still discoveries to be made. It is worthwhile to analyze some of the ele-

[4] "And makes us presume, at [the sight of] its proud roofs
  That all its inhabitants are gods or kings."

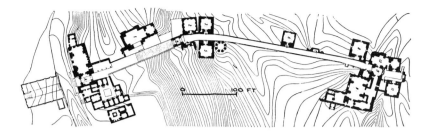

This group of mausoleums, only 600 feet long, offers ever new experiences of surprise and discovery to the visitor ascending the path because of the subtle changes in direction, both horizontally and vertically.

Figure 4
Shah Zindé, Samarkand.

A view of Shah Zindé, Samarkand.

Figure 5

ments contributing to this impression. The path is narrow, varying in width from 6 to 12 feet. It varies also in direction, not only horizontally but vertically as well, ascending at varying grades, with several flights of stairs interspersed, some long, some short. It is broken by two intermediate gates. In ascending, you again and again interrupt your procession, to turn off to one side or the other, into one of the mausoleums, and frequently inside you turn again into some chapel or niche. Always you leave behind some direction in which you have not yet gone and explored. Add to this the delicacy and the completely two-dimensional character of the glazed-tile decoration, which makes any volume look large and important, and you begin to understand why the experience seems so much beyond the normal human, so entirely "out of this world" (Figs. 4 and 5).

Figure 6
Bryce House,
Annapolis, Maryland.

This building of moderate size appears monumental because of the contrast of the low wings and the low brick wall in front, because of the high level of the first floor, and because of the comparison with the familiar size of the bricks, the window panes, and the steps.

Figure 7
Church and
monastery of the Superga
near Torino, Italy.

The church appears large because the common cornice of the nave relates it to the six stories of the monastery; its impression is enhanced because it is located on higher ground and closer to the beholder than the monastery. The cupola, rising from the cornice of the nave as from a base, appears truly majestic.

The enrichment of spatial experience by the change in direction, horizontally and vertically, is the main virtue of the "informal" design. But it may also be present in formal design, as in the Scala di Spagna in Rome and in the Place Royale group in Nancy. There are many means to enhance the visual importance of buildings and squares. Brinckmann devotes to them an interesting chapter.[5] The most widely used is a contrasting background: vertical versus horizontal lines, regular shapes versus irregular ones, large buildings versus small ones, which may appear even smaller if set lower or farther back, larger elements (floor heights, windows, columns) versus smaller ones, volume and body versus flat surfaces, and so on. Another technique is to relate these contrasting elements by guiding lines. Finally the presence of elements of familiar size, such as bricks or steps, "gives scale." Steps are particularly important because of their three-dimensional character and their association with movement in space; after all, the very word scale — *scala* — means stairs (Figs. 6 and 7).

There is an unending wealth of examples to illustrate these relations. It is interesting, for instance, to compare the imposing effect of a relatively small building, like the Palazzo Angelotti in Montepulciano, with the almost complete lack of impact of the world's tallest structure, the Empire State Building (Figs. 8 and 9).

Very important, and too generally neglected, is the role of the "floor," such as the pavement of a plaza. A unified design and a concave section can do much to convey the experience of the size and shape of a square, and adequate size of the elements of the floor may help to realize the size of both a square or street and the surrounding buildings.

With so rich an arsenal, it would seem possible to conquer the visual chaos of our great cities and to create form and order on the more than human scale on which they are built. That is what the men of the "City Beautiful" movement thought; why did they fail?

The monumental scale, as Corneille said, belongs to gods and kings. But where are our kings? Where are our gods? *Monument* comes from *monere,* to remember. What do we want to remember and to be remembered for all times? The monument, said Dean Hudnut in a profound witticism, does

[5] A. E. Brinckmann, *Stadtbaukunst* (Berlin, 1920).

Figure 8

Palazzo Angelotti, Montepulciano.

*The monumental impression of this rela-
tively small building is due to several factors: because the street is narrow, winding,
and drops down, the second story of the
Palazzo rises high above the four stories
of the houses in the background; the strong
plastic expression of the* rustica *and window treatment of the Palazzo and the deep
volume of its court contrast with the flat
surfaces of the houses.*

Figure 9

The Empire State Building, New York,
as seen from West 34th Street.

*In contrast to the Palazzo Angelotti, the
world's tallest building is quite unimpres-
sive because there is nothing against which
to compare its distance and size, and because the arbitrary variation of the heights
of buildings on the street destroys any
possibility of relating foreground and background by guiding lines.*

not remember. Worse, we suspect it to remember what was
not, as Swift's Houyhnhnms found out that humans are wont
to say the thing that is not. There are deep-seated ideological
reasons for the antimonumental trend of contemporary
architecture.

But there are practical reasons also. The great traditions of
civic design, which inspired the City Beautiful movement, organized the city as a system of streets on which people moved
and of squares on which they assembled. Palladio wrote:
"These principal piazze ought to be made of such size, as the
multitude of the citizens requires, that they may not be too
small for their convenience and use, or that, through the small
number of people, they may not seem uninhabited"; and a
nineteenth-century mayor of Brussels stated: "If a plaza has

no utilitarian destination, it is dead and deserted."[6] This alone would have killed our "Civic Centers." But in order to cope with the demands of traffic and with the impact of the surrounding skyscrapers, they have been extended to dimensions that can no longer be related to the human being; their scale is no longer "superhuman" but colossal and inhuman.

There appears to be a definite upper limit to the size of a plaza, as to the length of a street, which can convey a strong spatial experience. We know that the surrounding buildings, to be impressive, should be seen at a distance of not more than 1:3; this distance is nowhere exceeded on the Piazza and Piazzetta of Venice. But we cannot simply compensate for a larger surface by making the surrounding buildings higher. It is amazing how small the most impressive historical squares really are. The mighty oval of the Piazza San Pietro in Rome is only 430 by 650 feet. The measure of approximately 450 feet appears rather frequently in the most successful plazas, such as the Place Vendôme in Paris and Amalienborg Square in Copenhagen.

Where the small dimension considerably exceeds this measure, as on the squares along the Ring in Vienna, the Place de la Nation in Paris, the Civic Center in San Francisco, and the square in front of St. Isaacs in Leningrad, the spatial impression is weak, more that of a field than of a plaza, despite the great height of the structures. Leningrad, the latest and greatest creation of the classical period of civic design, is of particular interest because here the means of that period, the street with a *point de vue* and the monumental plaza, have been exalted to their limit and in some cases beyond. Yet, this vast urban composition, completed around 1830, covers only a very small part of contemporary Leningrad, and Leningrad is much more compact than an American metropolis of comparable size (Figs. 10 and 11).

What is most visible in the American metropolis are structures and spaces of an entirely different character and on an entirely different scale, of which the great bridges are the most outstanding examples. This is not the superhuman scale, because it is in no way commensurate with the human person; nor is it the inhuman scale of the overgrown apartment house, such as Stuyvesant Town, or the colossal scale of a public

[6]Charles Buls. *L'Esthétique des Villes* (Brussels, 1893).

Figure 10
Leningrad,
Uritsky Square.

In the great squares of Leningrad the extreme limits of the "superhuman" scale have been reached and in some cases exceeded.

building with a classical order blown up to five times life size. The great bridges, the airfields and hangars, the dams and reservoirs, the power stations and elevators, the expressways with their cloverleafs, are perfectly "right" in scale, which is neither "human" nor "superhuman"; it might be called "extra-human." It is a scale related more to the phenomena of nature, to rivers and lakes, to mountains and valleys, than to any creation on the "superhuman" scale, even though some of these may be just as big. They differ from the "superhuman" in three ways: they are utilitarian, not symbolic, not "dwellings of gods and kings"; they are the product not of human hands but of mechanical forces of nature, controlled by man; and they are perceived generally not in walking or standing but from a rapidly moving mechanical vehicle.

Related to, but not wholly of, these phenomena is that peculiar American invention, the skyscraper. It is hardly

230 URBAN DESIGN

ST. PETERSBURG

1. Isaac Cathedral
2. Kazan Cathedral
3. Winter Palace
4. Hermitage
5. Marble Palace
6. Fortress and Cathedral
7. Peter the Great's Cottage
8. Academy of Sciences
9. University
10. Academy of Arts
11. Mining School
12. Imperial Public Library
13. Foundling Hospital
14. Michael Palace
15. Taurida Palace
16. Old Arsenal
   a. New Arsenal
17. Smolnoi Church
18. Monastery of St. Alexander Nevski
19. Preobrajenski Church
20. Church of Holy Trinity
21. Roman Catholic Church
   b. Page School
22. English Church
23. Statue of Peter the Great
   c. Alexander College
   d. Rumiantsoff Obelisk
   e. Suworoff Monument
   f. Nicholas Monument
24. Markets
25. Kalinkin Hospital
26. Great Theater, Marie Theater
   g. Alexander Theater
   h. Michael Theater
27. English Club
28. Geographical Society
29. Leuchtenberg Palace
30. Summer Gardens
31. Exchange
32. Post and Telegraph Offices
33. Hôtel Benton
34. Hôtel Klee
35. Hôtel de France
36. British Embassy
37. Warsaw Railway Station
38. Peterhof Railway Station
39. Tsarskoe Selo Railway Station
40. Moscow Railway Station
41. The Point (Elaghin Island)
42. Isler's Mineral Waters

Figure 11
Plan of Leningrad.

While these squares are as large as possible, or larger, in relation to the human person, they are no larger than necessary to give rhythm and unity to the city of the eighteenth and early nineteenth centuries. But this city occupies only a very small part of the twentieth-century metropolis.

accidental that the skyscraper, like the two other outstanding vertical creations of architectural history, the Buddhist stupa and the medieval spire, was the child of a puritanical culture. It certainly was a symbol of power; it is seen by pedestrians; and the height of its floors and the size of its windows are inevitably derived from the size of the human body. We have never been quite sure whether it should be treated on a super-human or on an extrahuman scale. "The tall office building," said Louis Sullivan, "is lofty . . . the force and power of altitude must be in it, the glory and pride of exaltation must be in it." Power, glory, pride, exaltation—Sullivan saw the skyscraper as a monumental, "superhuman" creation; and as such, as a "cathedral of business," it has been treated in its heyday. But the United Nations Building—which might have a better claim to monumental symbolism than any other skyscraper—hides the elements relating it to human scale, the floors and windows, behind a uniform screen of glass—or of marble on the short sides. It is therefore completely extrahuman. Like Wachs-mann's gigantic hangar, it might be twice as big or half as big without looking really different. Le Corbusier's proposal for Algiers and Oscar Niemeyer's project for a huge apartment hotel in Brazil are, because of their greater size, even more unmistakably representatives of the extrahuman scale. The Algiers structure has no relation whatever to the buildings of the existing city, but it does have a strong and intimate rela-tion to the mountains and the sea.

Thus we deal in the modern metropolis with three different scales: the human, the superhuman, and the extrahuman. The metropolis is no longer a city; it is a region and can be con-ceived only as a vast urban landscape. A landscape is per-ceived mainly as a silhouette; even a high mountain, such as Mount Rainier seen from Seattle, appears at less than an angle of only a few degrees. The perception of volumes and spaces is not immediately sensual, as on the genuine urban scale, but more strongly mediated by associations. With few exceptions, the immediate sensation is that of wide-open spaces; the limits of space are "read" rather than felt. Can such an urban land-scape be conceived as a whole; can it be designed so as to produce a mental image?

The desire to grasp a city as a mental image is deep-seated and powerful. This image can be grasped in two ways: from the outside as a silhouette and from the inside as a sequence of open spaces, traditionally mostly streets and squares. In some small towns, like Montpazier and Richelieu in France, one can see from one gate to the other, grasping the whole length of the main street at one glance. But even in a city as big as Kublai Khan's Peking, Marco Polo derived strong satisfaction from the observation that "the streets are so wide and straight that you can see right along them from end to end and from one gate to the other." In the Renaissance the concept of the city as a unit was more consciously formulated. "The relation of the city to its parts is similar to that of the human body to its parts; the streets are the veins," wrote an Italian architect.[7]

It is evident that the enormous expanse of the modern metropolis can no longer be articulated by streets and plazas. If it can be articulated at all, it can be only as an urban landscape composed of the contrasting elements of built-up and open sections. Fortunate are those cities, like Hamburg and Leningrad, that are built around large expanses of water. Here the image of outer space and of silhouette may merge into one.

In the silhouette of the American city the towering center may represent the entire metropolis, as did the cathedral of old; though only once, in the magnificent pirates' den of Lower Manhattan has it been so concentrated as to grow fully to extrahuman scale, "a man-made mountain rising from the sea," as Fiske Kimball so aptly called it. Within the residential areas, which should as nearly as possible be pedestrian islands, the domestic human scale can and must prevail, and its intimacy may be enhanced by the outlook to the contrasting extrahuman scale of the surrounding urban landscape; and at the centers of community life the human scale may be exalted to the superhuman. But how can these built-up areas, outside the center, develop a silhouette that would set them off as important members of the body of the metropolis from the open parts of the urban landscape? The centers of their community life are low buildings; and tall apartment houses or industrial buildings, while they may be accents in the urban landscape, can claim no greater significance than the lower buildings that they appear to dominate.

[7] Francesco di Giorgio Martini, *Trattato dell' Architettura Civile e Militare* (1500); quoted from A. E. Brinckmann, *Platz und Monument* (1912), p. 30.

I have raised more questions than I have answered. Let me ask a last one. Maybe we are chasing a will-o'-the-wisp in our quest for a comprehensible form of the modern metropolis. At the end of the great period of civic design, and at the eve of the Industrial Revolution, the Abbé Laugier wrote: "Il faut de la régularité et de la bizarrerie, des rapports et des oppositions, des accidens qui varient le tableau, d'un grand ordre dans les détails, de la confusion, du fracas, du tumulte dans l'ensemble."[8] These words are strangely reminiscent of a much-quoted statement by Karl Marx, in which he contrasts the order, the organization, the co-operation within the individual factories with the disorder, the anarchy, the fight of all against all in the economy as a whole.

Commenting on an article I had written on "Form and Function in Urban Communities," Henry Churchill once wrote me that the form of our cities was a true reflection of their content. There is, no doubt, a true reflection of life, and one not without beauty, in the massed skyscrapers of New York's downtown area, in the dynamic hell of fire and smoke of Pittsburgh's Monongahela Valley, yes, and also in their counterpart, the aseptic tranquility of our upper-middle-class suburbs. As for the whole, there certainly are the "confusion, turmoil, tumult" for which Abbé Laugier called. Can we, perhaps, have civic design only in details, because we are citizens only in details? Can man design a city if it is not the City of Man?

[8] "There is need for the regular and for the bizarre, for relations and for oppositions, for accidents which give variety to the picture, for a great order in the details, for confusion, for turmoil, for tumult in the whole."

24

Scale in the Metropolis

Some observers of the urban scene in the United States think that the metropolis is already passé, that it is being engulfed by a larger unit, the "urban region," such as that which extends from Boston to Washington. However, there is really nothing new in the string of cities lined up along a favorable trade route or in the fact that the area between such cities is more intensely developed than the surrounding country. What is new is the character of the individual units out of which the "urban region" is composed. This unit is no longer a "city"; it is a "metropolitan region," though it is still called by the name of the historic city that forms its core: New York or Philadelphia, Montreal or Toronto.

The metropolitan region — or "metropolis" for short — is a new form of human settlement that has never existed before in history. Through 5,000 years of civilization man has lived in two main forms of settlement, opposed and supplementary to each other: the city and the country village.

This age-old pattern has been transformed by the Industrial Revolution and the ever-increasing division and specialization of labor, which is both its cause and its effect. Now all work not directly tied to the soil is increasingly polarized in ever larger and more diversified concentrations of population, while at the other pole the village breaks up into individual farms. This second movement has almost run its course on the North American continent; only in a few areas in Canada, chiefly in Quebec, do genuine country villages survive.

The first, and far more important, movement is only in its beginning, and most people still misinterpret the modern metropolis as just an overgrown city. But actually there are profound qualitative differences. Not only is its population larger but, as a result of the development of new means of transportation and communication, it is spreading out over a vaster and vaster territory; and this territory contains not only the elements of the old city—residences, markets, buildings for government, religion, and culture—but extensive areas devoted exclusively to work. It also includes large open areas for recreation as well as for agriculture.

It is, indeed, neither city nor country. This has alarmed many architects, planners, and critics who look for the city in the modern metropolis and cannot find it. No longer can it be identified from the outside by its silhouette, clearly set off from the surrounding fields. No longer can it be comprehended from the inside as a system of clearly defined spaces of plazas and streets. It appears as chaos; it seems impossible to give form and order to this endless sprawl. Faced with this phenomenon, unheard of and never seen before, we are inclined to escape and to refuse to admit that it is what it is. We wish that it would make up its mind to be either city or country.

It would be nice for architects and planners if it could be that way. City and country have existed for 5,000 years; we know what they look like and how to design in or for them. But nostalgia is a poor guide. Too often suburban design has failed by mistaking the suburb for a village and trying to recapture, in a conscious creation with its carefully thought-out technical solutions, the picturesque charm of the rural village, the product of the gradual and spontaneous mutual adaptation of men and nature. I am afraid that we shall equally fail if we mistake the metropolis for a city and try to recapture the urbanity that was the orderly framework in which citizens lived and in which they—and only they, on their own feet—moved around.

Ultimately both attitudes—the "rural" toward the suburb and the "urban" toward the metropolis—are eclectic. Like any eclecticism, they may create works of superficial charm, but not a genuinely true form. Just as there can be no genuine content without a form that contains it, so there can be no genuine form without the content to which it gives form.

If we can ever hope to find the form and scale of the metropolis, of the whole as well as of its many and diverse parts, and their mutual relationship, we must accept and understand it as it is actually developing before our eyes.

There are the residential neighborhoods, the world of the child, the aged, and the housewife. Their scale is the normal, intimate human scale of the village. From a short distance, just across the street or yard, close enough to recognize your neighbor's familiar face, you see in the same glance the whole of his house, without the effort of moving your head or craning your neck, or even moving your eyeballs. To be easily perceptible as frame and background of the normal human being as he lives his everyday life, this is the essence of the "human scale," the scale of the neighborhood.

But the adult moves out of the neighborhood to "the city" to meet and join with others for business, political, cultural, or solemn religious activity. By joining forces with his fellows he acquires a new dimension, the dimension of the citizen. The place where men meet to function as citizens, the agora, the forum, the piazza, has always been the core and essence of the city. This new force and dimension, the body politic, found its symbol and expression in gods and kings. Their houses are on a different, a "monumental" scale, which I choose to call the "superhuman" scale. It is still related to the human being, not to his normal size but to that attained by a proud effort. Where this relation is lost, the work is no longer monumental but merely colossal, not superhuman but inhuman, brutal, and senseless. Experience shows, and the physiology of human vision confirms, that there are definite absolute limits beyond which a building, a square, or a street becomes out of scale.

With the Renaissance and its ideal of *l'Uomo Divino*, "Man the Divine," man's house transforms itself into the *palazzo*, and the residential street and square into the symbols of "urbanity," which we admire in Paris, London, or Bath. Man's grandeur and dignity are the theme and inspiration of all design on the "superhuman" scale, the scale of the city. This realm of man the citizen is the realm of architecture with a capital "A." But the home and the neighborhood in the city, as in the country, always has been largely outside the realm of the architect—it was and still is the sphere of the craftsman-builder, lay or professional.

Western man of the mid-twentieth century does not think of himself as the representative of Divine Reason, sitting proudly on a throne or standing triumphantly on a rostrum. He thinks of himself rather as being buffeted by the animal drives of his subconscious, lying helplessly on the analyst's couch. Grandeur and monumentality ring false. It may be more than coincidence that the dissolution of monumentality in twentieth-century architecture has occurred at the same time as the dissolution of the city into the twentieth-century metropolis.

The metropolis contains more than the residential areas and the city, both areas whose character is determined by the relations between persons—in their daily lives in the one, in business and public affairs in the other. There are in the metropolis other elements that have no relation either to the "human" scale of the first or to the "superhuman" scale of the second. They are of two kinds: areas for industry and transportation, and areas for recreation. In both, man enters into relation not with man but with nature, though in opposite ways. In the one he is active, working to transform natural matter; in the other he is receptive to her beauty.

The great technical structures—dams, bridges, cloverleafs, docks, airports, blast furnaces, "cat-cracking" plants, grain elevators, etc.—can no longer be dealt with on the "human" scale of the village or neighborhood or the "superhuman" scale of the city. Their dimensions are determined not by the size of men but by the size of machines. Even the largest buildings on the "superhuman" scale were related to man by the elements designed for human use: steps, doors, windows, and floors. But the door of a hangar must fit not man but a giant plane. The cathedral or palace was built from units of brick or stone dimensioned to be handled by human muscle. The technical structure is built mainly by machines, that is, by the forces of nature controlled by the engineer's technology. The scale of such a structure, neither produced nor inhabited by men, is outside the human. Yet, as we all know, these structures can be perfectly "in scale." They have nothing in common with the brutality of the colossal that results when a building, conceived on the "superhuman" scale, is stretched to a size where it can no longer be related to the human person.

A building of "extrahuman" scale is not necessarily larger than one of the "superhuman" scale. What characterizes it is that its dimensions are not related to the size of man, and they may therefore be doubled or halved without essentially changing its visual impact. But while the scale of a hangar or bridge is not necessarily related to man, it is definitely related to surrounding nature. If this relation is disregarded, the structure will be "out of scale," but in the hands of a creative engineer-designer such as Robert Maillart it may achieve the perfect harmony of a great work of art.

The other element that is not on the scale of man but of nature, the large park, is also essentially a metropolitan phenomenon. Only with the rise of the modern metropolis has it become universal for the family to seek unfamiliar surroundings, picnicking in the forest or the meadows or on the shore of a lake, though, in Canada and the United States at least, rarely venturing far from that sacred chrome-plated image of the protecting and nourishing mother, the family car.

Thus we deal in the metropolis with elements on three different scales: the "human" of the neighborhood, the "superhuman" of the city, and the "extrahuman" of the great technical structures as well as of the great parks. It depends on their relationships whether they enhance or destroy each other.

The relation between the intimate "human" scale and the "extrahuman" scale is well known from the village embedded in a landscape. It is one of contrast — looking out from the smug intimacy of the familiar into the strange wide world of mountain, forest, or sea. It may be possible similarly to enrich the outlook from a neighborhood toward an impressive technical structure on the "extrahuman" scale, such as a bridge or a grain elevator, provided that it is seen at a distance.

The relation between the "human" and "superhuman" scale is equally well known and is generally a fortunate one. The monumental structures of the city rise from the quiet background of domestic streets; and one returns from the heightened intensity of the urban center to the relaxation of the neighborhood.

The real difficulty exists in the relation between the "superhuman" and the "extrahuman" scale. The technically determined forms of the engineering structures disrupt the spatial order of urbanity, and their dimensions devaluate any monumentality inherent in the "superhuman" scale. While most of the structures on an "extrahuman" scale remain outside the city area of urbanity, two intrude strongly: the automobile and the skyscraper.

While the beauty of a technical structure on the "extra-human" scale, such as a bridge or a hangar, may, like the beauty of nature, be appreciated from a moving vehicle, the relation of the "superhuman" to the human person can be fully established only with the person moving on foot. Similarly, a square can hardly be experienced as a festive outdoor living room when it is crisscrossed by automobiles. It may be that truly "urban" architecture can survive only in a pedestrian precinct such as a university campus or a civic center.

The skyscraper is a strange hybrid. Because it is inhabited by human beings, it contains all the elements relating it to the human scale—floors, doors, windows—and through most of its history it has been treated as a monument on the "super-human" scale. But its technical structure, its generally prosaic purpose, and frequently its colossal dimensions, which are no longer commensurate with the human person, conflict with the attempt to treat it as a monument. More and more we see it treated as "extrahuman." All elements related to the size of the human person—floors, doors, windows—disappear in or behind vast, uniform screens of glass or marble. The United Nations Secretariat building goes far in that direction; its dimensions could almost be changed without changing its character.

Whether the skyscraper is treated on the "superhuman" or the "extrahuman" scale, it cannot well be incorporated into the enclosure of an urban street or space. It makes sense only as freestanding sculpture. As such, it can play an important role in creating the image of the metropolis as a whole, as something more than the sum of its parts. The traditional city was perceived from the outside as a silhouette and from the inside as a sequence of spaces. The silhouette of the center is today the only visual expression of a North American metropolis, and it is a creation of chance rather than of design.

The vast periphery lacks points of concentration visually, just as and because it lacks them functionally. It is often said that the growth of the metropolis should be limited by a green-belt. But this goes counter to the dynamic nature of the metropolis. It is doubtful that its expansion could or should be stopped, but it should be possible to channel and organize it. The basic principles of such organization are the separation of built-up and open areas and the creation of subsidiary centers in the built-up areas. Where such a center exists, it can find its visual expression in a group of tall buildings. The planned suburb of Vällingby near Stockholm is an example of this approach, but there is none in North America yet.

The metropolis is too extended to be organized as a sequence of streets and squares. It can become visible only as a sequence of open and built-up areas. Thus perception of a silhouette and perception of a sequence of spaces are no longer separate aspects but intertwined. The silhouettes of the built-up areas surround and shape the open spaces; they merge into a new type of urbanized landscape.

The goal in designing the metropolis as an urbanized landscape is essentially identical with the goal in organizing it as a political body. It must be a unit that can be identified and with which its citizens can identify themselves. Many professionals must work at this task: architects, engineers, landscape architects, planners. But whether one designs a letter box or a railroad system, a bank building or a bathing beach, one always designs not only that one object but the metropolis of which it is a part.

25

Design with
the Automobile —
The Metropolitan Region

It has become fashionable to talk of "the exploding metropolis." The term implies a purely negative process, a violent destruction resulting in a formless heap of scattered fragments; and the automobile is identified as the powerful explosive that has wreaked havoc with the form of the city. The product of the explosion is accused of being "neither city nor country."

And so it is. The metropolitan region that is developing before our very eyes all over the world is indeed a completely new form of human settlement, which includes and merges urban and rural elements—a slowly emerging new form that must be dealt with on its own terms. For thousands of years men have dwelled primarily in two complementary—and antagonistic—forms of settlement, the city and the rural village. Both forms, particularly the city, were compact, separated from the surrounding country by a clearly defined edge, more often than not a city wall. Today, principally in North America, both have been transformed. At one pole the country village is dissolving into separate farms, and at the other, "urban" populations are agglomerating into huge "conurbations," the metropolitan regions. Both transformations have been brought about by new means of transportation, primarily the automobile.

We are nostalgic for the beauty of the traditional city. Seen from the outside, it could be clearly grasped as one unit with a rich and characteristic silhouette, lovingly reproduced in innumerable paintings and etchings. From the inside, it could be understood, more subtly, as a sequence and system of enclosed spaces of streets and piazzas, and these too have inspired painters since the days of Pompeii. This clear distinction of outside and inside has disappeared, together with the compactness of a community based on the human scale of walking distance.

It did not disappear overnight; the automobile has had forerunners. When the horse-drawn carriage became the general means of transportation of the English aristocrats in the eighteenth century, they built the extensions of Bath as a series of crescents stretching out into the landscape. You do not see Bath either from without as a silhouette or from within as a sequence as shaped spaces. The silhouettes of the crescents are the edges shaping the landscape. Here, for the first time in history, appears the urbanized landscape, prototype of the new and different visual expression of the urban region—unsurpassed to this day as to visual quality, although on a very small scale.

Subsequently other means of transportation had their impact on the region. The commuter railroads created isolated suburban clusters; the streetcars extended radial ribbons. But it was only with the adoption of the automobile as a universal means of individual transportation that the metropolitan region emerged full-fledged from the eggshell of the mother city. Now the region covers hundreds of square miles, in which areas "developed" for residences, industry, or business are interspersed with "open" areas: parks, farms, and forests. Law and politics, as well as language itself, still divide this vast region into "city" and "suburbs"; but the impact of the automobile has made these concepts obsolete, knitting the region together into one indivisible and interdependent economic and social unit.

Not only has the automobile created a new and vaster type of metropolitan region and created new visual elements on a different scale, but it has also brought about a new and different way of perceiving the regional environment. When one drives at fifty miles an hour, many of the things seen and perceived by the man standing or walking on his own two feet are never perceived. But the varying sights of the urban landscape seen along the driver's path build up into a sequence of spaces and silhouettes, a new mental image in which various parts of the region become interrelated. "For most people interviewed, paths were the predominant city elements," says Kevin Lynch in his perceptive study *The Image of the City.** Driving along such a path from the outskirts toward the towering centers of our metropolitan regions, we may now and then sense the possibilities of this approach to a comprehensive image of the region, but as yet we have nowhere deliberately used this new tool to relate expressways to the system of open spaces and building masses that constitutes the urban region.

Certainly every single path can develop only a part of the image of the vast complex that is the region. Only as a composite of many paths traveled at different times and with an understanding of their spatial relation to each other can memory gradually build up a total image. The creation and perception of the image of the region become a temporal art, like music or poetry, as well as a visual one. But it may be well to remember that the total image of the traditional city also exists only as a creation of memory, although a simpler one. It is often said that "beauty is in the eye of the beholder." That is a half-truth; beauty is in the memory of the beholder.

Only from one exceptional point in space and time can the complex total of the region be perceived as a single simultaneous image—from an airplane at night. From the blazing profusion at the center the lights gradually thin out toward the periphery; the colored strings of neon signs depict the commercial streets and the black patches the parks, forests, or lakes. Along the expressways and main arteries flows the stream of headlights. The dynamic element of community life—transportation, and its static elements, streets and structures—are expressed by one and the same medium: light. The apparent chaos of the urban region reveals its inherent structure as a jeweled embroidery on a ground of black velvet. Here technical achievements of the twentieth century—the electric light, the airplane, and the automobile—have combined to create an image of unique beauty, not only a thing of intense

*Cambridge, Mass.: Technology Press and Harvard University Press, 1960, p. 49; paperback edition, The M.I.T. Press, 1964.

sensuous charm but a genuine form that truly expresses its content.

We have so far considered only the metropolitan region in the narrower sense, roughly speaking, the commuting watershed of the big urban agglomeration. But the region extends beyond this core for hundreds of miles in all directions. A strange and remarkable reversal in the historic roles of city and country is taking place. In classical antiquity most of the world's work was done in the countryside, and the cities were primarily centers of consumption of the ruling leisure class; and even today this pattern survives in much of Spain, southern Italy, and Latin America. In contemporary North America, the world's work is increasingly done in the big metropolitan agglomerations, while a growing proportion of the people found in the countryside have retired there for rest and recreation; some are permanently retired, living on savings and pensions, but more are retired for a few summer weeks or months or just for a week end, living in summer cottages, lodges, motels, trailers, or tents. The automobile has made possible this new way of life and generated the growing demand for large national and provincial parks and wilderness areas, as well as for roads and camp sites.

The entire landscape of the region is changing under the impact of this flood. We see and protest its negative aspects: the despoiling of nature by roadside stands, billboards, and parking lots, and the destruction of the peace and beauty of a lonely lake by the intrusion of cars, motorboats, and shacks. But for millions of eyes and minds the images of the regional landscape would not exist without the automobile; and during the drive through a region, there emerges a memory image of the relation of its parts that did not exist before.

The ugliness of most of man's current works in this newly opened-up wider region is a challenge. It need not be so. Clusters of cottages or a motel might be focal points of a landscape, as are so many old villages or manors; and highways might articulate the natural forms of the earth as many paths and dirt roads do. The mechanical power of the automobile has created a new type of region and raised new questions. Only the creative power of the human imagination can answer them.

26

Continuity and Change of Urban Form

The city is not a work of visual art. It cannot be perceived
from one point and at one time. Its mental image can evolve
only as a sequence of perceptions. In this respect, it is akin
to the products not of the "spatial" but of the "temporal"
arts, to works of music or literature. But a symphony or a
novel is the work of one mind, created in a definite span of
time; once completed, it remains unchanged. Not so the city.
The polis is the body politic; the *civitas* is the community of
its citizens, interacting in co-operation and conflict. The city
is a historical process; change is its very essence. Generation
after generation, individuals and groups build, alter, destroy,
and replace the artifacts that are the visible city.

In the face of the massive solidity of these artifacts, it is
difficult to see the city as changing. Work with school children
in Philadelphia showed clearly that they viewed their environment as static; it did not enter their minds that it ever had been
or would be different. Adults have witnessed change and recognize it intellectually. But they find it hardly less difficult to
visualize it.

City planners and builders find it hard to resist the temptation to project a definite "once and for all" image. The men of
the Renaissance, who in their proud invention of the central
perspective represented infinity itself as the finite point of the
meeting of parallel lines, designed their ideal cities as encircled
by a definite wall; and the contemporary designers of "New

Towns" attempt to set an equally definite limit by an encircling "greenbelt." "New Towns" have been founded throughout history; probably no other name is more widespread throughout the world than Neapolis, Villeneuve, Neustadt, Novgorod, Yenishehir, or the equivalent. But it may be questioned whether there really can be a new town. Every town must be somebody's home town, and the essence of a home is familiarity, the habit of living together. There can be new houses but not new homes; and there can be new complexes of buildings and streets but no new towns. When a town is "new," it is not a town; and when it is a town, it is not "new."

A city exists in and through time, as well as in space. It changes — and yet it remains the same. We do not hesitate to say "the last time I saw Paris," or "Philadelphia in Benjamin Franklin's day." It is true that "nobody bathes twice in the same river"; but it is equally true that "old man river, he just keeps rolling along."

The "old man" is a person, a living being, an organism. If the undeniable beauty of cities cannot be understood as the beauty of a work of art, perhaps it can be understood as the beauty of a natural organism. Inevitably the word turns up in discussing the city. The city is not an organism; its citizens are not cells but free agents, and every part of its physical "body" is a product of conscious action, not of unconscious organic growth. Nonetheless, the analogy holds: a city, like a human person, has an identity, which persists even if not a single stone of its original buildings can be found.

In the course of about seven years every single cell of the human body has disappeared, but the identity of the person remains. What constitutes this elusive identity of a human person — or of a city?

THE MEANING OF IDENTITY

The most obvious means of identification is the name, superficial and external, but not without significance. Frivolous changes of name do occur, but generally a change of name denotes an important change of status. In our society, women generally change their names when they change their marital status; men and women frequently change their names when they change their national or social status. Similarly, the change of name from Nieuw Amsterdam to New York or from St. Petersburgh through Petrograd to Leningrad expressed profound changes in the life and character of those cities. Even the familiar change from "Smith's Corners" to "Elmhurst," realtor-sponsored though it may be, usually reflects a genuine change from rural village to city suburb.

However, a person who has changed his name never hesitates to say "when I was a child." The subjective sense of identity has deeper roots than the name; it is rooted in memory. A comparable collective memory exists in cities: tradition. The people of any community transmit to and accept from each other certain notions of how things are, how things are done, concepts of what is "normal" and "right." There are commonly accepted elements in their image of their city, their concepts of its districts and streets and houses and other buildings, and of the relation of each part to others. These concepts of "how things are done" are crystallized in customs and laws. Many Americans who saw the destroyed cities of Europe after the last war saw them as a *tabula rasa* on which something completely new and different could be built. But in most cases rebuilding followed the pattern established by lot and street lines. The concepts in the minds of men were not as easily destroyed as the solid structures. "The softest conquers the hardest," said Lao-tse. Gray matter is far more resistant and immovable than stone or concrete.

Concepts as well as artifacts are, of course, always changing in cities, but generally the new is colored by what it changed *from*. Sometimes a traumatic event may obliterate tradition. Because a city is not an organism, it is more susceptible to amnesia than is a human being. But just as an individual may recover from amnesia, so a city may recover and rediscover its tradition.

But identity exists not only subjectively, as memory and tradition. We say not only "when *I* was a child" but also: "I knew *him* as a child." While both the physical appearance and the behavior of the adult may bear no similarity to those of the child, we do not doubt the identity of his person. We define the elements that determine the specific characteristics of a person, as of any organism, as the "genes." As the person grows and matures, these characteristics unfold; he "becomes what he is." The changes that he undergoes during his lifetime do not obliterate his self; he becomes "more himself" than he was as a newborn infant.

Can we identify the "genes" of a city? Can we see them unfold through change to develop the "character" or "personality" of a city? Evidently, as in an organism, such determining elements exist in real life only in interaction. But we may diagnose them separately by considering *situation, site,* and *pattern.*

The situation of a city, or its relation to the surrounding **SITUATION** region, is the basic reason for its existence and development. Most cities develop either as centers of a region, from which they draw their substance and which they dominate and serve, or as gateways, crossroads, bridgeheads, or junction points between two different regions, in particular as transfer points between two different modes of transportation.

Situations may change. A gateway may cease to function, and many port towns have faded when their access channels have silted up to become insufficient, as technology changed. Other cities owe their existence to the creation of new crossroad situations, as do the many railroad junction towns. Central cities may be displaced or superseded by rivals, as Alba Longa was displaced by Rome as the head of Latium, and Vladimir was superseded by Moscow as the capital of central Russia.

Where a city continues for a long time as a center of its region, it becomes strongly identified with it as its symbol and acquires a deeply ingrained character of its own. Chartres is today, as it has been for more than thousand years, the center of the fertile plain of the Beauce.

But growing, developing cities modify, create, and re-create their own situation. St. Louis came into being as a gateway to the West, where goods and people transferred from the Mississippi River boats to the covered wagons and pack horses that explored the great Western plains. As the city grew, it developed railroads and roads to the east and west and connected them by bridges. River boats lost their importance, but the role of railroads and roads increased; and they all converge on St. Louis. The city has transformed its situation from a gateway to a center of the Mississippi Valley region. But the change has left a scar; as the city turned its back on the river, its waterfront has become decayed and blighted.

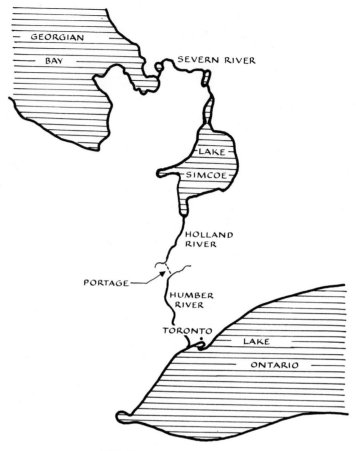

a. 1760: Canoes; waterways and portage.

Figure 1

Toronto originated as the junction point of the portage route to the Great Lakes to the north with the east-west waterway formed by Lake Ontario and the St. Lawrence River. Each subsequent change in transportation has repeated this pattern.

More typically, a growing city adopts technological change to re-create its situation on a larger sacle. This is particularly true of central cities that have become national capitals. The center of Russia might have been established at any place within a fairly broad area. But once Moscow had become the capital, it inevitably became the hub of the railroad, road, and airline systems. It has now even become the hub of the water transportation system, connected by canals with the five seas that wash the shores of European Russia.

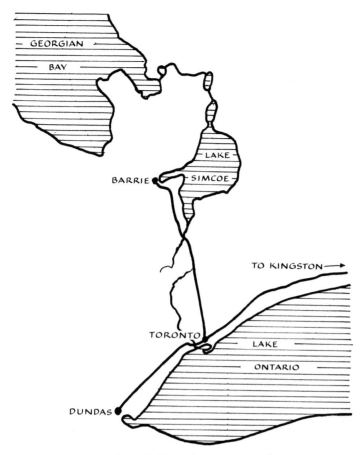

b. 1810: Horse-drawn carts; roads.

Even more direct is the continuing impact of the situation on cities that develop at junction points. The Huron Indians established Toronto (Fig. 1*a*), "the meeting place," on the shore of the east-west waterway formed by Lake Ontario and the St. Lawrence River at the point from which the best route, by canoe, went north to the Great Lakes: up the Humber River and after a short portage down the Holland River to Lake Simcoe, from which the Severn River flows into Georgian Bay, the easternmost extension of the Great Lakes. The early settlers used the same route. But when they brought their wheeled wagons, they supplemented the roads (Fig. 1*b*) running east and west to Kingston and Dundas, at the

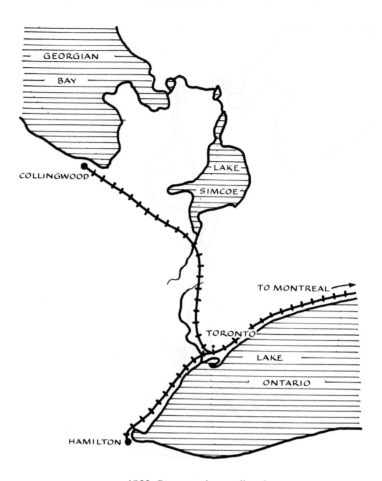

c. 1855: Steam engines; railroads.

lower and upper ends of Lake Ontario, respectively, by a
road running north to Barrie on Lake Simcoe, where goods
were transshipped on barges, which used the existing waterway to the Great Lakes. When steam railroads replaced
horse-drawn carts, the first line (Fig. 1c) was again built to
the north, to Collingwood on Georgian Bay, where goods
were transshipped to steamers plying the Great Lakes. Finally, with the coming of the motor vehicle (Fig. 1d), the
first expressway (Highway 400) was built to the north, past
Lake Simcoe, where it joins the Trans-Canada Highway,
which continues along the eastern and northern shores of
the Great Lakes, while other expressways (Queen Elizabeth
Way and Highway 401) follow the shores of Lake Ontario.

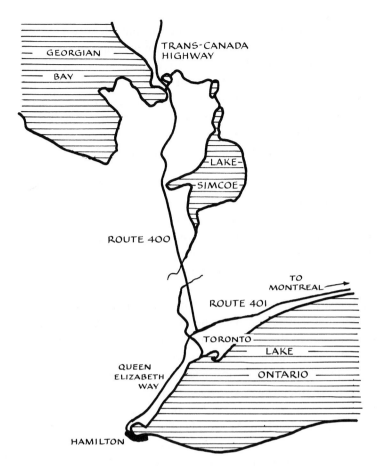

d. 1955: Motor vehicles; expressways.

The urban development of the Toronto area has always followed these lines of transportation in broad ribbons to the east, west, and north, bypassing areas to the northeast and northwest, which are equidistant from the center of the city. Thus the changes in the technology of transportation have served to continue the original situation and the urban form resulting from it.

The selection of the site is the first and most decisive act **SITE** in the history of a city, often hallowed by legend and by solemn foundation rites. A site was selected for its functional value: hilltops, islands, or peninsulas for defense, and bays, rivers, or fords for access. Such strong features of the natural site tend to remain and to give permanent identity to their cities. Changes may even increase their importance. The lakefront parks and the Outer Drive have made the shore of Lake Michigan more dominant in the image of Chicago than it was in the nineteenth century. The *quais* and bridges have identified the Seine more closely with Paris than it was in the Middle Ages, when it was hidden from view by the buildings that lined its banks and even its bridges.

But man-made changes may also modify or even obliterate the original site, once its function has become obsolete.When they stand in the way of the growth of the city, hills are leveled, and canals are filled in. The Aztecs had selected the island of Tenochtitlán because the surrounding lake served well as a protective moat, as a supplier of fish, and as access to the fertile lands lining its shores. But the lake was long ago drained, and its former bottom is covered by the streets and houses of modern Mexico City. Boston was founded on a peninsula, connected with the mainland by a narrow neck. But the bays at the side of the neck were filled, and the peninsula site disappeared, once the protective function of the surrounding water became obsolete. The founders of Moscow selected for their fortress—*Kreml'* in Russian—a triangular site, protected on two sides by the Moscow River and its tributary, the Neglinnaya Creek. The creek has long been buried in a sewer, and few of Moscow's citizens know that it ever existed, but the Kreml has remained as the heart of the city as has the Boston Common and the Zócalo of Mexico. In most cities, though not in all, the original site has remained as its heart, as a visible symbol of its continuing identity.

This is true even when it is no longer inhabited. Athens had been founded as the fortress center of Attica on a steep hill dominating the surrounding Attic plain. At an early date, its people left it to settle in a more convenient location at its foot. But, deserted by man, it remained the home of their gods. When Athens was destroyed by the Persians, its original function as the center of Attica had already been overshadowed by its new function as a commercial and maritime power, a gateway to the Mediterranean Sea. Quite logically, Themistocles proposed to rebuild the city around its port, at the Piraeus, but the Athenians refused to move away from the home of their gods. The duality of Athens and the Piraeus, center and gateway, has remained to this day. But the glorious rock, visible from everywhere on land and sea, orients everything around it: this is Athens.

Wherever a mountain dominates the site of a city, it bestows on the city its continuing identity, as in Montreal, where it also gave the city its name. At this very moment, the citizens of Montreal are rising to defend the dominant silhouette of the mountain from being obscured by skyscrapers.

The mountain, dominating the site of the city and symbolizing the continuity of its existence, may even be as far distant as Fujiyama is from Tokyo. The Chinese, in their elaborate ancient doctrine on the siting of cities, prescribe a location at the foot of a protecting mountain to the north. In their greatest creation in the art of city building, the Imperial City of Peking, the mountain was man-made, in the form of the "Coal Hill" at its northern end. Under the protection of the mountain to the north, every city, like every house, opens to the south. The streets, intersecting at strict right angles, are oriented to the four cardinal points, thus integrating and identifying the city with the cosmos.

The rectangular pattern, either checkerboard or gridiron, **PATTERN** exists, of course, not only in China. It is the most widespread and perhaps also the oldest conscious city plan. Certainly it has its roots in preurban patterns of land division. The great urban civilization that developed in the valleys of the Indus, the Euphrates and Tigris, the Nile, and the Hwang Ho were all based on field agriculture, and it is probable that the division of urban land into rectangular lots and blocks followed the methods developed for the allotment of fields. In Northern Europe, where the open field system and a different technique of plowing led to a division of fields into long narrow "hides," the lots and blocks of medieval towns also tend to have an oblong shape. The use of the plow in the foundation rites of towns in widely dispersed and different cultures confirms this relation of the urban pattern to the underlying agricultural way of life.

The French settlers of Quebec brought with them the division of land into long narrow strips, and the long narrow blocks of Montreal continue this tradition. On the other hand, the land of southern Ontario was parceled out in square "concessions" of 1,000 acres. On the dividing lines between the concessions a strip, one chain wide (33 feet), was left for public access. These "concession roads" now form the system of arterial roads in the Toronto area. From property lines they grew first to dirt roads and finally to broad concrete ribbons. The original genes formed the body, as it developed from the embryo into manhood, and are reflected strongly in tradition. Subdividers and road engineers in the area think in terms of concessions and concession roads; even the planning of subways has followed these concepts.

Not only in China but also in India and in the Roman world, the orientation of the grid was determined by the four cardinal points. The division of land on the North American continent followed this example, and the plans of American cities have been fitted into it. We may consider the concepts of the cardinal points as divine entities and of the city as an image of the cosmos to be ancient superstitions, but they actually dominate our image of the city. Almost all American cities designate their streets as north, south, east, and west. The people of these cities—and sometimes even their planners—are surprised when they are told that their city's "north" deviates far from the astronomical north. In Montreal the streets paralleling the St. Lawrence River are called "east-west," though they actually run from north-northeast to south-southwest.

Figure 2   Moscow.   *a*. Historical development.

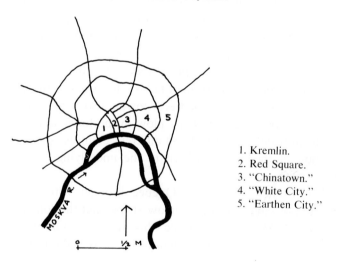

1. Kremlin.
2. Red Square.
3. "Chinatown."
4. "White City."
5. "Earthen City."

The "four cardinal points" are not the only concept of cosmology. Equally ancient and sacred is the image of the cosmos as a circle; and this image has also been reflected in cities. Here again, roots can be traced back to rural forms. The African kraal, the encampments of the Scyths and the Huns, and many other settlements are round. It is hardly an accident that descriptions as well as ruins of perfectly circular cities are to be found among peoples of pastoral cultures, such as the Hittites, Medes, Persians, and Arabs.

The circle is an enclosure and tends to predominate where defense is the primary consideration. But the city must communicate with the surrounding region, and roads spread out from its gates; as the city grows, a second wall, and sometimes a third and fourth one, encircle the new sections. Thus the pattern continues; nor does its influence cease when the walls are torn down. To the contrary, as walls and roads are replaced by streets, boulevards, and greenery, it is felt even

b. Subway system.

more strongly. In Vienna, the "Ring," a wide, tree-lined boulevard with many monumental public buildings and small parks, which has replaced the old fortification, is the most important element in the image of the city.

This "radiocentric" pattern, characteristic of many European cities, has found its most complete realization in Moscow (Fig. 2a). On the land side of the triangular Kremlin (1), a market square, known since the Middle Ages as the "Red Square" (2), developed. From here, three streets radiated. The settlement that grew along these streets, known as "Chinatown" (3), was soon enclosed by a wall that, together with the Kreml wall along the Neglinnaya Creek, formed a semicircle. As the city grew, this new "White City" (4) was again enclosed by a wall describing three quarters of a circle but terminating at the banks of the Moskva River. Only the next extension of the city (5) was enclosed by a completely circular "earthen" wall.

All these walls have disappeared and have been replaced by broad ring roads. Together with the old radial streets, all of which were widened to 200 feet during the 1930's, they form the dominant system of arterial streets. The railroads, radiating in all directions, all stopped at the line of the "earthen wall," where their terminals repeated the function of the gates; and they were later connected by an outer beltline (not shown). When a subway system was built, it again followed the radial pattern (Fig. 2b). A circular line, not included in the original plan, was added, responding to the inherent logic of the city's pattern.

Thus the "radiocentric" pattern, initiated in rudimentary form when "Chinatown" was built, not only has continued but has become stronger and clearer with every subsequent change.

With the radiocentric plan, growth and change inevitably confirm and strengthen the original center. It is different with the gridiron. In New York, while the financial center has remained anchored at the "wall" of pregrid Nieuw Amsterdam, the more important "uptown" center has constantly shifted to the north, from Canal Street to 14th to 23rd to 34th to 42nd. It is still on the move and is now entering the Fifties. Similar shifts along the main streets of the gridiron occur in many North American cities, albeit on a smaller scale.

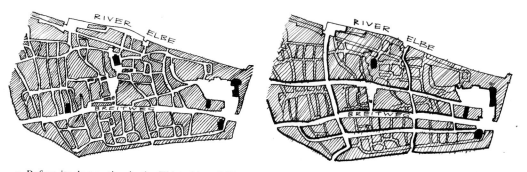

a. Before its destruction in the Thirty Years' War.   *b.* Reconstruction after the Thirty Years' War.   **Figure 3**
Magdeburg.

While the gridiron and radiocentric patterns are the most frequent and clearly defined ones, others are to be found. The simplest of these is that of a city developing along one main street. The medieval German city of Magdeburg had developed along the slightly curving "Breiteweg" (Broadway), roughly paralleling the river Elbe (Fig. 3*a*). In the Thirty Years' War, the city was systematically destroyed, and later rebuilt according to a new plan (Fig. 3*b*). This plan shows four new streets, two paralleling the rebuilt "Breiteweg" and two perpendicular to it; all are slightly curved. This is in complete contradiction to the universally dominant doctrine of the seventeenth century, which demanded a strict geometric pattern of symmetrical streets and squares. It is doubly remarkable because the author of the plan, the mayor of Magdeburg, was a man trained in the exact sciences, the renowned physicist Otto von Goericke.

The center of Magdeburg was destroyed a second time during the last war. Again a new plan was made. It differs considerably from the previous status; but again it shows the characteristic slightly curving streets. Once again this was in complete contradiction to the "Stalinist" concept of the City Beautiful, which was the official doctrine in East Germany at the time. Once again the continuing tradition proved stronger than the changing fashions of men.

The pattern of a city is formed not only by its streets but also by its characteristically different districts. Medieval Paris consisted of three parts: "la Cité," the original island, the seat of secular and ecclesiastic power; "la Ville," the burgher's quarter on the right bank; and "l'Université" on the left. A fourth, aristocratic district was added west of the

"Ville," when the kings built the Louvre at the end of the Middle Ages.

The "Cité" still contains the cathedral and also the "Préfecture," which runs Paris; the "Quartier Latin" on the left bank, with the Sorbonne and Montparnasse, is the Paris of the intellectuals; the "Ville," with its stock exchange, banks, and department stores, is the Paris of business; and the district extending from the Louvre along the Rue de Rivoli and the Champs Elysées is the Paris of luxury and fashion. The changes that have occurred in the course of five centuries have developed and articulated the original distinctive characteristics of these four districts.

Patterns of streets and of districts are not unrelated. In Manhattan, the only district outside of the old downtown that does not conform to the gridiron pattern is Greenwich Village. It is hardly an accident that it has become the favorite abode of nonconformists. The "genius loci" continues to maintain the identity of "The Village" as an entity in, but not entirely of, Manhattan.

INTERACTION OF SITUATION, SITE, AND PATTERN

We have so far dealt separately with these three factors shaping the city. It may be worthwhile to attempt to observe their interaction in two cities, Leningrad and Hamburg.

Leningrad. When Peter the Great decided to open "a window to the West," he selected a location at the easternmost tip of the Baltic, where the river Neva, divided into two arms by an island, falls into the sea. Inherent in this situation were two main directions: westward down the river to the sea, and southeastward to the vast Russian land. Inherent in the site was a focal point, the tip of the island.

Neither was recognized at first. The first plan provided for development on the northern bank, radiating from the fortress. It was rejected in favor of a second plan by the French architect Le Blond (Fig. 4a), which contemplated the main development on the island. On the south bank only a narrow sliver was included, and any additional building there was strictly prohibited.

But it was on this side that the Navy yard, called the Admiralty, was located, and the people who migrated to find work there came from the southeast. So did the country's highest ecclesiastical dignitary, the Metropolitan Bishop of

Novgorod, and to accommodate his journeys to the new capital, the road was paved. As the "Nevsky Prospect," it has become and remained the city's main street, terminating at the tower of the Admiralty. In the middle of the eighteenth century it was supplemented by two other broad avenues, also terminating at the same tower (Fig. 4b).

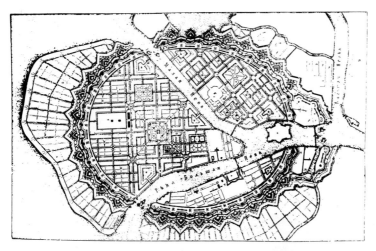

a. Le Blond's plan for St. Petersburg, 1717.

Figure 4
St. Petersburg-Leningrad.

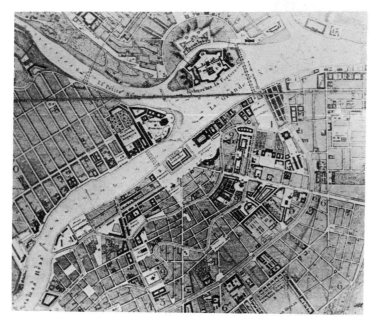

b. Center of St. Petersburg, about 1850.

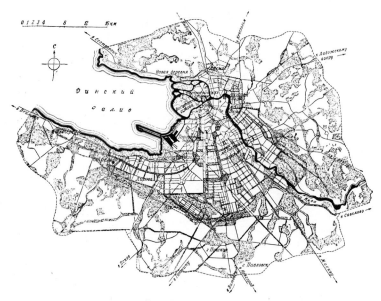

c. Leningrad, plan, about 1940.

d. Leningrad, the point of the island.

Two small arms of the Neva, the Moika and Fontanka, encircling the Admiralty, form together with the radials and the embankments of the Neva the basic structure of the city.

The plan for the vastly enlarged city (Fig. 4*c*), adopted around 1940, continues the theme. The city extends pri-

262　URBAN DESIGN

marily on the left bank to the southeast. The extension is organized around long, broad, and straight streets, converging toward the Neva at the point where the river divides.

The river is here flanked by the fortress on the right bank and by the Winter Palace and the Admiralty on the left. But the central focal point, the tip of the island, long remained unbuilt, as it was on Le Blond's plan. Only in the first half of the nineteenth century did it receive its form (Fig. 4*d*). Appropriate for a maritime commercial city, the stock exchange was built here. A great colonnade, surmounted by a huge pediment, is flanked by two enormous columns and further flanked by the two bridges that connect the island with the north and south banks.

Only with this change did the focal point of the site become the visible central landmark of the city. The "frame" of the "window to the west" was completed. To use a phrase coined by Louis Kahn, the city had "become what it wanted to be."

Hamburg. After Charlemagne conquered the Saxons, he established a bridgehead on the north bank of the Elbe. On a slight hill, protected on two sides by the swamps formed by two small tributaries of the Elbe, the parish church of St. Peter was built. Charles's successor established here an archbishopric to carry on "the apostolate of the north," and a cathedral was built next to the parish church. Thus Hamburg started life as a gateway from south to north.

With the rise of Lubeck, the leading city of the Hanseatic League, to the role of "Queen of the Baltic," Hamburg's gateway function received added meaning. From Lubeck, up the river Trave, and after a short portage down the river Alster, the shortest trade route to the Elbe basin went through Hamburg. Gradually Hamburg extended its trade down the Elbe to the North Sea and to the ports of the Netherlands, England, and France. When Lubeck lost its dominance over the Baltic trade and stagnated, Hamburg continued to develop its trade with the west. From a gateway from south to north it changed to a gateway from east to west, finally to become "Germany's gateway to the world." Today its location as the terminal point for ocean-going ships is the dominant factor in its geographic situation. But it is a man-made factor, created by changing, relocating, and deepening the channel of the Elbe over the centuries.

Meanwhile, the site had also undergone changes. The islands in the swamplands south and west of the town were, one by one, enclosed by dikes and settled. In the fourteenth century a dam was built across the Alster, transforming the swamps to the northwest into a lake. Finally, in the sixteenth century, a "New Town," built on a gridiron pattern, was added and was, together with the old town, enclosed by huge fortifications. Up to the beginning of the nineteenth century the city remained within this egg-shaped wall (Fig. 5a).

The two rivers had now developed their distinctive character. The Elbe was the harbor. But the Alster had been transformed from a river leading out of the city into a lake within the city. A local poet of the eighteenth century expressed this by saying: "The Elbe makes us richer by shipping; The Alster teaches sociability."

Both from the Alster Lake and from the Elbe River the city presented its silhouette, the tall spires of its five parish churches. This silhouette (Fig. 5a, bottom) has become deeply ingrained in the minds of its citizens as the image of their city.

In the beginning of the nineteenth century the walls were torn down, and tree-lined boulevards took their place; the deep moats remained but were embedded in a greenbelt (Fig. 5b). The trapezoid basin of the "Binnen" (inner) Alster was more clearly defined by tree-lined streets bordering it to the west and south. With the elimination of the wall the larger "Aussen" (outer) Alster was no longer separated from the city.

In 1842 a big fire destroyed a great part of the old city, which was rebuilt on a completely new rectangular plan (Fig. 5c). The definition of the Binnen-Alster was completed, a straight, tree-lined street replacing the irregular jumble of houses that had previously formed its longest side. But the transformation of the Alster did not stop there. The "Kleine" (little) Alster, south of the locks, had remained shapeless, its muddy bottom emerging at low tide. Now the locks were removed to its lower end, raising the water to the constant higher level of the Alster Lake. It was transformed into an oblong rectangle, shaped like an urban plaza by bridges at its two short sides, an arcade on its west, and a quay on its east. The quay opens up into a square in front of the new city hall, set at right angles to the "square" of the "Little Alster."

Many changes have occurred since 1842, and hardly a building remains from those shown on the plan of 1750 (Fig. 5a). But the model for the postwar reconstruction (Fig. 5d)

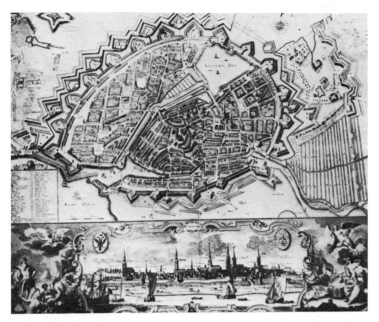

a. About 1750.

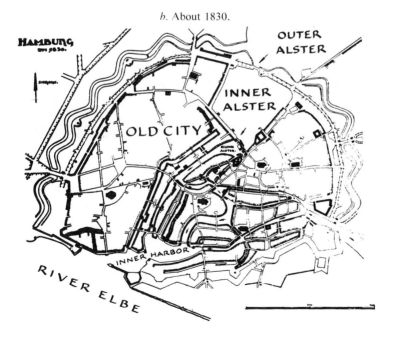

b. About 1830.

Figure 5
Hamburg.

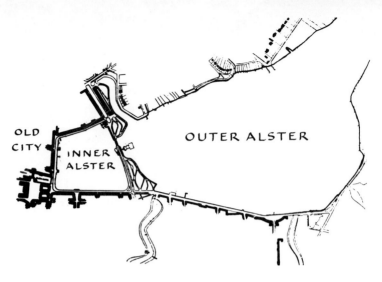

c. Plan for reconstruction around Alster Lake, 1842.

d. Model of reconstruction of central city, 1955.
The river Elbe is to the lower right; the Inner Alster is to the upper center; the Outer Alster is at the upper edge.

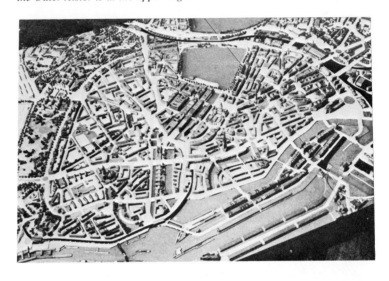

—now largely completed—shows the continuing identity of the central city, clearly defined by the surrounding ring roads, parks—and railroad tracks. The City Hall Square, as the crossing point of two subway lines more than ever the center of the city, is only a stone's throw from its point of origin, St. Peter's church. The development of the Alster as the com-

e. View of central city from Outer Alster Lake.

munity living room has been continued by extending the arcade farther down the bank of its channel.

The beloved image of the spires rising at the old place over the horizontal mass of the profane buildings, seen across the water, continues to identify the city (Figs. 5*e* and 5*a*), even though none of the present spires was actually built before the middle of the nineteenth century. This image was seriously endangered. Large commercial corporations, unable to expand horizontally in the densely built central business district, required office towers. But the city was not willing to destroy its silhouette. Instead, it is establishing a second "city" four miles from its center and has obtained agreement that the corporations will locate there.

MEMORY

The silhouette, more than any other image, encompasses the whole city. But it is not the whole image, which is a composite of many images, seen and experienced at different places at different times.

The artist who painted the auto-da-fé of Savonarola presented the Piazza della Signoria from the same point as did the photograph taken four centuries later (Fig. 6). The Piazza has hardly changed during these 400 years, but the two images differ radically. The painting shows the Duomo and

Figure 6
Florence,
Piazza della Signoria.

a. Sketched from a painting of about 1510.

b. Sketched from a photo of about 1910.

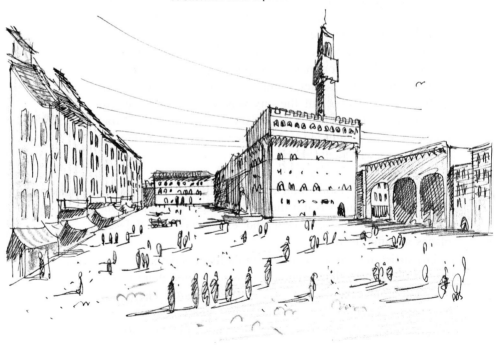

the Campanile, the Arno River, and the hills of San Miniato and of Fiesole. None of these can actually been seen from the Piazza, but they were constituent parts of the image that the artist carried in his mind.

So even the image of a city at a given moment exists only in memory. But in it and behind it lie memories of the history that has shaped the present life of the city and gives content to its form.

"Beauty," it is said, "is in the eye of the beholder." That is a half-truth. Beauty is in the memory of the beholder. Only memory can re-create the continuity through change, which is life.

27

A Visitor Looks at the Montreal Exhibition: "Expo — 1967"

We expect millions of men, women, and children to visit the Montreal exhibition. Why will they go there? What do they expect to see, do, or experience? Certainly, a variety of people expect a variety of things. And perhaps it is the variety more than any one thing that is the greatest attraction for most of them. But not for all, no doubt. There will be a few specialists who will come to study seriously some particular field. They will find their way; and if they are normal human beings, in addition to being specialists, they also, like all the others, will want to see the variety of everything there is to see.

The exhibition is dedicated to man and his world; and people will come primarily to see what man has done and can do, how he lives in different environments, in different countries, how he has adapted himself to his environment and his environment to his needs, what he has invented and created. Most of them will want "to take it all in." Some will try to do it in a single day. But even the majority, who plan to come back, will on their first visit frequently be driven by curiosity to find out what there is to see in every part of the exhibition.

It is therefore necessary to give them a clear orientation. This is, to some extent, facilitated by the fact that the site consists of three different parts, separated by bodies of water. The three areas will be devoted to different functions. But even within each of the three major sections there will be so much to see that orientation will be difficult. Therefore each section will need a major spine along which the crowds will be led to the major points of interest. The orientation, however, should not be too rigid and obvious; it should not reveal everything at one glance. The pleasure of surprise and discovery should remain. People should still be able to wonder what there is around the next corner and to find out for themselves. This, as Leon Batista Alberti observed 500 years ago, makes a place appear bigger and more interesting.

People will always be torn between the desire to see everything that there is to see and the impossibility of seeing it all. Probably the best solution would be to display a few of the most impressive and significant exhibits illustrating a given theme "on the highway." These main themes would inform visitors who are drawn on to see other themes. At the same time they would serve as gateways to the byways where the full array of exhibits are situated.

Most people want to see not only the creations of other people but also other living people. Watching the crowd as well as being part of the crowd is part of the attraction of an exhibition—but not all the time. There should be quiet "harbors" on the edge of the stream where one can sit and watch the crowd flowing by, looking out at it or down on it.

The average length of a visit at other such exhibitions has been found to be six hours. Being exposed hour after hour to

Expo 1967, the Universal and International Exhibition of 1967 in Montreal. **Figure 1**

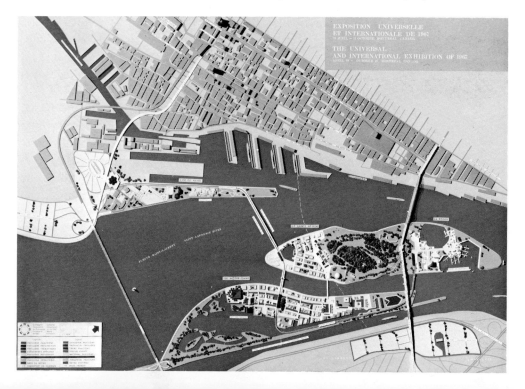

the variety, the excitement, the sights, and the sounds of an exhibition is, as most of us know from experience, extremely tiring for the head as well as for the feet. One needs some place to rest, to get a bit "out of it" for a while. Some such break may be provided by traveling from one section of the exhibition to the other, whether by walking across the bridges or by riding in some means of public transportation, which does not have to move fast. There is no more pleasant and restful way of travel than by water, and the location of the site makes it possible to use this widely. Perhaps there could be landings giving direct access to a lower floor of some of the main exhibition buildings, similar to the access to the Venetian palaces from the Grand Canal.

However, the relief of temporarily turning from a view *of* the exhibition to a view *from* the exhibition toward the water and the city and mountain beyond need not be limited to these occasions of travel from one exhibit to another. It could be one of the greatest attractions of our exposition and should be provided from the greatest variety of settings: out of the buildings, from balconies and terraces, from gardens and promenades, from ground level, and from high points.

No less important than the views *from* the exhibition are the views *of* the exhibition: from the city, from the south shore, from the bridges, and from one section to the other. From such places it will be important to create beautiful and significant silhouettes. Most important in this respect is the upper end of St. Helen's Island. This could be developed into the key point of the entire urban landscape of Montreal, similar to the "arrow" in Leningrad. The "arrow" is the point of an island that divides the "big" and the "little" Neva rivers. It was transformed into the key point of that city by the construction of the early nineteenth-century stock exchange, a building with magnificent scale and broad steps leading down to the water.

Actually, both images of the exposition—from the inside and from the outside—will exist in two variants: in daylight and at night. Walking through its spaces, looking out from its bright lights to the dark river, and in particular looking from the city to its symphony of lights—these images could be the most memorable of all impressions. They present a great and most unusual challenge to its architects.

VI

METHODOLOGY
OF PLANNING

28

Science and Planning

Life in the modern metropolis is full of strange contradictions. City dwellers are completely dependent on each other, and they seem to be more isolated and lonelier than ever. Ways and means of traffic are built with ever greater skill and at ever greater cost, and traffic jams become worse and worse. More and more people move to the suburbs to live in the country, and there is less and less country to live in.

While the most advanced technology and elaborate organization tackled all the individual problems of the city, such as transportation by rail and road, communication, water supply, and fire protection, no attention was paid to their interrelation and interaction—and the city as a whole became more and more chaotic. Men found themselves living in a new environment that they themselves had created without ever knowing or wanting it. Thus the modern metropolis reflects in the sharpest form the basic contradiction of Western society—the contradiction between our success in applying science to the relations of man to nature and our failure to apply science to the relations of man to man.

The first reaction to the big city was emotional. Along with praise of its bigness and glory went fulminations against "the Big Wen." Cities were and are accused of being parasites, consuming the strength of the nation. The accusation is threefold: biologic, economic, and social. It is claimed that the urban death rate exceeds the birth rate and that the city

UNDERSTANDING THE PROBLEM

remains alive only by constantly draining the countryside of its best stock; that the city consumes more than it produces, taking the goods of farm and mine without returning equivalent goods and services; and that it leads to moral and social disintegration, living on but gradually destroying the healthy traditions inherited from the village community. It was in answer to these questions that scientific investigation of the city started, each discipline studying its particular field, largely ignoring other aspects of the complex urban problem.

There is, indeed, much evidence that many cities during long periods did not reproduce themselves biologically. While in recent times this has been due to an abnormally low birth rate, caused by economic and social factors, in earlier periods—for which adequate statistical data are lacking—it appears to have been caused by an abnormally high death rate, the result of extremely unhealthy living conditions.

PUBLIC HEALTH IN THE CITY
The threat to the health of the urban population presents itself primarily in the form of pollution of water, soil, and air. Water-borne diseases, notably cholera and typhoid fever, were the great killers of the urban population in the nineteenth century. Progress in bacteriology and engineering has now enabled all large cities to provide an ample supply of safe water to their population. The elimination of epidemic diseases is one of the great triumphs of science, without which our modern big cities would not be possible.

The planning of a water supply system was undertaken by each city for its own needs. Frequently the sewage was dumped into a river that served as a source of water supply for another city farther downstream. But mechanical, chemical, and biological methods of sewage treatment have been developed and are being applied increasingly. The emphasis is shifting from mere *disposal* toward *utilization;* feeding microorganisms in fishponds, making fertilizers, capturing methane gas for fuel and fats for the making of soap. Planning is directed toward a permanent balance within an entire river system; this system comprises ground water as well as surface streams. Into the hydrological study enter such factors as: exhaustion by wells; the influence of planted and of paved surfaces on runoff of surface water and recharge of ground water; and the influence of changing levels of streams on the level of ground water. Better understanding of these relations has led to the modern planning practice of preserving the natural drainage areas of river valleys and developing them as parks, thereby also providing recreation and improving the atmosphere.

On the other hand, incineration of trash, while it has effectively stopped pollution of the soil, contributes to the pollution of the atmosphere. A sizable part of the Los Angeles "smog" has been found to be due to domestic incinerators. Pollution of the air has produced a specific urban "microclimate" unfavorable to health. A substantial portion of the sun's ultraviolet rays is absorbed by the city's atmosphere; the temperature and frequently also the humidity are higher in the city than in the surrounding countryside; some industries emit toxic gases or nauseating smells. Fresh breezes are kept out of many courts and streets by the walls of buildings, while in other places streets act as funnels for high winds. We are only beginning to measure the astonishing differences in climate to be found in different parts of a city or a metropolitan area and to understand their causes.

There are several ways in which planning can improve the microclimate. The first is by selection of a favorable site. It was an accepted rule of ancient Greek town planning that a new town should be built on a southern or eastern slope. Location of industry on the leeward side of the residential quarters and the planting of trees offer considerable protection; in the Soviet Union these measures are standard practice in the building of new industrial plants. Second, pollution can be checked at the source; the replacement of coal by oil or gas, more complete combustion, and the replacement of individual furnaces by more efficient district heating plants, as well as the capturing of soot and fly ash by filters on the smokestacks. Enforcement of air pollution control is greatly aided by scientific methods of measuring air pollution such as those which have been recently developed by the Franklin Institute of Philadelphia for the measurement of some obnoxious odors. Finally, there are positive measures for the improvement of the climate. Parks and trees can substantially modify the temperature and humidity of the air as well as the degree of pollution. Protection against undesirable high winds and access for desirable breezes can be greatly improved by judicious location of structures and trees. Notably in planning on a small scale, or "site planning," new methods provide much more favorable orientation to sun and winds than is possible by building parallel to the streets on the traditional gridiron pattern.

ECONOMY OF THE CITY Though factors creating specific health problems in the city — such as concentration of population and of industries at certain locations — are economic, those dealing with public health rarely inquired into the possibilities of a different distribution of economic activities. On their part, the economists were generally not concerned with the cost of illness or of the means needed to improve health. The problems that called their attention to planning were the costs of transportation, the emergence of depressed areas, the need to assess the demand for investments in the city and to understand the behavior of the real-estate market.

The theory of the location of industry, developed to select the best location for a given industry because of accessibility to raw materials, power, markets, and labor force, is being applied, inversely, to determine the industries suitable for a given city or region. In combination with the scientific exploration of the natural resources it serves as a tool for determining the economic resources of a region and for devising plans for their development. Economic geography approaches the same problem by classifying cities and regions according to their economic function, such as manufacturing, transportation, trade, or recreation. Of particular importance are studies of the "central" functions of cities, that is, the services they render to the surrounding region, the radius of service of each function, and the resultant optimum distances between service centers. Similar techniques are used to determine the most efficient number, size, and spacing of commercial, administrative, and cultural establishments within cities.

The economics of location are largely identical with the economics of transportation. Studies have extended from the design of roads and terminals for different means of transportation to the measurement of traffic needs, in particular by "origin and destination survey." Such surveys, by measuring where traffic originates and for what purpose (home to work, to shopping, to recreation, etc.), make it possible to simulate future traffic movement with the aid of computers and to design roads and parking spaces according to anticipated needs. More important, they indicate how traffic can be reduced by placing homes, factories, shops, and other facilities in such relation to each other that the travel distances will be minimized.

The relation of the various parts of the city to each other is its structure. Structure is important in its physical aspects, which are studied by urban geography, and in its economic aspects, which are studied by land economics. It is also, as a basis of human relations, the subject of sociology. The rapid growth of urban population created unprecedented problems of adjustment of behavior to new conditions. The mere size was new, and it is mainly in response to urban phenomena that scientific statistical methods were developed to measure trends in the size and characteristics of population. Analysis of trends makes it possible to predict future development. It also provides a basis for reserving the land areas and building the roads, schools, parks, etc., that will be required by the predicted population.

SOCIAL STRUCTURE OF THE CITY

The population of the city differs from that of the surrounding countryside. Both the natural selection of those who migrate to the city rather than stay in the village and their adaptation to new conditions are at work to create a new type of city dweller. Within the city there are groupings and regroupings along class and ethnic lines. Much study has been devoted to the understanding of these changes and the development of conditions that will guide them in the direction of co-operation rather than conflict. It is an unavoidable limitation of the social sciences that they cannot use the main tool of the natural sciences, the controlled experiment, in which all variables but one are kept constant. But the development of statistical methods for the analysis of multiple correlations has provided a substitute for isolating and measuring the impact of specific changes in the environment. It thereby creates a basis for planning changes in the environment directed toward changing human behavior.

The change from rural to urban life tends to dissolve the old ties of the family and village community, leading in extreme cases to "anomie," the absence of any norms of behavior. The development of new social ties can be enhanced by an environment that enables people to meet to and to co-operate, such as in community centers and common recreational and educational facilities. In Western countries this kind of community planning is focused exclusively around the residential neighborhood; in the Soviet Union it centers largely around the place of work. Recent investigations indicate that even such apparently minor details as grouping houses around a court rather than lining them up on a street have substantial influence on the formation of aquaintance.

PLANNING AS SYNTHESIS OF SCIENTIFIC DISCIPLINES

As social problems have arisen, each discipline — public hygiene, economics, sociology, technology — has devised methods to meet them without reference to factors outside its own field. But it has become more and more evident that the individual problems can only be solved together, because they are all interrelated aspects of one indivisible problem, the life of human beings within a definite space, which has to be viewed as a whole. A Scotch planner, Patrick Geddes, defined this approach as "synoptic," as the "together-seeing" of what he called the "trinity of land, people, and work." Geddes conceived the synopsis also as immediate sensual vision; and, indeed, planning as an art aims at co-ordinating all elements of the urban landscape into a harmonious whole. To the extent that planning is a science, it is the science of the interrelation of the various aspects of urban life and of the various sciences that study each of these separately.

A scientific survey of all aspects of an area is now accepted as the indispensable first step in planning. According to the extent of the area we may roughly define three levels: "regional" planning, dealing with large areas such as river valleys, states, nations, or even continents; "city" or "metropolitan" planning, dealing with large cities and their immediate environment; and "neighborhood" or "community" planning, dealing with sections of a city or with individual villages or small towns.

REGIONAL PLANNING

The most successful and best-known example of regional planning on this continent is in the Tennessee Valley. Many previous attempts to deal with river valleys had dealt with one or two aspects of the problem only and had frequently resulted in unforeseen and undesired results. The Upper Rhine, for instance, was reconstructed in the middle of the nineteenth century for purposes of navigation, flood control, and drainage. However, it had not been foreseen that the new straight and narrow channel would result in the scouring of the river bottom and a gradual lowering of the level of the stream and consequently, of the ground water level in the adjacent valley. This caused heavy damage to plant growth. Recently the situation has been made worse by another single-purpose project, a hydroelectric plant on the left bank, in French territory, which is diverting most of the water from the river bed.

By contrast, the Tennessee Valley was conceived and carried out as a multiple-purpose project for power production, navigation, and flood control as well as for fish breeding and recreation. In addition, the TVA has promoted industries as consumers for electric power and navigation and has improved agriculture as a market for industry as well as for electric power. Contour plowing, as well as reforestation, by decreasing erosion, in turn has slowed the silting-up of the storage basins that control floods and feed the power plants. Thus, the effects of the planned development on various aspects of the life of the valley support each other—instead of conflicting as they do in the Upper Rhine Valley, in the absence of comprehensive planning.

Similar to the TVA, but on an even larger scale, is the reconstruction of the Volga. A series of twelve dams is transforming the river and its main tributary, the Kama, into a series of lakes of a total length of about 1,500 miles. Besides serving for power production, navigation, flood control, and drainage, the reconstructed river will also irrigate about 10 million acres on the left bank in its lower reaches. In addition, the first link of the project, the Moscow-Volga canal, completed in 1937, provided the city of Moscow with an ample water supply, several lakes for recreation, and storage basins for equalizing the load on its thermoelectric plants.

The Greater Volga project is an integral part of the Soviet Union's national development plan for the relocation of its industry. This relocation, based on a continuing survey of both natural and human resources, has largely achieved its two main goals: (1) minimizing the need for transportation and (2) introducing elements of industrial and urban culture into formerly backward areas, especially in the non-Russian regions. Perhaps the most remarkable aspect of Soviet planning is the co-ordination of the construction of physical facilities—in industry, agriculture, medical care, etc.—with the training of people to operate them, thus minimizing the danger, on one side, of technological unemployment and, on the other, of underutilization of capital investment.

In Great Britain, technological unemployment has transformed some areas dominated by one depressed industry, such as textiles, into "depressed areas." In other parts, notably in the London region, there is overcrowding and encroachment of urban development on fertile agricultural land. The answer is being sought in plans for the redistribution of industry and population. The Board of Trade is encouraging industries to establish themselves in the depressed areas, now called "development areas." One of the incentives is the erection of well-planned, publicly owned "Industrial Estates" that lease factory space, supplied with all services, to manufacturers. The Ministry of Housing and Local Government guides the activities of the County Planning Boards, which allocate the land under their jurisdiction to development for the purpose for which they have found it to be best suited—agriculture, industry, housing, or recreation. It also organizes the building of New Towns, which are to receive the "overspill" of the overpopulated big cities. While both ministries have some remarkable achievements to their credit, they appear to be working sometimes at cross purposes, the Board favoring the establishment of industries where population is at hand, and the Ministry where it wants to attract new population.

Dependence on one industry, which suffered a severe depression, also provided the impetus for planning in Puerto Rico. The big cane sugar plantations that, under United States rule, had largely displaced the previous subsistence farms, dismissed scores of thousands of workers during the depression of the thirties, swelling the ranks of the unemployed, who already constituted a large part of the rapidly growing population. The solution was sought by land reform, by diversified agriculture, and by development of industry.

The Puerto Rico Planning Board, established in 1942, combined the planning of these economic activities with the planning of physical facilities; both island-wide and locally, it proposed roads, harbors, airfields, housing projects, schools, hospitals, and health centers. Acting as advisor to the governor and legislature, it co-ordinates the activities of all public agencies, in particular by working out the Commonwealth budget both for capital investments and for current expenditure for six years in advance. While the economic problems of Puerto Rico are far from solved, planning has undoubtedly contributed to a rise in living standards during the past ten years.

A comparable problem of imbalance faced the new state of Israel, where 80 per cent of the population was concentrated in and around the two big cities of Tel Aviv and Haifa. The national plan for a population of 2.5 million aims at agricultural development, chiefly on irrigated land, to provide 80 per cent of the nation's needs and 20 per cent of its employment. Of the 2 million urban population, half are to live in the three big cities of Tel Aviv, Haifa, and Jerusalem, and half in new or enlarged existing towns of about 50,000, each forming the center of one of the 24 planning districts into which the country has been divided. Forests and parks, highways, ports, and airports are designed to serve the planned future population of the various districts.

Planning for new settlement on an even larger scale is involved in the national plan for Poland, which includes settlement of the new western provinces by millions of migrants from the overcrowded central regions and from the area east of the Curzon Line, which was returned to the Soviet Union in 1945. The plan proceeds in three stages, characterized as reconstruction, industrialization, and urbanization. In the first, the emphasis is on agriculture, mining, and the reconstruction of existing industries; in the second, on the creation of new industrial centers and the development of small towns as service centers for the surrounding countryside; in the third, on the development of medium-sized cities, each to supply consumer goods and services to one of 29 regions of the country. In the process the population engaged in manufacturing is to increase from 22.5 per cent in the first stage to 30.0 per cent in the second, to stay constant thereafter, while the percentage of those engaged in services is to increase from 27.5 through 35.0 to 45 per cent. All detailed plans for industry, transportation, or housing are designed to serve this over-all goal of development.

Planning by stages also characterizes the development of the Northeast Polder, which comprises about one quarter of the roughly 800 square miles of the Zuider Zee, reclaimed by the Netherlands government from the North Sea, which had covered them for several centuries. There may be some questioning of a goal that, in the apparent interest of maximum agricultural productivity, provides for relatively large farms with twice as many farm hands as farm owners and for no industrial employment. But the accepted goal has been achieved smoothly and completely, thanks to careful forethought and attention to every detail. First, the hydraulic works were undertaken, followed by measures for soil improvement based on mineralogical, microbiological, and botanical research carried out by experimental state farms. In the second stage, forests and trees were planted, and roads, houses, barns, shops, schools, and churches were built. In the third stage, carefully selected families of farmers and farm laborers and of service and professional people were settled. The population is served by a central town of 10,000 people and by ten villages of 1,000 to 2,000 inhabitants, spaced at distances of four miles from each other. In order to avoid uneconomic duplication of services, the central town was developed ahead of actual need, before the entire area had been settled.

As a result of this careful planning, the Northeast Polder has prospered from the beginning, while in less well planned previous reclamations the early settlers suffered severe hardship and heavy losses, and were frequently forced to give up their hard-won farms.

METROPOLITAN PLANNING   The population of the Northeast Polder is much smaller, and that of Puerto Rico or Israel is no larger, than the population of a big city or metropolitan area. What makes metropolitan planning different from planning these regions is the concentration of population and the need for accommodating many diverse functions in a very limited space—a task of physical or spatial planning rather than of economic planning.

Basically, this requires a land-use plan that allots space to each function in such a way that all functions can be carried out with a minimum amount of money, time, and inconvenience. There is agreement on a few basic requirements: limitation of density, separation of areas and of roads according to function, and balance between places of work and places of residence. There is corresponding agreement on the evils of existing big cities: overcrowding and mixture of incompatible uses both on the land and in the streets, long distances between home and work, and lack of open space for recreation. Different schemes have been proposed as guides to a better organization of metropolitan areas.

Whatever the scheme, it can be realized only gradually as new areas are developed or old areas rebuilt. Where the municipality owns the land, as in most cities in Sweden and Finland and in the Soviet Union, the plan can be carried out directly. The same holds true for the British "New Towns." Outside of these, development requires the agreement both of the private landowner and of the British government, which owns the development rights. In most countries, including the United States, planning control is limited to the prevention of undesirable types of development by zoning, the encouragement of desired development by the provision of streets, utilities, and other services, and the erection of public buildings, including public housing projects.

Planning of public improvements is therefore one of the basic tasks of city planning. Among these, traffic needs generally appear as most urgent; they can be provided in time if development follows a plan that is able to predict the generators of traffic, that is, the number of people living in and the activities (industry, commerce, recreation, etc.) carried on in each part of the region. They can generally be best satisfied by a system of rapid-transit lines with bus feeder lines and parking spaces for private cars at their stations.

Streets are differentiated according to their function into three types: limited-access expressways for rapid movement between different parts of the region, approaching but bypassing the centers of concentration; collectors that carry traffic to and from the access point of the expressways and also for shorter distances between other points; and service streets that give direct access to the points of ultimate destination. The provision of parking spaces at or near these points of destination, either by legislative requirement or by public action, is a necessary supplement to the provisions for moving traffic.

A further step in the differentiation of traffic arteries is the separation of pedestrian and vehicular traffic, both within residential neighborhoods and in shopping areas. Together with the provision of ample parking space, this principle forms the basis of the modern shopping center, which is perhaps America's most original contribution to contemporary planning practice.

The size, spacing, and timing of all public improvements, schools, playgrounds, parks, health centers, etc., are based on an analysis of present and predicted future needs and are related to the land-use plan. In the evaluation and co-ordination of proposals of agencies exercising jurisdiction in various fields, such as education or recreation, the planning of an over-all program of public improvement is an important tool for the allocation of priorities and the achievement of greater efficiency and economy.

In general, the huge existing structure of a big city allows only gradual and partial realization, which may easily obscure the over-all planning goal. In an exceptional situation, the city of Warsaw has turned the catastrophe of its almost complete destruction into the opportunity for reconstruction on entirely new lines. Realization of the plan, which was concieved in its main outlines by courageous and imaginative planners before the war, has been made possible by public acquisition, through condemnation, of the entire city region of 700 square miles and is being pushed ahead with remarkable energy. The historical center is being rebuilt with a radical improvement of its street system and an increase of open space and public gardens. A large district for heavy industry is being created leeward of the city and downstream on the low eastern bank of the Vistula. A light industrial district adjoins the city center to the west. The high western bank of the Vistula is being transformed into a park, and the main residential districts parallel the river. Each district has its own cultural, administrative, and shopping center and its own zone for service industries. It is further subdivided into neighborhoods, separated from each other by small parks.

The planning of the neighborhood and of the residential district in the Warsaw plan follows the same basic principles that have been accepted by planners in all countries, though under different names and with different emphases. First is the replacement of the traditional system of small blocks and undifferentiated streets by the "superblock," with through traffic concentrated on peripheral streets and prevented or discouraged on all interior streets, which serve only for access to dwellings. Second is the provision of all facilities for the daily life of the family in the neighborhood, within easy walking distance so that the elementary school and playground, nursery schools, and kindergardens can be reached without crossing major traffic arteries. Third is the grouping of the buildings independently from the surrounding streets, which makes possible orientation to sunshine, prevailing winds, and pleasant views as well as adjustment to natural features such as hills, river valleys, rocks, and trees.

Within the framework of these principles there are wide variations, dependent on variations in habits and ways of life, in the size of the area and population of each neighborhood, the type of house, the grouping of structures, the design of access roads, and the kind and number of community facilities included. There is even greater variety in the planning of the next-larger unit, variously called a residential district or a community, which groups several neighborhoods around a common center for those facilities which cannot be supported by the individual neighborhood, such as a shopping center, high school, theater, library, or health center.

The principles of community planning have been successfully applied to a number of private and public developments in many countries. Radburn, New Jersey, and the "Greenbelt Towns" were pioneering efforts in the United States. Baldwin Hills in Los Angeles, Fresh Meadows in New York, and Park Forest near Chicago are more recent examples. The British New Towns are built up in rigidly defined neighborhoods, each surrounded by its own little greenbelt.

A more flexible approach characterizes the development of Vällingby in Sweden. In 1930 the city of Stockholm bought an area of about four square miles outside its limits, about ten miles from the city center. In 1949 this area was annexed;

planning had started several years earlier and was completed in every detail in 1951, when construction of the buildings got underway.

An industrial estate, built by the city between a suburban railroad and an express highway, provides employment for about half the population; the other half will find employment in Stockholm, which can be reached in 25 minutes by rail. The stations of the railroad, about a mile and a quarter apart, serve as centers for two new communities, one of 8,000 and one of 15,000 persons, both of which are now substantially completed. Together with a previously built third community, which is also centered around a railroad station, they form a semicircle around a 500-acre central park facing Lake Mälaren to the south.

On the outside of the semicircle a park belt separates these three communities from neighboring developments, and park strips separate them from each other, connecting the outer belt with the central park. Thus from every house both a community center and a large park can be reached in a short walk.

The center of the larger community serves as a cultural and administrative as well as a commercial center for the 60,000 to 80,000 persons of the surrounding area. It consists of a spacious plaza built over the railroad station. Adjacent is the high school, which also serves as a community center. Grouped around the center are a number of eleven-story apartment towers with apartments designed for families without children. The bulk of the population lives in three-story apartments not more than a third of a mile from the center. Beyond that is a zone of single-family houses extending to a distance of half a mile from the center.

The communities are divided into "superblocks" for about 3,000 persons, each of which contains a mixture of apartments, single-family houses, and also "collective houses" with housekeeping services for single persons or working couples. Parking courts and garages are arranged on the periphery of each superblock; the block interior is a neighborhood park with a playground for school-age children and five or six small play lots for preschool children in the immediate vicinity of the houses, most of which are grouped around courts opening on the neighborhood park. Pedestrian and bicycle paths connect these parks with each other and with the larger parks, underpassing the main roads.

The development was carefully timed. All of the streets and utilities, as well as district heating, were started one or two years before the buildings; each superblock was completed as a unit. As a result, all the physical needs of the inhabitants have been well served in an efficient and economical way. There is still much discussion on the effects of the physical plan of the neighborhood on the social relations of its inhabitants.

Some private developments applying the basic principles of neighborhood planning, such as Levittown, Pennsylvania, are very uniform not only in their dwelling type and physical appearance but, more importantly, in the characteristics of their population as to age, family composition, race, and income group. It has been pointed out that neighborhood planning may result in increased segregation by class, race, and other characteristics. On the other hand, co-operation and understanding between groups may be encouraged by a mixture of houses at different price levels, of single-family houses and apartments, of dwelling units designed for the needs of large and small families, of single persons, and of old people.

In England and also in Denmark a number of very attractive apartments and cottages have been built for old people as part of neighborhoods inhabited by "normal" families. Thus old people, when they can no longer maintain the house they needed when they were heads of larger families, can remain in their accustomed neighborhoods in contact with their friends and relatives, rather than being isolated in old people's homes. Community centers, like the Peckham Health Center in London, have attempted to strengthen family cohesion and emotional health by providing recreation for all members of a family in one spot, thus counteracting the centrifugal tendency inherent in the conventional pattern of urban recreational activities.

There can be no doubt that planning on all levels, from the neighborhood to the nation, has contributed to better conditions of living. But there is also no doubt that, by and large, accomplishments have fallen short of the possibilities.

PLANNING AND REALITY

Planning, the co-ordination of the activities of many men and groups of men, can be fully effective only in a functioning democratic society that is able to formulate common goals and to enlist the active participation of its members in their achievement. Planning presupposes knowledge; it cannot be effective if knowledge of facts or intentions is withheld in order to strengthen competitive positions. For this reason alone, war and war preparations with their inevitable secrecy are antagonistic to planning. In the sphere of physical planning the same antagonism exists; planning for work and living demands maximum accessibility; defense requires inaccessibility. In the past, location on hilltops and enclosure by walls have been largely responsible for making life in many cities unhealthy and inconvenient. Location far inland and dispersal into many small communities, sometimes proposed as protection against the atomic bomb, would be no less detrimental to a prosperous and cultured life.

Large-scale planning, either regional or national, has been most effective where public investment predominates. It is important to note that in Puerto Rico the investments of the Commonwealth government exceed private investments; the latter have not always been integrated into the plan but have often been made in fields or in locations where they did not have the best effect on the over-all development of the island. Similarly, in Israel the development of the new towns has been retarded because private investors prefer to build in Tel Aviv and Haifa. On the other hand, Great Britain and the Netherlands have achieved a degree of guidance of private investment, mainly through use of credits.

On the level of metropolitan planning, division of the area among many political units has been a very severe obstacle. Within the jurisdiction of a city, planning relies on the combined use of the police power for zoning and building codes and control of subdivision of land, of the taxing power for the financing of public improvements, and of the power of eminent domain for the acquisition of land for public purposes. A significant extension of the power of eminent domain has been acknowledged by the redevelopment laws enacted in recent years in most American states. These laws enable public authorities to condemn properties in blighted areas for the purpose of replanning the area. In a number of

European nations, similar powers extend to *all* urban land, not only to blighted areas. Evidently, planning is more easily accomplished and has produced the best results where the land is in the hands of one owner, whether this is a municipality as in Stockholm or Warsaw, a public corporation as in the American "Greenbelt" towns and the British "New Towns," or a private corporation as in Radburn or the garden cities of Letchworth and Welwyn. On the smaller scale of neighborhood planning, most achievements have been due to building by a single owner, public or private.

Public ownership in itself does not guarantee successful planning. Ingrained habits of short-range or narrow thinking often are serious obstacles, as exemplified by the differences between the British Board of Trade and the New Town Corporations. On the European continent, conflicts between the plans of the state-owned railroads and the cities have frequently seriously hampered urban development.

The main condition for successful planning is a common life for the entire community. Essentially, planning is the application of scientific method to the entire complex of human activities within the framework of a given physical area. Its success depends on the degree of acceptance of the scientific spirit by society.

29

The Conceptual
Framework of
Land Use

The term "land use" has found its way into the language not only of geography but also of many other disciplines: economics, sociology, public administration and law, engineering, and planning. Planners, accused of being Jacks-of-all-trades and thoroughly trained in none, when driven to the wall to define their special field of competence, tend to fall back on "land-use planning." Certainly, land use is an important concept not only for description and analysis but also for prescription and planning. Thus a discussion of various concepts involved in the precise meaning of the term "land use" is of considerable relevance to those who use it.

**USE OF THE LAND
AND USE ON THE LAND**

At first glance, land use appears to be a simple and unequivocal concept. If I am not mistaken, it originated in relation to agriculture. Farm land may be used for growing wheat or corn or for grazing cattle. That is simple enough. Here the emphasis is on the *use of the land,* of its productive capacity. What happens on the land depends on what is taken from the land.

In an urban environment—the area with which I am familiar and to which I shall limit my remarks—the emphasis shifts to *use on the land*. Certainly, physical characteristics such as slope, drainage, bearing capacity, climatic and scenic conditions play a role in determining urban land use, but their importance is secondary to the relation of a piece of land to human activities located on other pieces of land. For urban use land is a site rather than a factor of production.

This attitude is characteristically expressed in a widely used textbook by the definition "land use is concerned with the surface utilization of land," followed by a division of all land into two major categories, "developed" and "vacant," and supplemented by the remark "for our purposes, agricultural land is considered vacant land."[1]

CONVENTIONAL LAND-USE CLASSIFICATION

Mr. Bartholomew does not attempt to analyze or classify his blandly defined concept. Instead he proceeds to divide developed land into two types of subcategories, those "privately" and those "publicly" developed. This division reflects the dependence of land-use concepts on the practice of zoning, which on the North American continent has preceded and, for a long time, has dominated planning. Zoning, originally and essentially a device not for community planning but for property protection restricts the use of parcels of privately owned land in the interest of the owners of neighboring parcels; it does not cover land that is publicly owned and developed.

Thus, while the first division establishes its categories according to the criterion of purpose—"developed" or "vacant" for urban purposes—the second one introduces a completely different criterion—ownership. Other criteria appear in the third step, the division into subcategories. "Privately developed" land is divided into six subcategories: one-, two-, and multifamily residential; commercial; and light and heavy industry. The terms "residential," "commercial," and "industrial" denote the purpose or function of a piece of land. But the difference of the three residential categories refers not to different functions but to different types of structure. However, in the division of industry into light and heavy, the criterion is neither purpose nor structure (nor ownership). Heavy industry is defined as producing "objectionable" effects

[1] Harland Bartholomew and Jack Wood, *Land Uses in American Cities* (Cambridge, Mass.: Harvard University Press, 1955), second edition, p. 13.

such as smoke, noise, or heavy traffic. Here still another criterion is introduced: the effect of influence of the activities performed on a piece of land on its surroundings.

An even more mixed bag is presented by the subcategories of "publicly developed" land. Here we find: (1) streets, (2) railroad property, (3) parks and playgrounds, and (4) public and semipublic property. Subcategories 1 and 3 use the criterion of physical characteristics (roughly parallel to the structural charateristics employed to subdivide residential use), implicitly or explicitly associated with function or activity. On the other hand, subcategories 2 and 4 revert to the criterion of ownership. In the case of railroad properties this is clearly associated with function. However "public and semipublic property" includes land uses serving widely divergent functions and activities, from airports to cemeteries. Moreover, this subcategory goes beyond the boundaries set by its master category of "publicly developed" land by including "semipublic," which is defined as "used by large numbers." Here still another criterion appears—quantity, or intensity, rather than quality, or kind, of activity.

The authors of the textbook go on to explain that a golf course is "semipublic," while a beer garden is "commercial," though the number of people using the latter is likely to be larger, and though the same activities—social intercourse supported by consumption of alcoholic beverages—are carried on in both of them. Moreover, the beer garden, accessible to the public, falls in the same general category as the private residence as "privately developed," while the golf club, with access as severely restricted to its members and guests as the private residence, is classified as "publicly developed land."

CRITIQUE OF CONVENTIONAL LAND-USE CLASSIFICATION

The theoretical inadequacy, the inconsistencies, and the glaring contradictions of the conventional system have not escaped the notice of more sophisticated planners, such as Mitchell and Rapkin, Rannells, and Guttenberg.[2]

[2] Robert B. Mitchell and Chester Rapkin, *Urban Traffic, a Function of Land Use* (New York: Columbia University Press, 1954); John Rannells, *The Core of the City* (New York: Columbia University Press, 1956); Albert Z. Guttenberg, "A Multiple Land Use Classification System," *Journal of the American Institute of Planners,* August 1959.

These writers discard the criterion of ownership as irrelevant. They distinguish four criteria relevant to the classification of land uses:

1. Buildings or other improvements on the land.
2. Occupants or users of land.
3. Major purpose of occupancy of the land.
4. Kind of activities on the land.

They adopt the third criterion, "major purpose," as the most relevant one and introduce the concept of "establishment" in order to identify the major purpose. Establishments are defined as "individuals or groups occupying recognizable places of business . . . within or upon units of land" and, alternatively, as "units of land use, classified as to their major activities." However, in the case of units of land owned by units of government—"The Establishment" in the terminology of England's "angry young men"—they are forced to drop the criterion of establishment and limit themselves to the criterion of "major purpose [or activities]."

The major purpose of business establishments is identified on the basis of the Standard Industrial Classification Code used by the United States Census. This method of identification permits correlation of land-use data with census data and eliminates the division into "light" and "heavy" industry, which has never been satisfactorily defined. The Standard Industrial Classification Code for the classification of land uses is being adopted increasingly by land-use researchers in both the United States and Canada. For the nonbusiness establishments it is supplemented by the purpose of the establishment. However, in most of these cases, the physical structure customarily devoted to such purpose is substituted —such as "dwelling unit" for "residing," "school" for "education," "church" for "religious worship," etc. Thus the criterion of physical structure re-enters by the back door, as it were. Mitchell and Rapkin are well aware of this problem. How does one classify, for instance, a store-front church or a residence in a loft building?

They are, of course, also aware that different establishments may be found on one unit of land. As the unit of land, they and most other researchers adopt the parcel as the smallest identifiable unit. In this way the criterion of ownership re-enters by the back door in order to define the boundaries and hence the quantities of land devoted to various purposes. The quantities of land devoted to qualitatively different land uses and their spatial distribution, generally defined as "the land-use pattern," are of primary interest for land-use research, projection, and planning. In addition to the percentage distribution by land-use categories of all land within the universe under study and to the general pattern of their distribution, significance attaches also to the "grain," that is, the sizes of the units of land of various categories that are clustered or interspersed with units of other categories. The concept of the "grain" of land use has been defined and developed in particular by Kevin Lynch.[3]

A map, representing every parcel by major purpose or function, gives complete information on the quantity, pattern, and grain of land use by purpose. But, aside from the presence of establishments with different purposes on one parcel, which becomes particularly vexing in the center of the city where most of the parcels are occupied by multistory buildings, Mitchell and Rapkin also recognized that one establishment, while serving a single general purpose, may contain several activities. Each of these may occupy a distinct portion of the parcel occupied by the establishment; and the size, spatial pattern, and intensity of use of such portions may be significant factors in the understanding of land use. For instance, a parcel occupied by a large establishment of the electronics industry is likely to contain distinct pieces of land devoted to different activities, each associated with a different kind of physical structure: processing of materials (a factory building), storage of goods (a warehouse, or a storage yard), administration (an office building), storage of vehicles (a parking lot), recreation "green space", etc. Evidently, it is equally important for the understanding and analysis of land use to know how much land is devoted to office buildings, parking lots, or green spaces, and where these are located, as it is to have such data for different branches of manufacturing or of retail trade.

[3] Kevin Lynch and Lloyd Rodwin, "A Theory of Urban Form," *Journal of the American Institute of Planners*, Vol. XXIV, No. 4 (1958); Kevin Lynch, *The Image of the City* (Cambridge, Mass.: The Technology Press and Harvard University Press, 1960; paperback edition, The M.I.T. Press, 1964).

Evidently, land use can be classified under different aspects, or "dimensions," to use Guttenberg's term, and each classification will result in different quantitative and spatial patterns of distribution. Guttenberg and others[4] rightly stress that land-use classification must fulfill the basic requirements of any classification system: internal consistency and ability to be extended to include new phenomena.

Guttenberg distinguishes five dimensions. Three of these —function of establishment; type of activity; and type, size, and value of buildings—are practically identical with those employed by Mitchell and Rapkin, although the latter's "occupiers or users" category is omitted and appears indeed to duplicate "establishments." However, it is significant that in dealing with buildings, or rather more broadly with "site facilities," he not only lists the type of buildings, or their qualitative aspects, but introduces two quantitative aspects: size (in terms of floor area) and value. In fact, each of these represents a different quantitative aspect, each of which has to be measured and classified independently, with value applicable not only to the site facilities but, separately, to the site itself. It is true that a map of land values is generally considered to be something different from a land-use map. However, as site value largely determines land use and value of site facilities reflects it, they are very closely related to land use.

Quantitative aspects are also involved in Guttenberg's remaining two dimensions, listed as the first and last. The first, labeled "general site development," deals with the degree or intensity, of land use, from "vacant, unused" through "vacant, used" to occupancy by temporary and by permanent buildings (it may be questioned whether this can be distinguished from "site facilities"). The last, labeled "activity effects," deals with a variety of quantitive aspects. It attempts to answer such questions as "how much of a given activity, how much traffic, smoke, or noise does the activity generate; what is the service radius of the activity?" All these questions are valid and important for studies of land use. We found that the quantity of smoke, noise, etc., generated

[4] For example, Robert M. Sparks, "The Case for a Uniform Land Use Classification." *Journal of the American Institute of Planners*, Vol. XXIV. No. 3 (1958).

by an activity on a piece of land had been used to classify industries as "light" and "heavy." Most land-use studies employ, with good reason, service radius as the criterion for the classification of certain uses, such as shopping centers or parks, which are generally classified as "neighborhood," "community," "regional," etc.

It appears that land uses must be classified according to many different quantitative as well as qualitative aspects. Among the latter, purpose (or function) of establishment, kind of activity, and type of site facilities stand out. Accessibility, classified as "free," restricted by price, and "restricted by ownership," is also a significant qualitative aspect. Quantitative aspects requiring attention are the number of persons or other units, such as vehicles, that are present on a given piece of land (and the length of time and period of day or year at which they are present); size of site facilities, in terms of bulk or of floor area (including floor area zero, as for parking lots or tennis courts); and value of site and of site facilities.

ASSEMBLY AND PRESENTATION OF LAND-USE DATA

The multidimensional classification of land use can, by definition, never be fully presented on a two-dimensional map. At best, the interrelations between two aspects of land use can be presented on a single map. Wider possibilities are offered by transparent overlay maps. However, these are costly to reproduce and cumbersome to handle.

In addition, the study of different aspects of land use and of their correlations has as its base the assembling of many characteristics for small units, generally parcels, which then can be assembled in different combinations for different aspects. Because of their small size and great number these units cannot be presented well on maps for large areas. Therefore, presentation in tabular form is being increasingly employed. Once the characteristics of each parcel have been transferred to a punched card or tape, they can be easily tabulated and cross-tabulated in any desired way with the aid of business machines, in particular electronic computers. Electronic devices have also been successfully used for transferring data to maps, employing a small-meshed orthogonal grid for location of each item. In the field of traffic research —which is more generously financed than geography or planning—there has been much pioneering work, and land-use data has been employed to determine traffic generation.

While the detailed parcel-by-parcel data are of great value for certain purposes, such as tax assessment and detailed planning of housing or redevelopment projects, an understanding of the land-use patterns of cities and metropolitan areas can be derived only by studies employing larger-area units. Depending on the scale, the categories of land use will undergo some change; frequently some, such as streets or elementary schools, will be absorbed by the predominant use of the areal units in which they are located. Concomitantly, other concepts, such as land value and density will change their meaning with a change in scale of their frame of reference.

Assembly of land-use data by meaningfully selected and classified characteristics and their presentation in tabular and map form describes land-use patterns and identifies regularities both in space, in different cities or areas, and in time, where observations at several periods permit observation of change. The identification of typical patterns and consistent trends makes it possible to predict future land-use patterns that may be expected to develop if certain conditions are anticipated as given.

DETERMINANTS OF LAND USE

Highly consistent regularities have, in fact, been observed. The correlations of routes of transportation with topographical features and of certain categories of land use both with routes of transportation and with topography are familiar to geographers. Less attention has been paid to correlation of residential value with altitude above the lowest level to be found in a given urban area. Perhaps most remarkable is the concentric pattern that is found in North American urban areas both at any point in time and in the trend of change in pattern. The regular decrease in density, or intensity of land use, has been most fully recorded for resident populations; but it is equally valid for industry, commerce, schools, and other public institutions, even for cemeteries.

Such regularities are, of course, results of the working of the real-estate market, which have been extensively studied by land economists. In a free-enterprise economy, in which land is a commodity, land uses are allocated by the market.

While the observed regularities testify to an element of rationality in this process, the real-estate market is far from being a perfect market. It allocates sites to land uses exclusively on the basis of the benefits accruing – or expected to accrue – to the owners of that particular site. It cannot account for the benefits – or "malefits" – that the use of one site produces for the owner of neighboring sites or for the community.

As noted earlier, public intervention in the workings of the real-estate market occurred first and still occurs primarily to prevent malefits to neighboring property owners. Increasingly, it occurs also in order to prevent malefits and to produce benefits for the treasury of the municipality in which the land is located. In both cases zoning is the principal instrument. In both cases public intervention does not necessarily produce benefits for the entire urban community; frequently it produces demonstrable malefits.

Community planning attempts to minimize the malefits and maximize the benefits to the community. It uses prescription, also called "control" or "guidance," with the intention of producing the "best" land-use pattern. The goals are primarily the protection of future as well as of present neighbors, the economy of public services, and the enhancement of the amenities of the environment, mainly in terms of physical, mental, and social health, and of aesthetics. The means are primarily restrictions by zoning and subdivision controls. They are supplemented by promotion and by development of public transportation, sanitary, and community services.

It would, however, be fatuous to assume that any official land-use plan can prescribe a land-use pattern in disregard of market trends. Any realistic land-use plan is, of necessity, an amalgam of prediction and prescription, with the role of prescription decreasing the further the plan extends in space and in time. The resulting land-use pattern reflects the interaction of extrapolated market trends and of anticipated public policies. Here a neglected problem lies in the fact that the trends, which are extrapolated, also mirror the effect of past policies, which have changed over time. Will future policies modify the trend, or is their effect already included in the extrapolation? Only a careful evaluation of the effects of past policies can provide an answer.

The inherent contradiction between public planning and private ownership and development of land comes to the fore in the implementation of official plans. The plan, for example, may designate a certain piece of land as a shopping center. This designation creates a monopoly for the owner, or owners, of that piece of land and raises its price. As a result, a potential developer of shopping centers finds himself unable to buy the designated piece, acquires another one, and requests a change in designation that cannot reasonably be refused. The very act of designation has militated against the implementation of the designated land use.

Faced with this situation, Official Plans in Ontario have gradually shifted their methods of designating land uses. The earliest Official Plans showed definite boundaries for each use; later these were replaced by symbols indicating approximate locations. However, as this method also frequently proved impossible to implement, some of the latest plans have replaced symbols by "boxes." Such boxes will state that somewhere within a given area—usually delimited as a "neighborhood" or as a "community"—stated numbers of acres must be allocated to schools, parks, shopping centers, etc., respectively.

Such symbols or boxes will not be found in plans for British New Towns or for suburbs of Stockholm, where public ownership of land permits the allocation of specific pieces of land to specific land uses. Thus an apparently minor technical detail, the graphic presentation of land use on a map, can reflect and represent the basic social, economic, and political philosophy of a community.

30

Projection and Planning of Transportation and Land Use

In attempting to understand, predict, and plan the development of an area, two main approaches may be distinguished. The first relies on the extrapolation of long-term trends for large groups of observable phenomena; it may, as a further step, attempt to break down the resultant over-all picture into some of its component elements. The second method attempts to evaluate the motivations and actions of the various individuals and groups that interact in the development of the area and to build up a composite picture from these parts.

In predicting population and employment, for instance, the first approach usually applies one or more variants of the ratio method of projection. The second approach might start from evaluating the prospects of all "basic" industries actually or potentially operating in the area, then proceed by estimating the "multiplier" effect on "service" industries, and finally derive total population by estimating the number of dependents of those employed in each industry or all of these industries. In projecting land use, the first approach might extrapolate the trends of major land uses as to location and density; the second might delve into the various factors motivating all locators and derive future land distribution as the composite result of their actions.

Britton Harris has characterized the first approach as "static and descriptive," the second as "dynamic and be-haviouristic." This characterization should be qualified. A trend describes change over time as a dynamic process; and it describes the net result of the behavior of all agents that have brought about the changes. What is meant by the denial of the dynamic and behavioristic character of the first approach is primarily the fact that it cannot—as does the second approach—explicitly study the effects of *new* forces that are not reflected in the observed trends. It is concluded that projection of trends is invalid if and when such new factors start to operate. In particular, it is assumed that extrapolation of trends must be modified to take into account decisions of public policy.

I consider this line of reasoning faulty. A trend, as a description of the net result of all past behavior, reflects the impact of many new factors, including public policy decisions, which have started to operate during the period described by the trend. Therefore, if it is claimed that a new factor, which will be operative in the future, requires a modification of the extrapolation of a trend, it is not sufficient to prove that this particular factor has not operated in the past. It must be demonstrated that its impact will be different from the impact of all the factors that have shaped the trend in the past.

This problem can be illustrated by an example. The population of the Toronto metropolitan area has been projected, by use of the ratio method, to grow from 9.5 per cent of the population of Canada in 1958 to 10.5 per cent in 1980. It was suggested that this figure should be raised because of the anticipated impact of the opening of the St. Lawrence Seaway—the result of a public policy decision. However, it was decided that the impact of the Seaway was not likely to be greater than had been the impact of the establishment, generally by public policy decision, of other new transportation facilities by road, rail, air, water, and pipeline during the period from which the trend of relative population growth had been derived.

To summarize this point, the difference between the two approaches can be defined simply. The second approach deals with dynamic and behavioristic factors explicitly, while the first one takes them into account implicitly. The first employs aggregation, the second disaggregation. The advantage of the second approach of being able to deal explicitly with known new factors, in particular public policy decisions, is obvious. The less obvious advantage of the first method is its ability to account for not only known but also unknown future factors and policy decisions. It is not as simple as it looks.

While the aggregative and disaggregative approaches start from opposite ends, there is, of course, no reason why both should not be applied to the same problem, in the hope that they will meet in the middle and produce the same result. If the end results are different, it becomes necessary to reconcile them, and this involves deciding how much confidence is to be placed in one or the other method. It seems to me that this decision depends on the extent—in time and space—of the "universe" under study. In dealing with a short-term employment forecast for a small community, for instance, it will be preferable to use estimates of future employment in all existing or proposed establishments. In dealing with a long-term population forecast for a large metropolitan area, on the other hand, extrapolation of a long-term trend is more likely to reflect the impact of the many unknown private and public decisions that will be made.

The claim that a projection can account for future public decisions is based on a hypothesis that may be formulated as follows: people pursue the same goals as *citizens through the political process* that they pursue as *buyers and sellers through the market*. This statement implies the further hypothesis that the weight of various groups in the political process is proportional to their weight in the market. Both hypotheses warrant exploration and discussion.

It may be worthwhile to review the development of research in the fields of transportation and land use in the light of the foregoing considerations.

TRANSPORTATION RESEARCH   In the development of transportation research four steps can be distinguished, extending the field both in space and in time. The methods developed at each step retain their importance and are integrated into the methods developed at later steps.

During the first step, research was directed mainly toward measuring present traffic at specific points or on specific lines, with the general purpose of "eliminating bottlenecks."

Because experience showed that the corrective measures undertaken on the basis of such limited research were soon made ineffective by growing traffic, attention shifted to prediction of future traffic volumes by means of extrapolation of growth trends of traffic volumes and/or of such factors as car ownership, population, employment, etc. Also, in this second step, observations of changes in traffic behavior resulting from the opening of relief routes led to the development of "indifference" curves.

Simultaneously, it became obvious that study of individual routes or channels had to be extended spatially to comprise the total system of traffic movements within a given area. During this third step, the technique of the *origin and destination survey* was developed. On the basis of such a survey a system of desire lines can be developed, and predictions can be made as to the volumes of traffic that would use various existing and proposed routes—if the desired movements from each origin to each destination remained constant.

Thus the need for a fourth step became evident: the development of a system for predicting future origins and destinations, desire lines, and traffic volumes. This required the development of methods simulating traffic behavior on the basis of the analysis of a great volume of observations of behavior, made possible by the use of electronic computers. The observations, derived primarily from "origin and destination" surveys, concern the "trip generation" of various units of land use, population, etc., and the choices of destinations made by individuals of various characteristics for various purposes. The choices are dependent on the friction of space in terms of route distance, travel time, and cost, as well as their choices of route and mode, dependent on the same and other variables. From the results of these observations, expressed in mathematical terms, a "model" of travel behavior is built. By "feeding" into the model various assumptions on land use and transportation facilities, traffic volumes on each link of the system can be predicted.

Transportation research, as seen in this very rough outline of the present "state of the art," has developed fairly sophisticated scientific methods. There are, of course, a number of weaknesses calling for further research. Some are mentioned here:

1. Truck trip generation of various land uses.
2. Pedestrian trips, in order to measure the correlation of total trip generation for various purposes with population characteristics, such as income, household composition, age, and sex.
3. Travel behavior of persons by industry, by occupation, and by sex, in particular for length and mode of work trips.
4. Variables determining modal split between private and public transportation, in particular the impact of levels of fares and of parking fees.

LAND-USE RESEARCH In contrast to the scientific methods employed in traffic research, the basic data that are processed by these methods — that is, the projections of land use — are still derived mainly by "handicraft" methods, by intuition more or less trained by experience. This state of affairs has stimulated attempts to construct land-use models.

Land-use prediction requires three steps:

1. Estimates of total population and industry in the area.
2. Estimates of the quantity of land requirements of population and industry, based on assumptions of densities and service standards.
3. Knowledge of the location of land uses and of the distribution of population and industry within the area.

Steps 2 and 3 interact and can be developed only together. In the development of estimates for each of the steps both aggregative and disaggregative methods can be used.

Implicit in any prediction concerning distribution and density of land uses is the assumption that they are correlated with travel time. In other words, it is assumed that all locators strive to minimize time and to maximize space (that is, minimize land cost); that in this process they are willing to "trade" time for space and vice versa; and that the resultant competition produces a distribution by which each locator achieves an optimum balance of time and space.

Thus, while transportation research predicts traffic flows and transportation planning designs transportation facilities on the basis of land-use distribution, land uses can be distributed only on the basis of travel time, which in turn depends on transportation facilities — the well-known "chicken-and-egg" relation. Therefore, a comprehensive plan, dealing with both land uses and transportation facilities, attempts to achieve a "balance" of transportation and land use. The balance is tested by a process of iteration, alternatively assuming land use and transportation as independent and dependant variables, respectively.

However, while traffic desire lines can be derived with a fair degree of confidence if distribution of land uses and models of travel behavior are given, it is questionable whether land uses can be predicted if only transportation facilities and models of travel behavior are given. But, to my knowledge, it has never been tried.

All attempts at constructing land-use models that I know about have implicitly or explicitly assumed some land uses as fixed. By treating these as "trip destinations," a distribution of "trip origins" has been derived (or vice versa).

I shall outline two of these: a very crude and primitive one that I sketched several years ago as a result of a study of the long-term trend of the distribution of population and density of the Philadelphia area; and a far more sophisticated one that Britton Harris is presently developing for the Penn-Jersey Transportation Study.

The first study showed a very consistent long-term trend in the distribution of relative population densities by concentric rings up to 25 miles from the center of Philadelphia as a function of the rate of population growth of the total area within the 25-mile circle. I suggested that this trend could be expressed by an equation of predictive value.

It may be worthwhile to spell out the assumptions implied in this hypothetical model:

1. Population density is a function of travel time; as travel time increases, demand and density decrease.

2. Travel time is proportional to straight-line distance, on the average (this does not preclude differences in travel time — and also in density — between different sectors within each concentric ring).

3. The only travel time relevant to population distribution by concentric rings is travel time to the center. (This does not

imply that there are no other destinations for work, business, shopping, etc., but that these are distributed by concentric rings by similar gradients as is population.)

As noted, this model deals only with distribution of population by concentric rings, not within each ring. Its results are therefore insufficient to determine the location of traffic generators in a manner useful for transportation planning. This has been attempted by a different model, developed by Ernest Jurkat, which represents the past density trends of individual areas correlated with the density trends of the ring in which each area is located. In this model industrial, commercial, and other areas were determined by conventional, nonmathematical planning methods.

The Penn-Jersey study attempts to overcome the "chicken-and-egg" problem by breaking the prediction period down into a sequence of small units, each probably two to five years long. The land-use distribution and the transportation facilities existing at present are assumed as "givens" for the first period. If, then, land uses are distributed by a gravity model representing travel-to-work behavior (trips for other purposes can also be dealt with by this model), distribution of residences of the labor force at the end of period 1 is determined by the distribution of its places of employment at the beginning of the period. The distribution of the places of employment at the end of the period is determined by the distribution of places of residence at its beginning. This is a very much over-simplified description of the Penn-Jersey model, which can handle also other physical and social data influencing the decisions of locators. In the present context the focus of interest is on "the first egg."

On the basis of the distribution of land uses thus projected for the end of period 1, several changes in the system of transportation facilities can be tested and one or more variants of changes adopted. The land allocation process is then repeated for period 2, etc.

If exclusive reliance were put on this model—which is not the case in the Penn-Jersey study—it might have a built-in bias toward such changes in the system of transportation facilities that can be brought about by a series of small additions to capacity. It is not likely that the addition of traffic demand occurring during any one of the short periods would indicate the need for a major improvement such as the creation of a rapid-transit system. The basic concepts of alternaive systems of metropolitan organization—comprising both land-use and transportation facilities—will still have to be developed exogeneously and a priori.

The transportation study that was undertaken in metropolitan Toronto tested a hypothesis of land-use distribution and transportation facilities that was developed a priori as a draft of a comprehensive plan for the metropolitan planning area for the year 1980. The tests show, for several variants of transportation services (commuter railroads, extension of subways, express buses) and of fare structures on these services, the traffic flow on each link of each element of the transportation system. Where the tests indicate either overloading or underuse on any link, that is, imbalance of land-use and transportation facilities, changes can be made either in the transportation facilities or in the distribution of land uses. Other changes, proposed for any reason, similarly can be tested by this model as to their impact on the total system.

In considering the use of the transportation system as a tool to bring about a desirable distribution of land uses—usually referred to as a desirable form of metropolitan development—two questions have to be answered. First, what are the desired goals; and second, how effective are transportation facilities in determining land use? I shall deal first with the second question.

We all know that different modes of transportation result in different forms of land development. Specifically, a significant difference should be noted between the effects of individual (private) and collective (public) means of transportation. Individual transportation, whether on foot, on bicycle, or in a private automobile, is "door-to-door" transportation. Where it is predominant within a fairly densely populated, or "urban," area, it will always be supplied by a network of paths in all directions allowing door-to-door movement at fairly uniform speeds. It is, as the Germans call it, "area"—as opposed to "linear"—transportation. Consequently, travel time is roughly proportional to straight-line distance, and growth tends to occur fairly evenly in all directions. There is no definite "structure" in the relation between developed and undeveloped land,

IMPACT OF TRANSPORTATION ON LAND USE

or in the distribution of densities on the land, except for a gradual decrease of density from the center toward the periphery.

Any trip by public transportation, on the other hand, always involves at least two changes of mode between modes of usually greatly varying speeds. The transfer points (stations or stops) become points of attraction for locators; a sequence of transfer points becomes a line of attraction. Where the technology of transportation favors widely spaced stops and great differences in the speeds—as in the combination of walking and riding steam-propelled commuter trains — a "point" or cluster pattern of settlement results. Where stops are close together and the difference in speed between the two modes—riding and walking—is moderate, as with streetcars and buses, linear patterns emerge.

When and where public transportation is the predominant mode of persons' movement—as is still the case in most of Europe—a definite·structure can be created by the location of transportation lines alone. Areas not served by these lines are kept "open" simply by lack of accessibility. However, where car ownership and paved roads are so nearly universal as to make accesibility merely a function of straight-line distance, as in contemporary North America, the impact of the location of transportation facilities on the structure of land use is much more limited. It may have a modest influence on the distribution of densities; but any substantial modification of the pattern of ubiquitous "sprawl," in particular the preservation of open space, can be brought about only by far-reaching measures of direct public control that require a strong consensus of public opinion concerning the goals of metropolitan development.

31

Limitations of Simulation
of Future Behavior

The ultimate purpose of all planning work is to recommend decisions, generally involving investments, to public or private action agencies. Decisions are always based on a prediction of their consequences, whether this prediction is made explicit in detail or merely implied in a general way. If a decision is made by tossing a coin, the probability that the prediction will come true is 50 per cent. If a prediction is based on informed judgment, the probability that it will come true is increased by a sizable percentage, but it is not possible to measure the size of the percentage. Any decision involves a choice between alternatives. The correctness of the predictions concerning the results of the chosen alternative can be measured, but only after the investment has been made. The correctness of the predictions concerning any of the rejected alternatives always remains unknown.

The use of computers to simulate future traffic behavior makes possible far more detailed predictions of the results of a number of alternatives than can be made by any other method, and thereby increases the probability that the predictions are true and that the decisions based on these predictions will be correct. With an investment of one billion dollars even an increase in probability by as little as 1 per cent is likely to result in saved costs or increased benefits of the magnitude of 10 million dollars. The justification for the expense in time and money required to construct computer models rests in this increased probability of true predictions.

Therefore, the Metropolitan Toronto Planning Board has undertaken a study of traffic expected in 1980, using simulation techniques. In this study the distribution of land uses, population, and employment, laid down in the draft of the Official Plan, was treated as fixed. Also assumed as fixed were the correlations between variables such as number and density of households and of jobs, income level, time and cost distance, street capacity, trip generation and distribution, and choice of mode and of route. These correlations had been derived from the analysis of a vast array of observations of past behavior and were expressed in the form of mathematical equations. Systems of transportation facilities, income levels, speed and fares of transit, and parking costs were varied in different simulations.

As usual in all such studies, land-use data were averaged and summarized for areas, and travel paths were represented by a limited number of links and nodes. Simulated traffic loads represented average hourly loads during a two-hour workday morning peak period.

The study has produced very valuable results. In addition, it has produced, as a fringe benefit, some insights into the limitations of simulations that may have some general validity.

WHAT THE COMPUTER CAN AND CANNOT DO

There is a popular notion abroad that electronic computers are "thinking machines." Actually they can perform only a very few of the simplest of those operations of the human brain which we call "thinking." They can perform three operations:

1. Add and subtract figures.
2. Differentiate between zero and other numbers.
3. Memorize numbers.

In the performance of these three operations the computer is vastly superior to the human brain. But it can undertake these operations only after having been instructed by men how to apply them in a long series of carefully programmed steps. Any errors of judgment in the formulation of these instructions, as well as any inadequacies of the data that are being processed, will be reflected in the results produced by the computer.

These results consist of arrays of many thousands of numbers. These numbers have to be arranged, mapped, and compared, in order to derive a meaningful interpretation of the results of a set of computer runs. This interpretation inevitably requires a certain degree of human judgment.

As will be evident from these short remarks, the computer is a very potent and valuable instrument used by fallible human beings, not a superior brain endowed with some superhuman power to see the future in a crystal ball.

Of necessity, any prediction of future human behavior can be based only on experience of past behavior. In Toronto adequate observations were available only for the year 1956. It was not known whether behavior would remain constant. The correlations between behavior and the factors that had been found to determine behavior might change, in which case the equations expressing these correlations would be valid no longer. Fortunately, a comparison with travel behavior observed in a number of metropolitan areas in the United States over a period of 15 years indicated that these correlations are indeed relatively constant.

CHANGES IN TRAVEL BEHAVIOR

However, this by no means precludes the possibility of future changes. If and when observations made in different years in the same area should show such changes, it would be possible to project trends of behavioral change. This would reduce the chances of erroneous predictions, but it would not eliminate them. Trends may change, and new trends may appear at any time in the future. Here lies a first and basic limitation of all simulations of future behavior.

As noted earlier, in all models land use has been kept constant, although it is well known that changes in the transportation system will generate strong pressures toward changes in land use. These changes in turn will generate different traffic patterns.

IMPACT OF TRAVEL ON LAND USE

The draft Official Plan had, of course, attempted to anticipate the probable effect of the tranportation facilities included in that plan. Insofar as facilities finally adopted differ from those in the draft Official Plan, it must be expected that land uses and densities will differ from those presented in the plan. Moreover, other changes, particularly in density, may occur for a variety of reasons beyond the control of the Planning Board.

While the models, being based on the assumption of a given fixed land-use pattern, could not, by definition, reproduce the changes that might be expected to result from changes in transportation, they do give some indication of the direction and order of magnitude of the pressures that are likely to produce such changes. These indications are contained in the results of the traffic assignment programs.

VARIATIONS WITHIN PEAK-HOUR PERIOD

A serious difficulty arises from variations of demand within the two-hour peak period that has been simulated in the models. Observations show that the load on transit facilities during periods of a quarter of an hour or longer may exceed the average of the two-hour peak period by as much as 50 per cent. The load may be further increased when weather conditions cause people to switch from driving to transit riding. Observations on roads generally show variations of only 10 to 20 per cent during a two-hour peak period. This is evidently due to the fact that during the whole length of such periods most roads are used close to the limits of their capacity. On roads not used to capacity variations up to 50-70 per cent have been observed.

TRIP DISTRIBUTION

A key part of the models consists in programs that simulate the number of trips that people will make between any one zone and all other zones under given conditions. If one of these conditions is changed anywhere, the trip distribution is changed in the entire system. For instance, if a new express-way reduces the traveling time between zones A and B, more trips will be made between A and B and correspondingly fewer trips both between A and C, D, etc., and between B and C, D, etc.

The increased trip volume between A and B found by a trip distribution program is then assigned by a second program to the various facilities that can be used to make trips between A and B. This may lead to the result that the addition of a new facility, such as a commuter railroad line between A and

B, may show an increased rather than a decreased volume on roads connecting A and B. This result may not be as absurd as it appears to be at first glance. Assume, for instance, a person working in zone A in the central city making a choice between suburban residences in zones B and C, respectively, which have equal road access to A. If zone B, in addition, has access by suburban railroad, he is likely to choose zone B, but may still drive to zone A.

Under the conditions of fixed land-use distribution assumed in the models, this effect is probably overstated. It implies that some other person, who would otherwise have lived in B and worked not in A, now lives in some other zone. In reality, it is more likely that the new commuter to zone A will be added to those who would have lived in zone B under the previous conditions (without the commuter railroad). In this way an increase on all facilities between A and B indicates strongly that the land-use plan should assign higher volumes of residents and of jobs to zones A and B, respectively.

The effect of changed accessibility on trip distribution is, of course, a long-term effect that works itself out only as and when people change residences or jobs. In the short run, immediately after a new transportation facility becomes available, the old pattern of trip distribution still prevails, and the change will consist only in a shift of travel from the old to the new facility. This can be measured by "freezing" the trip distribution. In evaluating the different results of "free" and "frozen" trip distributions, respectively, this difference between long-term and short-term effects must be kept in mind.

SIMPLIFICATION OF ZONES

In order to process the hundreds of thousands of households and many thousands of other establishments that are places of origin and destination of work trips, it was, of course, necessary to summarize them in zones, assuming that all trips to or from each zone have their origin and destination in the point of gravity of their zone. This involves a certain, relatively minor, possibility of distortion. A number of trips have their origin and destination within the same zone. These short "intrazone" trips are not represented by the model.

Two conclusions must be drawn from these considerations:

1. The total number of passengers and vehicles will be higher than shown in the results of the models. This difference

is likely to be negligible on expressways and on rapid-transit lines but may be significant on arterial roads.

2. Because short trips are made predominantly by automobile (pedestrian trips are not represented in the model), vehicle person trips will be more strongly underrepresented than transit trips, resulting in a certain distortion of the "modal split" between vehicle and transit trips in favor of transit. This has to be borne in mind in comparing the modal split predicted by the model with the modal split actually observed in the past. Similarly, the "submodal" split between expressways and arterial roads will be slightly distorted by understating the number of trips on arterial roads.

SIMPLIFICATION OF THE ROAD SYSTEM

For the same practical reasons that apply to zones, the many existing roads that can be used by vehicles had to be summarized into a simpler system of arterial roads. For this purpose the capacity of arterial roads was increased by the capacity of parallel roads that, by their location, may serve the same trips as do the arterials. The traffic loads shown on the arterials can therefore not be taken literally.

SIMPLIFICATION OF SURFACE TRANSIT SYSTEM

A similar but much more serious problem was encountered in dealing with surface transit. On the basis of information supplied by the Toronto Transit Commission, probable bus headways were determined on the basis of the future density and distance from downtown of each zone and simplified into three concentric zones with peak-hour headways of 2, 3, and 6 minutes, respectively, with 10-minute headways being assumed for the balance of the Planning Area.

However, it was not possible either for the Toronto Transit Commission or for anybody else to determine on which particular streets bus lines would be run in 1980. It was therefore technically necessary to assume that buses would run on all arterial roads at the headways previously described, although in practice these headways could be maintained only in the most heavily traveled direction. Furthermore, as the location of lines was not known, it was impossible to determine where transfers would be required. Consequently, it was impossible to introduce "transfer penalites" for waiting, as has been done, for instance, for transfer between two subway lines. Consequently, in all preliminary models, more frequent and faster surface transit has been assumed than can be expected realistically, resulting in a considerable over-statement of the number of passengers that are shown on surface transit.

In the final model of the recommended plan, an attempt has been made to correct this overstatement by increasing the relation of bus speed to vehicle speed from the observed ratio of 12:17 to 10:17. This may be adequate for the system as a whole but does not eliminate possible distortions in individual sections of the area.

The most important factor in the distribution of trips is the journey to and from work. In simulating these work trips, it was assumed that everyone is equally able and willing to fill any job. This assumption was inevitable because it is quite impossible to predict the spatial distribution of the supply and demand of a vast number of different skills—many of which do not even exist at present—in 1980. But it is, of course, far different from the situation in the real world.

SIMPLIFICATION OF JOBS AND LABOR FORCE

As parking cost is an important factor in determining the individual's choice between private and public transportation, it has also been introduced into the models in the form of a time equivalent (10 cents' parking fee equal to 2 minutes' traveling time).

SIMPLIFICATION OF PARKING COST

It has been assumed that in 1980 the all-day parking fee in the central business district will average $1.50 (in 1956 dollars). Parking fees in other areas have been scaled down from this level in proportion to the predicted levels of demand.

It is, of course, known that not all persons parking their cars in a given area pay for that service. Some park on the street and some in facilities provided by their employer. However, as it is impossible to estimate the percentage of all parkers in a given area who would enjoy these privileges in 1980, it was necessary to assume that all would pay the full cost. This would be the case if prohibition of all-day parking were strictly enforced on all streets and if appropriate government action were to force all employers, including nonprofit-making organizations, to charge the full cost of parking facilities to their employees. The method used in the models inherently implies these policies.

Income was estimated in terms of "purchasing power of transportation services." This implies that the relation between the cost of supplying various forms of transportation services will remain constant, the same as it was in 1956.

In the past this relation has been far from constant, and it is likely to change in the future, because the real cost of any product changes with changes of productivity in the particular industry producing that commodity or service. In the recent past, increases in productivity in the oil industry have reduced the real cost of gasoline. On the other hand, there is only a limited scope for increases in productivity in the transit industry, because the major part of its cost consists of wages. The assumed constancy in the price relation between private and public transportation probably can be maintained only if an increasing part of the cost of public transportation is borne not by the rider but by the public purse.

MARGIN OF ERROR

As is evident from the foregoing, there remain considerable areas of uncertainty.

If this is disappointing, it should be recalled that all sources of uncertainty enumerated in this discussion are present also in every other method of estimating future traffic, together with many sources of error that have been eliminated by the use of explicit and exact mathematical simulation models. The margin of error has been substantially reduced by their use.

This is all that can be expected from any method. No magic wand exists or will ever exist that can conjure up a completely exact and reliable image of the future. Uncertainty about the future is simply the corollary of the freedom of human beings to make their own decisions.

32

Are Land-Use Patterns Predictable?

The relationship between land use and traffic generation has been identified sufficiently well to permit us to estimate the origins and destinations of urban travel. Indices of land use, population, and employment help us to predict traffic patterns; however, to make this travel prediction, the planner must assume certain future spatial patterns of land-use distribution.

Such a land-use forecast is based presently on a "plan" evolved largely from judgment, and thus traffic analysts, who utilize scientifically based methods, must derive their results from a nonscientific basis. It is natural, therefore, to seek a scientific procedure for land-use forecasting.

One way to forecast future events is by extrapolation of past trends. Such extrapolation is possible if two conditions are fulfilled:

1. The number of independent variables must be small. That is, it must be possible to eliminate most of the endless number of variables that actually influence events, either because their influence can be shown to be negligible or because it can be shown that they are so closely correlated with the selected independent variables that the latter can be substituted for them.

2. The observations must cover a sufficiently wide and varied universe over a sufficient period to enable one to pre-

dict, with an acceptable degree of probability, the limits within which the observed correlations are valid.

On the implicit assumption that both conditions can be met, a number of independent variables have been used in an attempt to construct models of land use and population distribution.

SPATIAL RELATIONSHIPS The horizontal dimensions of space on the earth's surface are certainly a basic determinant of population distribution. Investigating the settlement pattern in Southern Germany, Walter Christaller uncovered a definite pattern, a hierarchy of "central places."[1] The smallest central places served an area with a radius of about 2½ miles. A cluster of the smallest central units was again served by a larger center, and so the pattern continued. Since circles do not dovetail, they may be modified into hexagonal areas. The result is a system of small-scale honeycombs within larger honeycombs. If horizontal space were the only factor, such a pattern of land use would develop. However, as Christaller recognized, this pattern is modified by political, topographic, and transportation factors.

Donald Bogue, analyzing the more recent settlement pattern of the United States, assumes 67 major metroplitan centers as "given" and investigates their influence on their sphere of dominance, measuring concentric zones of varying distance from the center.[2] He also measures the influences of sub-centers and major transportation arteries on individual sectors. Dependent variables are density of urban, rural nonfarm, and farm populations, and employment in manufacturing, wholesale trade, retail trade, and services. Sectional differences in over-all population density and economic development and other geographic factors are deliberately ignored. A fairly consistent pattern emerges.

Christaller, a geographer, and Bogue, a demographer, concentrated their studies on quantitative factors. Park and Burgess, sociologists, investigated differences in the social and

[1] Walter Christaller, *Die Zentralen Orte in Suddeutschland* (Jena: Gustav Fischer, 1933).

[2] Donald J. Bogue, *The Structure of the Metropolitan Community* (Ann Arbor: University of Michigan, 1949); also, Hans Blumenfeld, "The Dominance of the Metropolis" (Comment), *Land Economics,* May 1950.

economic characteristics of the population by concentric zones. They found that social-economic status increased with distance from the center. These findings were confirmed, for instance, by an analysis of the 1940 census data for the city of Philadelphia. While population density (whether measured over-all, gross, or net) decreased for all zones from the center to the periphery, dwelling-unit value and percentage of home ownership increased regularly to the zone of most rapid growth, which in the preceding decade had occurred between 7 and 8 miles from the center. Beyond this zone, residential value and home ownership decreased again.

The Park-Burgess pattern, valid for North American cities of the twentieth century, is a reversal of the older pattern developed in European cities during the preceding centuries. Thus, any theory can be valid only within the limits of a given social-economic structure and may change in scale or direction with future change of this structure.

Concepts based on differences related to the distance from center necessarily obscure the differences between sectors in each zone. Homer Hoyt found that certain sectors in United States cities show common characteristics through several concentric zones. Here, the determining factors appear to be: (a) rail and water transportation lines that attract industry; (b) predominant wind directions that attract high-income groups to the windward side, with lower-income groups residing on the leeward side. Again, these factors may be changed by historical developments, such as changes in means of transportation or in the class structure of society.

Both the concentric circle and sector theories deal only with the two horizontal dimensions of space. Small heed has been paid the vertical dimension. However, an investigation of the 1940 census data for the Philadelphia metropolitan district indicated a consistent correlation between altitude and average (contract or estimated) rental value of dwelling units. Each additional dime of monthly rent corresponded to a foot in elevation above sea level.[3]

Much earlier, in 1927, the North Jersey Transit Commission had reported that a close direct or positive correlation existed between ground-level elevation and land values.

[3] Hans Blumenfeld, "Correlation Between Value of Dwelling Units and Altitude," *Land Economics,* November 1948.

Surprisingly, my investigation of Manhattan between 59th and 110th Streets, showed a similar correlation between rents and ground-level elevation, though the height of the buildings frequently exceeded the maximum difference in ground-level elevation. Each north-south row of blocks between Riverside Drive and Park Avenue was investigated, using the rental data of the 1940 and 1950 census. Figure 1 presents the 1950 data for the row of blocks immediately west of Central Park. In addition to altitude, high rents were evidently related to two more variables: nearness to subway stations and proximity to the city's core. The latter is a significant exception to the Park-Burgess pattern.

Value of dwelling units may be an important factor in estimating traffic volumes. High values are correlated with high car ownership and high generation of vehicular trips. High values are also generally correlated with lower densities although the Manhattan Westside study found a significant exception.

Figure 1 Correlation of rent and altitude, New York, 1950. (*Note: The western boundary of the blocks is Broadway from 60th to 66th Streets, Columbus Avenue from 66th to 100th, Manhattan Avenue from 100th to 110th.*)

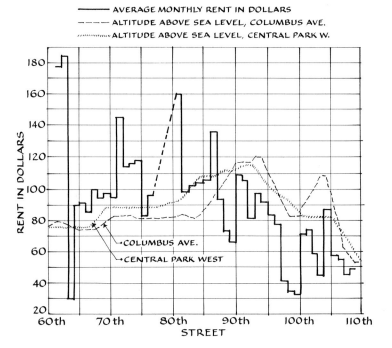

Correlation between altitude and value of dwellings can be observed in numerous United States and foreign cities. But most often the pattern appears to be of recent origin. In Paris, for instance, the influence of a reverse older pattern is still noticeable, with the aristocratic Faubourgs St. Germain and St. Honoré located in the valley and the working-class slums of Belleville and Menilmontant on the heights.

The theories we have discussed thus far afford a valuable insight into the correlations important for constructing any model of future distribution of land use and population. These theories, however, do not yield quantitative forecasts because they reflect correlations at a specific time and do not account for trends through time.

An attempt has been made to quantify the secular trend of distribution of population and over-all densities. Data from the decennial census counts of the period 1900 to 1950 for the Philadelphia metropolitan area have been assembled and analyzed for concentric zones up to 25 miles from Philadelphia City Hall.[4]

The same method was utilized to measure the corresponding trend in the Toronto metropolitan area. The data were less reliable though and were available only for 1929, 1939, 1949, 1954, and 1955. Data for the area beyond the 8-mile circle, extending up to 18 miles, were available as a residual only. Nevertheless, the Toronto trend was remarkably similar to the trend in Philadelphia.

Dr. D. A. S. Fraser of K.C.S. Data Control Ltd., Toronto, was engaged to express these trends in a mathematical formula. It was found that the formula had to be limited to zones of suburban growth, from 4 to 18 miles in Philadelphia and from 3 to 8 miles in Toronto. Both the older core area, already fully developed at the beginning of the periods of investigation, and the outer, semirural, areas were omitted because of different trends. Several formulas were devised. The simplest is verbally expressed as follows: A concentric zone of a given density moves outward at a rate equal to 0.85 of the percentage growth of the total area population during the given period, multiplied by the mileage distance of the initial

[4] Hans Blumenfeld, "The Tidal Wave of Metropolitan Expansion," *Journal of the American Institute of Planners*, Volume XX, No. 1 (Winter 1954).

density zone from the center. For example, if total population during a specific period grows by 10 per cent, and if at the beginning of the period densities x and y were found at 5 and 10 miles, respectively, from the center, then at the end of the period density x will be found at 5.425 miles and density y at 10.85 miles from the center. If total population grows by 20 per cent, density x will be found at 5.85 miles and density y at 11.70 miles from the center.

The constant 0.85 was found for Toronto; the corresponding constant for Philadelphia was found to be 0.83. The amazingly close relation of the two figures is probably coincidental. However, it is not improbable that the constants for most North American metropolitan areas vary within only a narrow range. It might be beneficial to test this hypothesis by similar investigations in other areas.

An attempt was made to use the 0.85 formula to forecast 1980 population densities for concentric zones between 3 and 8 miles from the center of Toronto. Resulting population figures for these five concentric zones yielded an excessive total and provided too little of the assumed total area population for zones under 3 and over 8 miles from the center. Note that the area total is built into the formula only as an independent variable, not as an automatic limit upon the sum of the zone results. Consequently, these results were adjusted downward proportionally to fit the total. The adjusted zone results served as controls for the population figures of each zone. The latter figures had been derived previously by the traditional method of estimating carrying capacity of each segment of each zone on the basis of natural conditions, historical trends, and existing zoning regulations. Application of the controls resulted in some adjustments.

It is evident that practical application of the results of the analysis of population trends by concentric zones is currently limited. Some reasons for this limitation are obvious:

1. The formula is based on the trend as observed during the first half and second quarter of the century respectively. The trend may change.

2. The formula is applicable only to the belt of suburban growth, and results must be adjusted to independent population estimates for inner, urban, and outer, semirural, zones.

3. Conclusions are valid only for each concentric ring as a whole, but yield no information on population densities (which may vary greatly) within the individual segments of each zone.

Densities are influenced by natural and political boundaries, as evidenced by the Philadelphia area study. In addition, the existence of secondary centers affects the density within individual segments, though, unexpectedly, this does not affect the density of entire concentric zones.

The concentric-circle theory may be regarded as a special case of correlation of population distribution with centers of employment—the case, that is, where there is only one such center. It should be possible to find the correlation of population distribution with several centers of employment. This requires a reversion of the gravitation formulas now used to determine the distribution of a given purchasing power among several shopping centers at given distances between the shopping centers and the several units of purchasing power.

At first glimpse, such an exercise may appear to be of purely theoretical value. Location of employment, even more than location of population, is dependent on individual decisions and therefore may be considered to be even less predictable. However, the location choice of industrial and commercial employment is more strictly limited by transportation facilities and other relatively permanent factors than is the choice of residence. Therefore, it can be predicted with greater confidence.

In the Toronto area, an attempt to correlate population distribution with a limited number of major employment centers is under way. The results thus far, although promising, are only fragmentary. If a satisfactory formula to express the presently existing correlation can be conceived, it may serve as a basis for calculating future population distribution of employment centers.

DISTRIBUTION OF NONRESIDENTIAL LAND USES

Few attempts have been made to construct models of nonresidential land uses. Adequate data have not been available for the construction of time series and the derivation of trends.

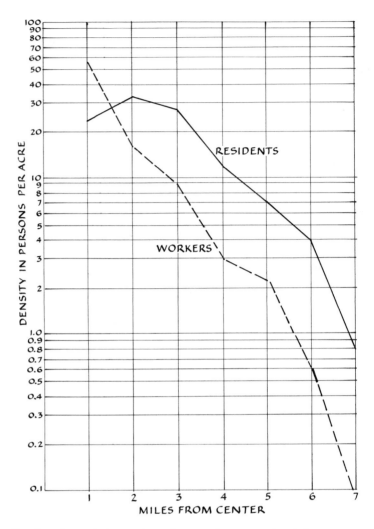

Figure 2   *Density of population and employment by concentric circles, Toronto, 1956.*

However, some valuable material is available for the indispensable first step.

Figure 2 illustrates the density of population in 1956 at place of residence and at place of employment in metropolitan Toronto. The zone within one mile of City Hall is primarily an area of employment. In the other zones the slopes for the employed population closely parallel those for the resident population. It appears that distribution of employment is correlated as consistently with distance from the center as is distribution of residence.

By calculating employment patterns, it is possible to arrive at approximate estimates of future trip distribution by concentric zones. Such estimates may be used as a control for the sums of trip predictions based on other methods for individual segments of each zone.

However, since space requirements for employment activities differ widely, a gross estimate of total employment cannot serve as a basis for a prediction of the land required for employment areas. The most pertinent and extensive of land requirements are those for the manufacturing industries, which must be investigated separately.

Figure 3 depicts the relative density of residential population and manufacturing employment in 1940 and 1943, respectively, for seven concentric zones in the city of Philadelphia. The decrease in manufacturing employment density, although rather consistent, is less drastic and not so regular as the decline in population density by distance.

Density of population and of manufacturing employment, Philadelphia, 1940-1943.   **Figure 3**

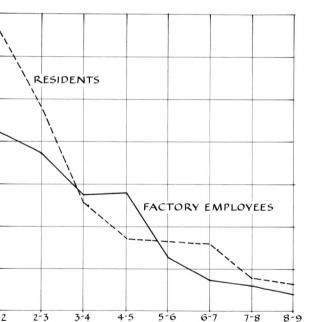

These densities express only the relation of persons employed in manufacturing to the total area of the zone. To derive the area in manufacturing use, the area required by each manufacturing worker must be known.

In the industrial districts of the Philadelphia metropolitan region in 1944 the number of persons employed per gross industrial acre averaged 51.4 within 2 miles of City Hall, 23.8 between 2·and 5 miles, and 15.7 over 5 miles.[5] Thus the decrease in density from the center to the periphery, or the increase in land used per capita, holds for both residence and employment space. This finding in the Philadelphia study is remarkable because the area between 2 and 5 miles contains extensive tank farms and railroad yards, and the outer area contains about a dozen fully matured industrial towns.

The percentage of the total area of any zone used for manufacturing is related to the number of industrial workers per square mile of total area. It is also related to the amount of industrial land used per worker. As we have shown, the number of workers per square mile decreases and the land used per worker increases with distance from the center. However, these two trends do not cancel each other out. A study of land use in the Philadelphia metropolitan district in 1944[6] showed that within 5 miles of City Hall industrial land use accounted for 19.3 per cent of the total area, between 5 and 10 miles for 2.3 per cent, and beyond 10 miles for 1.2 per cent.

Institutional land use is considered to be the third most important land-use category. The Philadelphia study also provided information on the gross land area used for educational, health, welfare, and penal institutions, and for cemeteries. Only areas of about 15 acres or more were listed as "gross land area" of specified use. Smaller land parcels, such as neighborhood schools and playgrounds, were included in the "gross area" of the predominant surrounding land use. Table 1 presents the correlation of institutional land use, as defined, with population and gross residential area in three concentric zones.

In the zone beyond 10 miles, several large institutions were

[5] Derived from *Industrial Land Use Plan,* Table VIII and Map 3, (Philadelphia City Planning Commission, 1950).

[6] *Land Use in Philadelphia Metropolitan District 1944* (Philadelphia City Planning Commission, 1949).

Miles from Center	Per 1,000 Population (1940)	Per 100 Acres of Gross Residential Area
0-5	1.22	9.3
5-10	4.39	9.3
Over 10	27.10	35.8

operating farms as well as performing their standard functions, and farming could not be separated from the areas of the institutions. Therefore, such areas are not comparable with those in the two inner zones. Within the limits of this study, comparison between these two zones reveals that these land uses have a constant relation to residential land, but not to population. In the 5–10-mile zone, about three and a half times as much institutional land is used to serve a similar number of people as in the 0–5-mile zone.

This is surprising, because a person's need for institutional services is not dependent on the location of his residence. Many services are supplied by various levels of government; and official governmental standards require that certain areas be allocated in relation to the number of persons served, for example, a specified school acreage for a certain number of students. However, in Philadelphia, the net acreage of public schools in 1944 for each 1,000 students was: within a 1-mile circle, 0.78; within 1–5-mile circles, 1.52; within 5–10-mile circles, 3.15.

Institutional densities, like residential and industrial densities, follow the pattern of regular decline from the center toward the periphery. This is true because as demand for land and prices of land decreases or increases, *all* land uses expand or contract with the price. Therefore the trend of population distribution by concentric circles can serve as a guide in forecasting the distribution of all land uses.

POSSIBLE DEVELOPMENT OF LAND-USE MODELS

The findings discussed here can serve only as very broad guides. The use of each segment of land is dependent on a great many variables: topography (altitude and slope), soil, climate, relation to transportation facilities and to centers of employment and of service, existing development and occupancy, zoning, etc. As stated earlier, the first condition for constructing a model is to reduce the number of these variables.

Apparently, the net result of these variables is expressed rather accurately by a curve representing the population density over time. In addition to past densities, distance from the center and time periods are used as variables in this method. This reduction to a sum of three variables fulfills the first condition. As the family of density curves is based on observations in several metropolitan areas over several decades, the second condition — validity within the limits of the area and period of prediction — also appears to be fulfilled.

This discussion of land use models leads to two conclusions:

1. With more research it may be possible to develop useful land-use models.

2. No matter what degree of success city planners attain in constructing models, models can only supplement, not supplant, the careful evaluation of the impact of the changing needs and intentions of all people and agencies in the community upon the evolving land-use pattern.

33

The Economic Base of the Metropolis: Critical Remarks on the "Basic-Nonbasic" Concept

SUMMARY

1. The concept divides all employment in a community into "basic" or "primary" employment, working for export, and "nonbasic" or "secondary" employment, working for local consumption.
2. This method purports to serve two goals:
    a. Concentration of attention on the most important industries.
    b. Prediction of future total employment and population, which are to be derived from future "basic" employment by means of a "basic-nonbasic ratio" and of a "multiplier."
3. The method seeks the answer to two different questions, which it fails to distinguish:
    a. What is the balance of payments of the community?
    b. What are the most "critical" industries, that is, those most vulnerable to outside competition and most capable of expansion into outside markets?
4. The confusion is increased by a widespread dual bias:
    a. A "mercantilistic" bias in favor of money-earning versus consumption-satisfying activities.
    b. A "physiocratic" bias in favor of food and raw materials versus manufactured goods and services.
5. The attempt to identify "basic" activities by the widely accepted method of proportional apportionment is misleading. The attempt to do it by actual market survey is

costly and ends up by revealing the inherent contradictions of the method.

6. The method neglects the import side of the ledger, which is equally as important as the export side, both from the "balance of payments" and from the "criticality" point of view.

7. As a result of its confusion of these two points of view, the method is unable to solve the problem of "indirect primary" activities. If a consistent "balance of payments" approach were used, the problem would cease to exist; if a consistent "criticality" approach were used, these activities would fall in line with all other activities.

8. The method fails to integrate into its conceptual scheme any payments received or made other than those for work performed.

9. Employment is not a usable unit of measurement for a "balance of payments" approach, which must use "value of product" and other value terms.

10. The proportion of "basic" activities increases with increasing division of labor between communities and decreases with increasing size of community and with increasing division of labor within the community.

11. The "basic-nonbasic ratio" is meaningful only in small and simply structured communities; the larger and more complex, that is, the more "metropolitan" the community, the less applicable are the ratio and the entire method.

12. The "multiplier" varies not only with the "ratio" but also with the "family coefficient" of both the "basic" and "non-basic" employed and with the percentage of the population that is not employed.

13. Because of these complexities the "multiplier" is not a useful tool for population prediction in a metropolitan area.

14. The identification of the "export" activities of each locality could be an important tool for a national agency planning industrial location. However, if local planning agencies use it as a guide to promotion, it will either be ineffective or, if effective, result in a harmful distortion of the national locational pattern.

15. A large metropolitan area exists, survives, and grows because its business and consumer services enable it to

substitute new "export" industries for any that decline as a result of the incessant vicissitudes of economic life.

These services are the constant and permanent, hence the truly "basic" and "primary," elements of the metropolitan economy; while the ever-changing export industries are the "ancillary" and "secondary" elements. The relation assumed by the method is, in fact, reversed.

THE CONCEPT OF
THE ECONOMIC BASE

The terms "economic base" and "basic" industry or employment are being increasingly used and discussed in planning and related fields. This concept claims that all economic activities of an area can and should be divided into two fundamentally different and mutually exclusive categories, "basic" and "nonbasic."

Apparently, the first American planner to formulate the concept was Frederick Law Olmsted, who said in a letter of February 21, 1921: "Productive occupations may be roughly divided into those which can be called primary, such as carrying on the marine shipping business of the port and manufacturing goods for general use [i.e., not confined to use within the community itself], and those occupations which may be called ancillary, such as are devoted directly or indirectly to the service and convenience of the people engaged in the primary occupations."[1]

Haig and McCrea, in conformance with this concept, state: "It has been urged that a distinction should be drawn between 'primary' and 'ancillary' activities: that primary activities be given precedence in the city plan."[2]

In the same year M. Aurousseau wrote: "The primary occupations are those concerned with the functions of the town. The secondary occupations are those concerned with the maintenance of the well-being of the people engaged in those of a primary nature. The more primary citizens there are, the more secondary, in a relation something like compound interest."[3]

[1] Quoted in R. M. Haig and R. C. McCrea, *Regional Survey of New York and Its Environs*, Vol. I (New York, 1927); p. 43, footnote.

[2] *Op. cit.*, p. 42.

[3] M. Aurousseau, "The Distribution of Population," *Geographical Review*, Vol. XI, 1921, pp. 567 ff. Quoted by Robert E. Dickinson, *City, Region, and Regionalism* (London, 1947).

Here we find the two ideas that have determined the further application of the "basic-nonbasic" concept:

1. Planning and promotion, with preference to be given to "basic" activities.
2. Prediction, with total future population being derived from "basic" employment by application of a "multiplier."

The bias in favor of the "basic" activities, implicit in such terms as "basic," "primary," "town-building," "town-growth," versus "nonbasic," "ancillary," "service," "secondary," etc.,[4] is made explicit in such statements as: "the first task of ... Letchworth and Welwyn ... was to secure that 'basic' industries would be attracted; the inhabitants ... could not ... live by taking in each other's washing."[5]

We shall return to the question as to whether, when, and why people can or cannot "live by taking in each other's washing." For the development of the concept the second application—for population prediction—has been even more important. It was broadly used by Homer Hoyt in his work for the FHA. The method, as developed by Hoyt, includes five steps:[6]

1. Calculate employment in each basic industry.
2. Estimate ratio of basic to service employment.
3. Estimate ratio of population to employment.
4. Estimate future trend of basic employment.
5. Derive future total employment and population from future basic employment.

This has become the accepted formula: frequently steps 2 and 3 are omitted in favor of a rule-of-thumb formula of "population to basic employment equals seven to one."

Hoyt started by assuming that employment in manufacturing was "basic," that all other employment was "service," and that their ratio was roughly one to one. For the purposes for which Hoyt developed his formula—a quick, rough-and-

---

[4] An exception is the use of the terms "surplus" and "domestic" in the sophisticated study by John M. Mattila and Wilbur R. Thompson, "Measurement of the Economic Base of the Metropolitan Area," *Land Economics,* August 1955, pp. 215-228.

[5] J. H. Jones, "Industry and Planning," in E. A. Gutkind, *Creative Demobilisation,* Vol. II (London, 1944).

[6] See A. M. Weimer and Homer Hoyt, *Principles of Urban Real Estate* (New York, 1939).

ready housing market estimate—it was serviceable. However, he soon discovered, first, the difficulties of identifying "basic" activities and, second, the existence of wide local variations in the "basic-nonbasic" ratio.

Hoyt defines his criteria for a "basic" activity as follows: "those industries and services which produce goods for people living outside the urban region being studied, and which bring in *money* [my emphasis, H.B.] to pay for the food and raw materials which the city does not produce itself."[7] Similarly, Richard U. Ratcliff defines "primary or city-building activities" as those "which bring into the community purchasing power from outside."[8] A Swedish geographer differentiates between "exchange (*bytes*)" production, which is regarded as "primary," and "own (*egen*)" production, which is considered "secondary,"[9] and a Swedish planner has used this distinction to develop his method of population prediction.[10] Perhaps the most straightforward explanation of the concept of "basic" workers was given by Andrews, who calls them "the wage earners of the community family."[11]

IDENTIFICATION OF "BASIC" WITH "EXPORT" ACTIVITIES

The concept sounds simple and convincing enough: in order to live a community, like a family, has to earn money. The number of families is determined by the number of bread-winners; the number of "housewives" who "service" the breadwinners, and of dependents, can be derived from the number of the former.

There are certainly cases where the concept is fully applicable. Take, for instance, a copper-mining village with 1,000 miners. There will be, say, 600 people employed locally in retail trade and consumer services; if the family coefficient is 2.5, the population will be 4,000. If the company hires another 1,000 miners, it is safe to predict that they will be followed shortly by about 600 more "secondary" employed

[7] *The Economic Base of the Brockton, Massachusetts Area* (Homer Hoyt Associates, published January 1949), p. 4.

[8] Richard U. Ratcliff, *Urban Land Economics* (New York: McGraw-Hill, 1949), p. 42.

[9] W. William-Olsson, *Stockholms Framtida Utveckling* (Stockholm's future development), (Stockholm, 1941).

[10] Fred Forbat, "Prognos for Näringsliv och Befolkning" (forecast of industrial activity and population), in *Plan* (Stockholm, 1948), No. 9.

[11] Richard B. Andrews, "The Urban Economic Base," in *Land Economics*, 1953, p. 161.

persons and that the population will increase to 8,000. Inversely, if the company lays off 500 miners, the population will in due course shrink to 2,000. It is also safe to say that no attempt to promote development of any or all branches of "secondary" activity will make a noticeable impact on the economic life or the population size of the community.

Now, let us define the specific conditions of this experimental case:

1. There is no possibility of substitution of another "basic" activity for copper mining.

2. There is no source of income from outside other than wage payments.

3. Earnings of all "basic" employed are roughly equal (or at least average earnings for any group which may be added or subtracted are equal).

4. The family coefficient of all groups in basic employment is the same.

5. None of the product of any "basic" industry can be sold locally: or, looking at the same phenomenon from the other side, all goods and services (other than those which because of their physical characteristics can be supplied only locally) are being supplied from the outside.

It is evident that every one of these five conditions is the exact opposite of conditions characteristic of a metropolitan area. A metropolis is not simply a sum of villages, and it cannot be analyzed by adding up studies of its parts.

LIMITATIONS OF THE "BASIC-NONBASIC" CONCEPT IN TIME AND SPACE

As has already been pointed out, the literature on the subject is pervaded by a conviction that the "basic" activities are more important than the "nonbasic" ones. Emphatic statements abound. "Basic employment is the same as . . . destiny."[12] Harold McCarthy goes so far as to call "the base . . . that group of occupations whose presence . . . is not predicated on the existence of other types of production."[13]

[12] *Working Denver: An Economic Analysis by the Denver Planning Office, 1953* (Department of Planning, City & County Bldg., Denver 2, Colo., 1953), p. 27. We shall frequently exemplify our critique of the "basic-nonbasic" concept by reference to this excellent study, because it has developed the concept more completely than most others. The senior author of this study was Maxine Kurtz.

[13] Quoted by John W. Alexander, "The Basic-Nonbasic Concept of Urban Functions," *Economic Geography* (Worcester, Mass., July 1954).

This is evidently untrue. No "basic" industry in a modern city could function without such services as water, transportation, and communication. Some students of the subject are aware of this. "Urban-Growth and Urban-Serving Employment . . . are both equally essential," says Victor Roterus;[14] and the U.S. Chamber of Commerce speaks of "a chicken-and-egg relationship," adding, "industrial growth stimulates the remainder of the local economy and the existence of the community makes possible industrial growth."[15]

Here a new and important point is being made: the community with its services is the basis of industry, as well as vice versa; and it is startling to find that this point is being made by a promotional pamphlet of the Chamber of Commerce rather than by planners. It is the more startling as — along with the goal of "strengthening" or "broadening" the "economic base" — the American planning profession also proclaims the goal of the "self-contained community." The Greeks had a word for it: autarchy.

Evidently, the two goals are mutually exclusive. In a completely self-contained, or autarchic, community, nothing has to be bought from outside, and consequently nobody works to earn money for outside payments. There is no "basic" employment: in fact, all people live by "taking in each other's washing."

On the other hand, the higher the percentage of the labor force in "basic" employment, the greater the dependence of the community on outside markets and on outside supplies, and the less it is "self-contained."

It may help to clarify our concepts to look at extreme cases. The copper-mining village comes as close to maximizing "basic" employment as any community is likely to come. An employed bachelor, who does not make his own breakfast or sew on his own buttons, would be the perfect example of 100 per cent "basic" and no "service" activity.

At the other extreme, a subsistence farm — or a truly "self-contained" community like the ancient Indian village — has no "basic" employment. All occupations are "concerned

---

[14] Cincinnati City Planning Commission, *The Economy of the Area* (Cincinnati, December 1946), p. 22.

[15] U.S. Chamber of Commerce, *What New Industrial Jobs Mean to the Community* (Washington, 1954).

with the maintenance of the well-being of the people," which, according to the quoted definition by Aurousseau, is the criterion of "secondary" occupations.

Also, and perhaps more significantly, the global community of mankind is engaged exclusively in "secondary" or "service" activities. A large nation is not far from this extreme; the "basic-nonbasic" ratio for the United States is probably about 1:20. The generally accepted applications of the "basic-non-basic" method—preferential promotion of "basic" (export) activities and prediction of future population by applying a "multiplier" to expected future employment in export activities—would be as patently absurd for the United States as they are sensible for a copper-mining village.

We may tentatively derive from the juxtaposition of these extreme cases a first statement: the applicability of the "basic-nonbasic" concept decreases with increasing size of the community.

Size, however, is not the only factor to be considered. Let us return to the case of the subsistence farm. By any acceptable usage, farming is its "basic" or "primary" activity. If the farmer or his wife engage, during the slack season, in some cottage industry, selling the product for cash, such activity is to them strictly "secondary" or "ancillary." Here the concepts appear reversed: production for own use—"taking in each other's washing"—is basic, and production for sale is ancillary. This is characteristic of a "natural" economy, while the reverse holds true for a "money" or "exchange" economy, which is dependent on division of labor. Hence our second statement: applicability of the "basic-nonbasic" concept increases with increasing specialization and division of labor between communities.

Still another aspect may be illustrated by the ancient Indian village community or, for that matter, by a village in medieval feudal Europe. Here a good deal of economic activity was for "export," for the Lord of the Manor, the Church, or the King. But far from being basic in the sense of being indispensable for the economy of the village, this activity is the only one that contributes nothing to it. The reverse of this picture is the town that receives these payments without having to compensate by any "export" activity or employment. Richard U. Ratcliff quotes H. Pirenne as saying that the early medieval fortress town "produced nothing of itself, lived by revenue from the surrounding country, and had no other economic role than that of a simple consumer." Another historian characterizes the "economic base" of such cities as follows: "The principal, constituent elements of the town were those who are able by *power and wealth* [my emphasis, H. B.] to command a means of subsistence from elsewhere, a king who can tax, a landlord to whom dues are paid, a merchant who makes profits outside the town, a student who is supported by his parents. These are 'town builders.' . . ." [16]

Here the "basis" for the economy of the town is not "persons employed in producing goods and services for export," as the "basic-nonbasic" method assumes, but "power and wealth." It may here be recalled that in the *"tableau économique,"* which Quesnay, founder of the "physiocratic" school of economics, developed in the eighteenth century, the urban middle class was called *"classe stérile,"* as serving the ruling class rather than working for the "producing" class, the farmers. Thomas Jefferson shared this physiocratic view.

In our context it is important to keep in mind that "nonbasic" activities are supported by money gained from the outside regardless of its source, which may be "power and wealth" rather than any "basic" employment. To the extent that this is the case, the "basic-nonbasic" ratio loses its meaning.

We may therefore formulate a third statement: the greater the amount of "unearned" income (that is, income derived from sources other than payment for work performed) flowing into or out of a community, the less applicable is the "basic-nonbasic" concept.

We shall later deal with attempts to assimilate "unearned" income to the concept of "basic" activities. Leaving aside this aspect, for the time being, and concentrating our attention on the relation of "basic" and "nonbasic" employment, we may accept as valid the existence of two opposite historical trends noted by Forbat in his aforementioned article:

1. Replacement of local crafts by large-scale industry work-

---

[16] F. L. Nussbaum, *A History of the Economic Institutions of Modern Europe* (New York, 1933); quoted by Andrews, *op. cit.,* p. 161.

ing for a national and international market; hence greater share of "basic" employment.

2. Increase in services; hence greater share of "nonbasic" employment.

Both trends result from increasing division and specialization of labor, the first between communities and the second within the community. It should also be noted that the increase in services refers not only to services to consumers, which are generally the result of commercialization of functions formerly performed by the household, but also to services to business, which were previously performed as auxiliary services within other businesses, but have now become so specialized and complicated as to require special establishments.

This specialization of business activities reaches its highest development in large and mature communities. As mentioned before, the same communities also are nearest to "autarchy," because they contain the greatest number of branches of production.

Therefore let us summarize: the "basic-nonbasic" ratio is highest in small, new communities and lowest in large and mature ones.

MERCANTILISTIC AND PHYSIOCRATIC OVERTONES OF THE "BASIC-NONBASIC" CONCEPT

The difference between "basic" and "nonbasic" activities is the difference in their role in the balance of payments with the world outside the community. Strangely, and rather inconsistently, the "economic base" studies dominated by this concept pay practically no attention to the other side of the ledger: no attempt is being made in these studies to differentiate between those locally consumed goods and services which are produced locally and those for which payments have to be made to the outside world. Yet, rationally, the money earned by "basic" activities is merely the means to make these payments, not an end in itself.

The idea, underlying the "basic-nonbasic" method, that the acquisition of money from the outside world is the "basic" purpose of the urban or metropolitan economy has its historical precedent in the mercantilistic school of economics, which regarded only gold and silver as true wealth. While in a study of the United States economy it is today taken for granted that increased production of goods and services for the home market is the goal, in the "economic base" studies of American cities these activities are regarded merely as supporting the "basic" ones working for export.

This is, of course, explainable by the role played by size that has already been discussed. If the slogan "export or die" is true for sizable countries like Great Britain or Germany, it is even truer for a single city or region that evidently cannot produce everything it consumes. In particular, many base studies stress the need for earning money in order to pay for imports of food and raw materials. "Basic Employment ... goods or services in exchange for food and raw materials ... [is] the critical or crucial employment ... ; without it the city ceases to exist."[17]

Here, as in many similar statements, there is the implication that the export activities are "basic" because without them the city could not buy food, which is a "basic" necessity, while New Yorkers would not "cease to exist" without such locally supplied goods and services as millinery or theater performances. But they would very rapidly cease to exist without water supply, which is also a "service" or "nonbasic" activity.

The belief that there is something particularly "basic" in the production of food and raw materials also has its historical precedent; the antagonists and successors of the mercantilists, the physiocrats, believed in the superiority of farming and mining over other branches of production.

If the classification of economic activities attempted by the "basic-nonbasic" concept is to acquire scientific validity and practical usefulness, it will have to discard all explicit or implicit notions that earning money or buying food is specifically "basic." It should be clearly understood that we are dealing exclusively with a difference in the market; the appropriate terms would be "export" and "home market" activities.

There is reason to pay attention to this difference. A product or service that has to compete in the national and international market is more vulnerable than one that, like local transportation or a corner drugstore, by its physical nature is protected against ouside competition; it is, for the

[17]New York Regional Plan Association, *The Economic Status of the New York Metropolitan Region in 1944*, p. 3.

same reason, also more capable of expansion by invading outside markets. But, by and large, the share of the national product that is sold locally is just as vulnerable to competition as is the part that is sold outside.

From the point of view of vulnerability by outside competition as well as of ability to expand into outside markets, both of which we may identify as "criticality," the only meaningful distinction is between activities that, *by the nature of their product,* have to and can compete with outside producers, *regardless of the location of their actual sales,* and those that do not compete; and it is just as important to measure the imported and the locally produced share of total local consumption as it is to measure the exported and the locally consumed shares of total production.

DEVELOPMENT OF TECHNIQUES OF MEASUREMENT

Manufacturing versus Services. The first studies, those made in the twenties for the New York Regional Plan Association and in the thirties by Homer Hoyt for the FHA, assigned entire activities to the one or the other category according to their predominant market; as Frederick Law Olmsted put it in the letter quoted earlier, "primary [18] are goods for general use (i.e., *not confined to* [my emphasis, H.B.] use within the community itself)." Consciously, they were satisfied with a rough approximation; subconsciously, they were guided by the criterion of competitive character rather than by that of actual markets of an industry.

Such a rough approximation by allotment of broad categories to the two classes of activities was also used—but only as a first step—by the 1944 study of the New York Regional Plan Association. As "basic—producing *in whole or in part* [my emphasis, H.B.] for persons living outside of the Region..." are specifically enumerated: manufacturing, wholesale trade, banking and insurance, transportation, administrative offices, hotels and amusements, federal and state employment. As "service—producing *entirely* [my emphasis, H.B.] for persons living within the Region" are enumerated: retail trade, professions, personal services, local transportation and utilities, construction, local government, business and repair services, real estate and local banking.

[18] The concepts of "primary" and "secondary" used in this type of study should not be confused with the concept of "primary," "secondary," and "tertiary," meaning "extractive," "processing," and "service" activities, as defined by Colin Clark and other economists.

Parenthetically, it may be noted that many of these last-named activities do not produce entirely for the local population, but they also serve many persons living outside the Region.

There is reason to believe that the motive for concern with "basic" activities was their competitive and therefore critical character. Had the authors of the New York Regional Plan study accepted this criterion, they would have sought further refinements along lines which will be indicated later. However they, like all others using the "basic" concept, interpreted it as meaning "export" and consequently sought to refine it by measuring the portion of each particular product or service which was sold outside the Region.

The measurement of this "exported" portion is easy in dealing with a national economy where exports and imports are counted at custom lines. In dealing with areas within a nation, however, no comparable data are available, and other methods have to be developed.

Proportional Apportionment. The method used by the New York Regional Plan study and most others is to assume that the community consumes a share of the total national production of each category of goods and services that is proportional to its share of the national population (in some cases purchasing power or other yardsticks are substituted for population). The surplus in excess of this proportional share is assumed to be exported or "basic." Frequently the relation between the actual and proportional share of a given category of production is expressed as a "location—or localization—quotient." The "location quotient" is the percentage of employment in a given local industry of total local employment, expressed as a ratio to the percentage of national employment in the same industry of total national employment or

$$\frac{ei}{et} \cdot \frac{Ei}{Et}$$ (e = local employment; E = national employment, i = employment in industry, t = total employment). "By means of the localization quotient ... the extent to which an activity is basic ... can be determined."[19]

The same method was applied by Victor Roterus in the Cincinnati study: "Urban-serving employment [was] calcu-

[19] Harold M. Mayer, "Urban Nodality and the Economic Base," *AIP Journal,* Summer 1954.

lated by assuming that the population will consume its proportionate share of the national production."

This is a most questionable assumption. The Philadelphia area's share in the production of weekly periodicals may about equal its share of national population and/or purchasing power. But it does not follow that all copies of the *Saturday Evening Post* are consumed in the Philadelphia area and that Philadelphians never buy copies of the *Reader's Digest*. They do (unfortunately).

The method of proportional apportionment is based on the completely fallacious assumption that categories of goods and services — however fine the breakdown — can ever be uniform. International trade statistics show that most countries are both importers and exporters of the same categories of goods. The same certainly holds true to an even greater extent for the exchange of goods and services between areas within the nation.

Of course, if the location quotient is very high, it stands to reason that most of the product is exported. However, in such extreme cases the importance of that particular industry will be a matter of general knowledge. No location quotient has to be calculated in order to find out that Detroit exports automobiles or that Brockton exports shoes. On the other hand, if an area produces its "normal" share of, say, electrical machinery, it would be completely erroneous to assume that this is a "nonbasic" industry working exclusively for the local market. It is entirely possible, and indeed quite probable, that most locally produced electrical machinery is exported, while at the same time most locally consumed electrical machinery is imported. Mattila and Thompson unwittingly demonstrate the fallacy of the method by presenting a completely absurd result: the "proportion of surplus ["basic," H.B.] to service ["nonbasic," H.B.] workers," calculated by means of the "location quotient," is given as 1:1.99 for Chicago and as 1:4.47 for Philadelphia![20] Are we to believe that one "basic" worker supports 2 "nonbasic" workers in Chicago and 4½ in Philadelphia?

This is not to say that the location quotient does not deserve careful study. By analyzing it, much can be learned about market areas and about competitive advantages and disad-

[20] Mattila and Thompson, *op. cit.*, p. 226, Table III.

vantages. But as a measurement of the share of "basic" activities or employment it is completely misleading.

Breakdown of Markets by Survey. The obvious inadequacy of this method has led several researchers to embark on the difficult and time-consuming attempt to follow up the actual sales of each establishment in the area under investigation. In Alexander's study of Oshkosh[21] establishments employing 75 per cent of the labor force were asked for the percentage of their sales that was local; the same percentage of their employment was then allocated to the category of "secondary" employment. The same approach was taken by Maxine Kurtz in the Denver study.

In addition to its high cost this method obviously encounters two obstacles: first, unwillingness to disclose one's market and, second, ignorance of the location of one's customers. The first obstacle appears to have been overcome fairly successfully both in Oshkosh and in Denver. Interviewing of cash customers of retail stores and other techniques have been used to narrow the gap of ignorance. The result of the studies is a reasonably accurate measurement of local and outside sales.

However, this is still far from finding the answer to the question: how does the community earn the money to pay for the imports it needs? If we leave aside, for the time being, the question of modifying the needs for imports as well as the possibility of paying for them by money derived from sources other than export, the main shortcoming is this: we know the *gross value of the exported goods and services.* What we want to know is the *"value added" by the community.* A flour mill may export 10 million dollars' worth of flour; but if it has to import 8 million dollars' worth of grain, it earns no more than 2 million dollars for the community. Employment probably has been adopted as the only available, though extremely rough, approximation to "value added." However, those using the method are apparently unaware of this relation and of its implications.

If "value added" is sought, other difficulties arise. Assume that the grain has been grown locally. If it is sold in the local market, to the local mill, by definition its production is a "non-basic" activity. Yet the payment received for its sale (in the form of flour) is a net earning of the community, a "basic"

[21] John W. Alexander, *Oshkosh, Wisconsin, An Economic Base Study* (Madison, Wisconsin: Wisconsin University Press, 1951).

support of its economy. Or, to take another example: a community exports a million tons of steel. If this steel is produced in an integrated metallurgical plant, the "value added" is the difference between the cost of ore, coal, etc., and the value of the steel; and all employment in the plant is considered "basic." But if the same steel is produced in a steel plant that buys its pig iron from an independent local blast furnace, then only the value added by the steel plant is considered "basic," and the value added by the blast furnace is, by definition, "nonbasic" because it is sold to a local customer. Thus the distinction between "basic" and "nonbasic" is a function of the inner organization of the industry: the higher the degree of specialization and differentiation (the breakdown of a process into parts performed by several independent establishments), the higher is the "nonbasic" share. This, incidentally, is one of the reasons why "nonbasic" activities appear to loom so large in metropolitan areas, where the process of differentiation reaches its apex.

This difficulty has given birth to the concept of "indirect primary" activities and employment. "Indirect primary" refers to all goods or services sold to a local establishment, which in turn exports its products. But the steel mill not only buys locally produced pig iron; it equally buys locally produced power, water, trucking services, banking services, local police and fire protection. Moreover, it buys locally produced labor power, which in turn buys locally produced bread and movie shows. Once "indirect primary" activities are admitted as "basic," where can the line be drawn? The economy of an area is an integrated whole of mutually interdependent activities; the distinction between "basic" and "nonbasic" seems to dissolve into thin air.

"Criticality" or "Balance of Payments"? Confusion is worse when confounded. The more we attempt to refine the "basic-nonbasic" concept, the deeper we get involved in contradictions. Whenever that happens, there is reason to assume that there is something wrong with the formulation of the question.

Let us return to the origin of the quest. It may be fairly illustrated as follows. If General Motors closes shop at Flint, no efforts to promote the development of department stores will save the town. On the other hand, if a Flint department store closes down but the General Motors plant continues to operate as before, it will soon be replaced by other stores. Therefore, the thing to worry about, the "base" of the Flint economy, is the automobile industry; once that works, the "services" will take care of themselves. Also, once we know how many people General Motors is going to employ, we should know pretty well how many people there will be in Flint.

Unquestionably true. But why is the situation of the General Motors plant so much more critical than that of the department store? Aside from the difference in size, which is extraneous to our problem, it is because the General Motors plant has to compete with all other automobile plants in the United States and in the world, while the department store has to compete, in the main, only with other stores in Flint (though its customers might purchase some goods in Detroit, or from a mail-order house in Chicago).

The difference in "criticality" is determined by the extent of the area of potential competition. In actual practice this is, of course, a range of areas from the locality through ever-widening regions to the national and international markets. A development and refinement of the "critcality" approach would have to go in two directions. First, as much attention should be paid to the *actual and potential* source of locally consumed goods and services as to the markets for local products; second, the potential area of competition should be broken down into areas of varying size.

Actually, both steps have been undertaken by many "economic base" studies. Most studies pay particular attention to industries with a location quotient smaller than one, assuming that here may be opportunities for new local industries to compete with outside suppliers. And most go into detailed analysis of their market areas; the Denver study, for instance, found that 54 per cent of the sales outside the metropolitan area were made within the "region," defined as Colorado, Wyoming, and New Mexico.

This is contrary to the "basic-nonbasic" theory, which demands concentration of attention on the "basic" industries, those with a location quotient larger than one, and which regards all export activities as equally "basic," regardless of the size or location of the export market. Thus, the practice of the economic base studies has been generally more sensible than the theory that they claim to follow.

In our case the theoretical weakness lies in the confusion of the question of "criticality," that is, the question concerning *potential competition* with the question of *"balance of payments,"* which is concerned with *actual sales*. Both questions are valid and important; but either can be clearly answered only if the two are clearly separated.

The concept of the "balance of payments" is well understood, but the assembly of the relevant data is exceedingly difficult. Apparently, the only attempt ever made was the famous "Oskaloosa versus the United States" study undertaken by *Fortune* in April 1938. In this study "a city of 10,000 people has been treated as if it were a little nation."

A "balance of payments" study evidently must use dollars as units of measurement, not persons. The widespread use of the categories of "basic" and "nonbasic" *employment* — a consequence of the attempt to use the concept for population prediction by means of the "multiplier" — has no place in a study of this type. What matters is not how many persons work at supplying the outside world but how much money they receive from it. For this reason some studies have used payrolls (and net earnings of self-employed persons) rather than number of persons employed. But payments for goods and services go only partly into payrolls, partly into profits, interest, taxes, etc. The appropriate measurement would be the one applied in international trade statistics: gross value of goods and services exported and imported. To these would have to be added taxes and disbursements of larger governmental units, as well as interest and dividend payments in both directions. However, the latter are "practically unobtainable," according to Charles L. Leven of the Federal Reserve Bank of Chicago.[22]

Nevertheless, the New York Regional Plan study of 1944 did make an estimate that "nearly one-third of the region's basic income was derived from dividends, rents, interests, and profits." It would seem that with the amount of labor and ingenuity that went into the Denver study, for instance, it might be possible to arrive at estimates realistic enough to

[22] Charles L. Leven, "An Appropriate Unit for Measuring the Urban Economic Base, *Land Economics,* November 1954. This is the most concise study of the subject known to this writer.

construct a model of "Denver versus the U.S.A." As Victor Roterus wisely remarks, no economic base study can achieve more than a rough approximation.

The attempts to "refine" the "basic-nonbasic" concept have destroyed its usefulness for the identification of "critical" industries, while making no more than a very partial and dubious contribution to identifying the balance of payments.

To repeat: there is a need for two types of studies, related, and using much of the same material, but different in their conceptual framework:

1. A "criticality" or "variability" study, analyzing all actual and potential branches of production in the area from the point of view of the size and character of the area in which they compete and their consequent vulnerability to outside competition and potentiality to expand into outside markets.

2. A "balance of payments" study, including *all* types of payments, and giving equal weight to both sides of the ledger.

Replacement of Imports by Local Production. One of the purposes of the distinction of "basic" and "nonbasic" activities "consists in concentrating investigation on those industries and services which . . . bring in money to pay for the food and raw materials which the city does not produce itself," to repeat Homer Hoyt's formulation. But if the city itself were to produce the goods that it now imports, the effect would be the same. Why should not investigation be concentrated on those industries and services which do *not* produce a surplus for export but, on the contrary, show a deficit in supplying the home market? Evidently, if Brockton, rather than increasing its capacity to produce shoes worth a million dollars annually, would build a clothing plant to supply its inhabitants with a million dollars' worth of clothing, which they now have to import, the improvement of the town's balance of payments would be the same. It may here be noted that this might not be possible in Brockton because the local market may not be large enough to support an efficient plant. But it would certainly be possible in a large metropolis. The larger the community, the greater the possibility of substitution for declining industries, hence the less significant the identification of "basic" activities.

Actually, even the Brockton study examines the possibility of substituting new industries for the "critical" shoe industry. Similarly, the New York Regional Plan study concentrates its attention on "industries in which New York's share of employment is far below its proportion of population and income," stating that "these industries might be explored to ascertain why they have not expanded to a greater degree in the Region,"[23] and the Cincinnati study considers specifically "local industries not meeting local demands." Charles L. Leven, in his afore-mentioned article, agrees that "efforts might be more profitably directed at establishment of local industries [supplying] local exporters."

The important point, in our context, is that the "basic-nonbasic" method is of no help whatsoever in identifying such industries. It rather tends to deflect attention from them and to confuse the picture. Half a loaf is certainly better than no loaf; but half a balance-of-payments study may well be worse than none.

The reverse substitution is no less important: the replacement of local production by imports. As Fred Forbat has pointed out, this is one of the long-term trends of industrial society, a corollary of increasing specialization and division of labor between regions. However, it still remains possible to substitute local production for imports; especially where the growth of the community creates a previously nonexistent large market, imports may be replaced by locally produced goods and services. In this way growth induces further growth. "He who has, to him shall be given" is a basic law of economics.

Moreover, the effects of "basic" employment on the balance of payments may vary widely. It is generally assumed that the opening of an establishment that exports part of its products will always improve the balance of payments of an area. However, if such an establishment is a branch plant of an outside firm and works mainly with imported material, and if the part of its products that is sold locally displaces the products of a local industry working largely with local materials, then the net effect may be the opposite.

This may be an extreme case not likely to occur in the United States. But it may be fairly typical of the impact of the establishment of branch plants of modern international

[23]New York Regional Plan Association, *op. cit.*, pp. 19, 20.

concerns in underdeveloped countries; here the result is frequently aggravated by related effects on income distribution. The resistance of these countries to such apparently beneficial improvements by foreign investors may not be entirely due to shortsighted nationalistic prejudices.

Indirect Primary Activity. The problem of "indirect primary" activity has attracted the attention of many students of our subject. Fred Forbat[24] refers to a study of a new oil refinery in Aarhus, Denmark, undertaken by the economist B. Barfod.[25] Barfod found that "the company's purchases of goods and services from local suppliers gave livelihood" to 70 persons for every 100 persons employed in the refinery. He classes these as "indirect primary" and derives the expected number of "secondary" employment by assuming that there will be 80 additional "secondary" workers for every 100 new workers in *all* "primary" employment, "direct" and "indirect" combined.

Andrews, in his series of articles in *Land Economics,* repeatedly returns to this question. He recognizes that "linked activity...the chain of production...makes *all* activities basic" and calls this a "very serious blindspot...unless the anachronisms [? H.B.] of this situation can be reconciled."[26] When dealing with a concrete example, however, he says: "Rigidly, we would classify the automobile-starter factory as a service activity...realistic[ally it] should be considered basic in that there exists only an organizational line between the starter and automobile manufacturer."[27]

Andrews seems to be unaware that "crossing an organizational line" is only a synonym for "sale" and that any method that—like the "basic-nonbasic" method—counts sales consists in counting line crossings. He adds, however, the very pertinent remark that "the number of links involved may very well be in direct ratio to community size." But he again fails to draw the conclusion: that the applicability of the "basic-nonbasic" concept is in inverse ratio to community size.

Ullman also wrestles with the problem. He says that "a

[24] Fred Forbat, "Synpunkter pa Lokaliseringsmultiplikatorn," in *Plan* (Stockholm, 1948), No. 9.

[25] B. Barfod, *Local Economic Effects of a Large-scale Industrial Undertaking* (in Danish) (Copenhagen: E. Munksgaard, 1938). I have not been able to locate this study.

[26] Andrews, *op. cit.,* 1953, p. 260 ff.

[27] *Ibid.,* p. 347.

city with large basic plants might appear to produce many basic workers whereas ... many small plants each feeding the other ... appear to have many service workers." He then tries to compromise by stating that "some intermediate producers are classed as basic if they contribute directly to an export industry," but concludes finally that "in this light all activities appear indivisible."

Alexander is also troubled by the problem: "since these castings [made in a local foundry, H.B.] are fabricated into axles which are exported, it could be said that this ... production is for the primary market. However, this leads to complications, and the arbitrary decision has been made to classify each activity on the basis of its own direct sales."[28]

We have already shown that the complications are implicit in the ambiguity of the question. If the question is, instead, clearly directed to the balance of payments, the decision to count only direct sales is by no means arbitrary, but a matter of course. Nobody thinks of including the steel industry in the export statistics of American automobiles, because the "value added" by the steel and all other "indirect primary" industries is, by definition, included in the gross value of the automobiles. Dollars, not persons employed, are the correct yardstick.

If, on the other hand, the question is directed to the "criticality" of each establishment, i.e., to the range of its potential market and its potential competitors, the "indirect primary" activities fall into place alongside all others.

Interurban Transportation. Practically all studies, while treating local transportation as "nonbasic," regard all other transportation as "basic." However, actually only those transportation activities which serve movements between two outside points earn money from the outside. A tanker, bringing oil from Venezuela to a refinery in the Philadelphia Area, exclusively serves and is paid by the Philadelphia plant. Its work might be called "indirect primary," but, as we have seen, that does not remove it from the "nonbasic" class under any consistent definition.

Normally, of the total exchange of goods between two points about half will be paid at each end; thus 50 per cent should certainly be classified as "nonbasic." The point might well

[28] Alexander, *op. cit.*, p. 12.

be made that the entire interurban transportation system performs a service for, and at the expense of, the local import and export trade and should be classified as such.

From the point of view of competitiveness, or "criticality," interurban transportation (except for the portion serving movements between two outside points) is strictly noncompetitive; nobody but some form of transportation can move goods and passengers into and out of the city. It is true, of course, that if transportation is very poor, other branches of production may move to other areas that are better served by transportation; it thus may profoundly affect the competitive position of the area as a whole. It was probably this thought that caused people to classify it as "basic." Yet in this respect it is not principally different from supply of water, power, housing, or any other local service.

Public Employees, Students, etc. A field in which the confusion of the "criticality" and the "balance of payments" approach has led to particularly glaring contradictions concerns those persons whose income, while clearly contributing to the economy of the community, is derived neither from sales to the local community nor from sales to the outside world. Andrews, Maxine Kurtz, Forbat, and others allocate employment in government institutions according to the population served (local or outside population); and they allocate the staff of universities in proportion to the number of local and "foreign" students.

From the balance-of-payments point of view, which these researchers are trying to apply, this does not make sense. From this point of view, the only thing that matters is the source of the income, not who is benefited by the work performed. The income of *all* federal employees is a net gain to the community, whether they deliver letters to local residents or work on projects to deliver milk — or atom bombs — to the Hottentots; just as all taxes paid to the federal government are a net loss to the community. Similarly, if the university professor is paid by state contributions, by the G.I. Bill of Rights, by an outside foundation, or by outside parents of his students, his income is a gain to the community. But it is not if he is paid out of city funds, out of contributions of local alumni, or out of money earned by his students in the community. The home residence of his students is irrelevant.

Evidently, these researchers were led astray because in the back of their minds, but not formulated, was the "criticality" approach. In a city of a certain size, post offices, local courts, elementary and high schools can, indeed, be taken for granted; but the city has to compete with other cities for a state university or for a regional office of the national government and also has to compete with them for students at its university.

Discrepany between "Basic" Employment and Outside Earnings. If a given community with a given level of living depends for 50 per cent of the goods and services it consumes on outside sources, its size is evidently limited by the amount of money it can pay to the outside. It is the standard assumption of the "basic-nonbasic" method that in this case 50 per cent of its employment would have to be "basic." The contribution to the "economic base" is assumed to be proportional to the number of persons employed in each branch of "basic employment." "Wholesale trade accounted for ... 12% of its total basic employment ... *therefore* [my emphasis, H.B.] ... about one-eighth of the economic base."[29]

This comfortable "therefore" contains — and conceals — a number of unspoken assumptions, which should be spelled out:

1. Average wages are roughly the same in all branches of production (the Denver study does touch on this question).

2. The ratio of "value added" to payrolls is roughly the same in all branches.

3. The proportion of the "nonpayroll" section of "value added" going to local owners is roughly the same in all branches.

4. Moneys paid or received by the community other than payments for goods and services balance out.

It is improbable that any of these assumptions correspond to the facts of life in a metropolitan area.

From the Denver study, for example, it can be seen that average annual wages in wholesale trade varied from $3,100 in "petroleum bulk stations" to $4,300 in "manufacturer's branches without stock."[30]

[29] *Working Denver, op. cit.,* p. 4.
[30] *Ibid.,* p. 68.

Sales per employee varied far more than average wages: in retail trade from $8,150 in "eating and drinking places" to $35,800 in "automotive"; and in wholesale trade from $28,000 in "auto and equipment" to $610,000 in "farm products (raw)."[31] These differences reflect largely, but hardly entirely, differences in markup. If we assume, for example, that the markup was 20 per cent in "auto and equipment" and 2 per cent in "farm products," the markup, or "value added," per employee would still vary from $4,700 to $12,000.

Evidently, the greater part of the $12,000 represents return on capital, and how much it will contribute to the purchasing power (the "economic base") of Denver versus the outside world will depend entirely on the share of the capital owned by Denverites.

Andrews recognizes the importance of this factor of "absentee ownership" of capital, saying: "If a dollar-flow measurement device were employed, the loss would be clear . . . [and] the community receiving the profits would count them."

Andrews, not employing such a "device," does *not count* these losses. But he *does count* the gains in the receiving community, where he classifies the income derived from investments in other communities as "capital export."

This is indeed a classical example of the confusion resulting from the attempt to achieve greater precision by refining a basically confused concept. The *export of capital* puts the community in the red; it is the *return on the capital* — and return of the capital — that produces income. Nor is this return contingent on previous "export" of capital by the community; the wealthy residents of Palm Beach derive their income from capital that was not exported by Palm Beach, but either was exported from New York and other places or was not "exported" at all but was accumulated out of the returns of "outside" investments. Andrews' concept of unifying all sources of income of the community under the term "export of goods, services, and capital" is an unfortunate attempt to force strange bedfellows into the procrustean bed of the "basic-nonbasic" concept.

Other important factors affecting the balance of payments of a community are the ratio of payments to disbursements

[31] *Ibid.*, p. 74.

of state and federal taxes and the "terms of trade," that is, the price relations between imported and exported goods. Assume, for example, that the work of 10,000 persons employed in export industries is required to pay for the food imported by a community of 150,000 persons. If food prices were cut in half, these 10,000 workers could pay for the food for 300,000 people.

Because of these many factors, "basic employment" is a very inadequate yardstick for the measurement of the economic base of the community.

The "Basic-Nonbasic" Ratio. As has been noted before, the attempt to distinguish "basic" and "nonbasic" employment has been made primarily in order to find the ratio of the second to the first.

Jones had made the rather naive assumption that "the majority of the town . . . are employed in providing goods and service . . . for other communities. It could not be otherwise."[32] In fact, it is otherwise. In most cases the ratio is considerably greater than unity, but it differs widely.

Roterus and Calef, in the afore-mentioned article, succinctly state the reason for the difference: "The basic-nonbasic ratio is a measure of the degree of economic interdependence."

It has been noted that the ratio is generally higher the larger the community. The reasons may be summarized as follows:

1. A greater completeness of all branches of production; the community is more nearly "self-contained" than a small one.

2. Greater "roundaboutness" of production; the productive process is divided into a greater number of organizationally independent, though economically interdependent, units.

In addition, in most metropolitan areas there is:

3. Higher average income, commanding more consumer services.

4. A concentration of "power and wealth," drawing unearned income from the outside and spending it for local services.

The New York Regional Plan study of 1944 found the abnormally high ratio of 2.2 "nonbasic" for every one "basic"

---

[32] Jones, *op. cit.,* p. 125.

employed. However, the study also states that nearly one third of the region's "basic" income is derived from sources other than the export of goods and services. If it is assumed that a proportional number of service workers were supported by this source of income and only the remainder are related to the "basic" workers, the ratio is about 1.5, practically the same as the one found in Denver, which was 1.53.

The ratio also changes over time; nor can these changes be easily explained. In Cincinnati, for instance, between 1929 and 1933, the decrease in the number of factory workers was 29 per cent above the national average, but the decrease in retail sales was 6 per cent below the average for the nation.

A slightly different and rather interesting approach to the question of "service" employment has been taken by Swedish planners and geographers who have attempted to find the number of service workers required to serve a given population in communities of various types. Here the distinction of "basic" and "nonbasic" is used as a tool for identifying those industries which have to be studied directly and individually, while a global average figure is used for the prognosis of all "nonbasic" employment. Forbat found that in the three towns of Kristinehamn, Skövde, and Landskrona secondary employment varied only from 20.92 to 22.39 per cent of the total population. Even this slight variation was due entirely to variations in agriculture, construction, and domestic service; after elimination of these three categories the range was 16.37 to 16.49 per cent.

These are three towns with a population between 15,000 and 24,000. For villages of about 2,000 population, Forbat found the proportion of service workers to be 15 per cent, and for Stockholm to be 27 per cent. This correlation of percentage of service workers with size is in accord with American experience.

Sven Godlund contributed to the discussion the concept of an "index of centralization," which is defined by the percentage of the total population employed in retail trade and consumer services. He found this to vary with size from 6.5 per cent in regional centers down to 3.5 per cent in villages, with even lower percentages in "special urban settlements," mainly industrial satellite towns.[33]

[33] Sven Godlund, *Studies in Rural-Urban Interaction* (Lund, Sweden: Lund Studies in Geography, 1951).

The "Multiplier." Investigation of the "basic-nonbasic" ratio is used to find the "multiplier," that is, the ratio of total population to "basic" employment. The multiplier is determined not only by the "basic-nonbasic" ratio but by three additional factors that are not always clearly recognized:

1. Family coefficient of basic employed.
2. Family coefficient of nonbasic employed.
3. Percentage of unemployed (including dependents) population.

Frequently a global ratio of population to employment is used. However, this ratio may vary considerably if any of these three factors change or if their relative weights change.

In Denver, for instance, the ratio of population to "basic" employment—the "multiplier"—was 7.8 in 1940. Between 1940 and 1950, however, there were only 4.6 persons added to the population for every one person added to "basic" employment. It is evident that a population prediction based on the number of additional "basic" employed and using the "multiplier" found in 1940 would have overstated the decennial population increase by 70 per cent.

Variations in the family coefficient between various "basic" industries are very significant. In the anthracite mining regions of Pennsylvania, for example, the addition of a mining job would usually mean the addition of a family. The addition of a hosiery job generally means employment of a female former dependent of a miner's family.

Generally the family coefficient is low in industries with high female employment and in communities with a high rate of employment and with low percentages of the population in the extreme age groups, that is, children and old people.

Forbat[34] found that the family coefficient in the Swedish countryside varied from 1.54 for textile workers to 2.49 for construction workers; for Stockholm both figures were considerably lower, 1.30 and 2.06, respectively. He also found that the family coefficient in trade and service employment averaged 1.7 to 1.8.

Forbat has developed a formula that takes into account the differences in the family coefficient for different types of employment. The formula is:

[34] Fred Forbat, "Untersuchungen über den 'Lokalisierungsmultiplikator'" (Investigations on the "Localization Multiplier"), in *Raumforschung & Raumordnung* (1953), No. 2, pp. 97-101.

$$P = \frac{Ep \cdot Cp}{1 - Rs \cdot Cs}$$

P = population
Ep = employed, primary
Cp = family coefficient of primary employed
Cs = family coefficient of secondary employed
Rs = secondary employment as percentage of population

If Ep equals 1, the "multiplier" becomes:

$$M = \frac{Cp}{1 - Rs \cdot Cs}$$

By applying this formula, Forbat found the following multipliers:

Villages:	2.1 to 3.2
Towns:	2.5 to 3.7
Stockholm:	2.3 to 3.3

These are large variations. They would be even larger except for the fact that high service employment and low family coefficient are generally associated, because both are correlated with high female employment, and that their influences tend to cancel each other. Thus, the multiplier is low in villages, despite a high family coefficient, because the villages depend for services largely on neighboring towns; it is low in Stockholm, despite high service employment, because the family coefficient is low.

A further difficulty in deriving the "multiplier" stems from the fact that there is a sizable and highly variable group in most communities that is neither in "basic" nor in "nonbasic" employment and is not part of the families of either group. These are the "independent nonworkers," who may derive their income from a great many sources: investments, pensions, social insurance, relief payments, etc. Forbat classifies these as "primary" ("basic") because their number is not dependent on the number of those in other "basic" groups. In the little town of Skövde their number was equal to one quarter of all other "basic" groups. In many American cities it may be even higher. On the other hand, in new or rapidly growing communities their number is low, in some cases practically zero. Also, their number may vary widely and abruptly with changes in the labor market.

Swedish statistical data make it possible to derive a separate family coefficient for this group that is, of course, lower than that for employed persons. In Stockholm, for example, it was 1.30 versus 1.63 for employed persons; in the Swedish countryside, 1.43 versus 2.14.[35]

American statistics lump "independents" and "dependents" in the categories "unemployed" and "not in the labor force." They also present no data from which family coefficient for specific industries in specific localities could be derived. In attempting to apply the Forbat formula to American cities, I have therefore substituted for both Cp and Cs (family coefficient for "basic" and "nonbasic" employed) what might be called a "community-wide family coefficient" that is, the ratio of total population to "basic" employed. The resultant multipliers are 5.5 for Philadelphia and 6.46 for Denver the latter being practically identical with the 6.6 found by Maxine Kurtz.

The fact that these figures are about twice as large as those found in Swedish towns is only partly due to the different classification of the "independent nonworkers." In a letter to me, dated September 26, 1955, Forbat has recalculated the "multiplier" for five Swedish towns on the basis of the "community-wide family coefficient." The resulting figures are between 3.5 and 4.1. The difference between these multipliers and those found for Philadelphia and Denver are due, first, to the fact that in Swedish cities employed persons average 49 per cent of total population against about 40 per cent in American cities, and, second, to an unusually high percentage of "basic" employment, which in the five Swedish towns was 53.3 to 60.0 per cent of all employment. This, in turn, is partly due to actual differences in economic structure and partly to differences in classification. Forbat classifies *all* "big" industry (as distinct from handicraft industry) as "basic." This method appears quite permissible in small towns but would lead to very serious distortions if applied, for instance, to the New York garment industry.

Barfod, in the afore-mentioned study of the impact of a new oil refinery on the population of Aarhus, apparently ignored all these problems. He found a "multiplier" of 8.8 for every person in "direct basic" employment and of 5.5 for

[35] *Ibid.*, p. 100, Table 2.

every person in all (including "indirect") "basic" employment.

The enormous range in multipliers—from 2.1 to 8.8—found by various methods shows that the multiplier is not the simple, unequivocal device for population prediction that it appears at first sight.

Population Prediction. One of the purposes of developing the "basic-nonbasic" method was its alleged usefulness for population prediction. Future population was to be found by multiplying future "basic" employment with a figure that could supposedly be derived from past experience.

We have seen that past experience does not and cannot yield any figure applicable to future experience unless a great number of variables are known, in addition to the future number of persons in "basic" employment. The most important variables are:

1. Average level of living of the community.
2. Percentage, in terms of value, of the goods and services constituting this level that have to be purchased from outside.
3. Net gain or loss to the community from money flow due to causes other than payments for goods and services.
4. Family coefficient of persons in "basic" employment.
5. Family coefficient of persons in "nonbasic" employment.
6. Percentage of total population who are neither employed nor dependents of employed persons.

These variables make it difficult to determine the multiplier for any community. But in metropolitan areas it is even more difficult to predict the figure to be multiplied: the future number of persons in "basic" employment.

The illusion that "basic" employment is more easily predicted than many other variables stems from the fact that future employment of individual enterprises is, indeed, frequently known with reasonable certainty. If a new steelworks requiring 5,000 workers is being built, it is highly probable that after its completion there will be 5,000 steelworkers living in the community. If the community is and will remain a company town, it is indeed possible to find its population by adding to the steelworkers and their dependents those persons and their dependents who service the steelworkers.

But in a metropolitan area there are many plants, big and

small, that open up or shut down, expand or contract their employment. We have seen that "basic" employment, by definition, is critical, competitive employment. It is the part of the economy that is most vulnerable, most likely to disappear or contract as a result of outside competition, and also most dynamic, most likely to spring up or grow as a result of invasion of outside markets. As the most vulnerable and most dynamic part of the metropolitan economy, "basic" activities are its most variable, least predictable element.

In addition, there is the practical impossibility of measuring "indirect primary" employment. Moreover, as Walter Isard and others have emphasized, a new "basic" industry attracts not only those which supply it, but also those which it supplies—not only "indirect primary" but what we might call "primary indirect" activities. Here another complication arises. Assume that a new steel plant, producing a million tons of steel, attracts, over the years, steel-fabricating plants that buy half of its production. Then one half of its workers must, by definition, be transferred from the "basic" to the "non-basic" category, because they now work for the local market. In other words, the more the steel plant contributes to the community's economic base—in the common-sense meaning of that term—the less "basic" it becomes according to the standard formula.

Some, like Isard, believe that, while application of the multiplier formula for prediction of the entire metropolitan population may not be practicable, it can be used to estimate the population to be added as a result of the impact of a specific known development, such as the new steel plant at Morrisville, Pennsylvania.

Isard's study of the impact of the Morrisville plant clearly shows two difficulties inherent in this method:

1. Within what area will the added population live?
2. To which figure is the "new" population to be added?

The first difficulty is relatively minor: the region of impact comprises several metropolitan areas.

The second difficulty is fundamental. Obviously, it makes no sense to add the "new" population simply to the present one, or to what the present one would be as the result of natural increase, at the end of the impact period. The addition must be made to a figure predicted on the basis of past trends. But these trends reflect the dynamic nature of the metropolitan economy, the never-ceasing shrinkage of old industries and expansion of new ones. In the Philadelphia area, for example, they reflect the coming and growth of the oil-refining industry, an event closely comparable to the coming of the steel industry, and both are even due to the attraction of the same locational factors. Thus the figure derived from the trend already anticipated the coming of new industries, and if their impact is added separately, it will be counted twice. It is impossible thus to isolate the impact of single factors in and on the metropolitan complex.

It is worth noting that even the Denver study, which had lavished so much care and ingenuity on the identification of "basic" employment, finally bases its prediction of the future growth of the economy and population of the area not on these figures, but on long-term trends and on estimates of the importance of locational factors.

We may conclude, therefore, that as a tool for predicting the population of metropolitan areas the "basic-nonbasic" method is useless.[36]

Promotion of "Basic" Industries. The other main purpose for developing the "basic-nonbasic" method is its alleged usefulness in concentrating attention on those industries whose promotion will do the most good for the well-being of the community, which is supposed to depend primarily on improvement of its balance of payments.

We have already pointed out that the method, strictly applied, tends to divert attention from many industries that might contribute most to an improvement of the balance of payments, namely those whose products the community now imports but might produce itself. We also noted that most authors of "economic base" studies have had the good sense to forget their theory and to give a good deal of attention to just these industries.

But suppose communities did succeed in advertising their locational advantages for all those industries which are not by their physical nature restricted to a local market and who

[36] Forbat, who has probably developed the "multiplier" method of population prediction more successfully than any other planner, informs me that he recently advised against applying it to a big city, because "in the economy of the big cities there evidently exists a different hierarchy."

therefore have a choice. What would be the effect on the national distribution of industry? Would it be more efficient than it is now?

There are two possibilities. If *all* communities do an equally effective job of industrial promotion, their efforts will cancel each other out, and the net effect will be zero. If only some communities do a good job, industries will learn of and be attracted by their locational advantages. By the same token, they will ignore and neglect equal or greater locational advantages in communities that do less or nothing for promotion. The net result can only be a less efficient national distribution than would result from the functioning of the market without benefit of local planning.

Location of industries working for the national and international market is a legitimate and most important function of national planning. Local planning organizations could make valuable, indeed indispensable, contributions to such national planning by discovering the potentialities and limitations of their areas.

Without such a national plan the value of their promotional efforts is highly dubious. Most likely they will be ineffective; if effective, they are more likely to do harm than good to the nation.

We can conclude that as a guide for the concentration of local promotional efforts the "basic-nonbasic" method is not a useful tool.

This is not to say that all results of the work done in the framework of this method are to be discarded as worthless. They can be of great value, first, for the development of "balance of payments" studies and, second, for the exploration of the "criticality" of various industries.

The Real Economic Base of the Metropolis. What, finally, is the relative importance of "basic" and "nonbasic" activities in a metropolitan area?

We have seen that the percentage of persons employed in "basic" activities decreases as a community becomes more "metropolitan" quantitatively and qualitatively — that is, the larger it is and the greater the variety and differentiation of its activities.

The more metropolitan the community, the more its inhabitants do "live by taking in each other's washing." Still, it remains dependent on the outside world for many goods and services and will have to pay for the major part of these by the products of its export industries. Is it not legitimate to worry about these more than about the "nonbasic" ones?

Certainly, from the point of view of sales there is no reason to worry about the "local service" industries, because they cannot be replaced from the outside. For the same reason there is good cause to worry about them from the point of view of the welfare of the consumer. If the Philadelphia subway system goes out of business, it cannot be replaced by the New York subways. Inversely, from the point of view of sales there is every reason to worry about the "competitive" industries; but from the point of view of the consumer's welfare there is no reason to worry about them. Their goods and services can be replaced by purchasing them from the outside; and the money they earn from the outside may be earned by other competitive industries that may be substituted for those which are lost.

The *ability to substitute* one activity for another is the crucial point. Most economic base studies touch on it in one form or another.

The Denver study says: "Gold mining created service jobs, but when it 'petered out,' catastrophe was averted by local enterprise substituting for the erstwhile gold mine . . . ghost towns are evidence, however, . . . the substitution did not always occur." However, it does not inquire under which conditions substitution does or does not occur.[37]

Part of the answer is given by Alexander, who explains that Oshkosh owed its origin to sawmills, which later disappeared but only after having attracted the millwork industry. "The reservoir of labor persisted and became the dominant factor in the survival of the woodworking industry."[38]

Homer Hoyt adds other factors: "What does Brockton have to offer as attractions to existing and new industries? . . . Adequate power and transportation; decentralisation; skilled machine operators; a location within the world's greatest concentration of buying power; and proximity to a great pool of technical knowledge."[39]

These advantages can be summarized under three headings:

[37] *Working Denver, op. cit.,* p. 27.
[38] Alexander, *op. cit.,* p. 34.
[39] *The Economic Base of Brockton, op. cit.,* p. 6.

1. Labor force of various skills; its presence is dependent on *local consumer services:* housing, schools, stores, local transportation.

2. *Business services,* including transportation with its terminals.

3. *Markets,* local and regional.

The more developed these three factors are, the more favorable are the conditions for substitution; and it is easy to see that all three are strongest in metropolitan areas, and the stronger, that is, the more metropolitan the area is, the larger and the more diversified.

The competitive advantage of a large home market is too well known from the field of international trade to require further elaboration.

The importance of a large and diversified labor force also needs little comment. Only some special aspects may be mentioned here. Edgar M. Hoover, Jr., says: "the more abnormal the sex and age requirements or the more pronounced the fluctuations, the more [such industries must be] located near others with complementary labor demands or in a large diversified labor market,"[40] that is, in the metropolitan area. Hoover also shows that the big city is the natural habitat of the small plant that is most strongly dependent on the services of other plants. The average number of wage earners per manufacturing establishment in industrial areas in 1937 was 43 in central cities, 61 in major satellite towns, and 95 in the remainder of industrial areas.

The reason for this concentration of small plants in big cities is "external economies." Hoover says: "Many of these 'external economies' are based on the availability of more and more specialized auxiliary and service enterprises, with increased concentration of the main industry . . . the availability of service enterprises makes possible a very narrow specialization of function in relatively small plants."[41]

This development soon reaches a point where the "primary" industry is as dependent on the "auxiliary" ones as these are on it, "Often the number and variety of ancillary establish-

[40] Edgar M. Hoover, Jr., "Size of Plant, Concern, and Production Center," in National Resources Planning Board, *Industrial Location and National Resources* (Washington, 1943), p. 251.

[41] Hoover, *op. cit.,* p. 245.

ments clustered around some primary industry is such that the locational dependence of the primary industry on the ancillaries, though small in respect to each one, is great in respect to the total."[42]

It is this high development of "business services" and other "secondary" industries that, together with the availability of labor of all kinds, enables the metropolis to sustain, expand, and replace its "primary" industries.

It is thus the "secondary," "nonbasic" industries, both business and personal services, as well as "ancillary" manufacturing, that constitute the real and lasting strength of the metropolitan economy. As long as they continue to function efficiently, the metropolis will always be able to substitute new "export" industries for any that may be destroyed by the vicissitudes of economic life.

We have seen that such substitutions may occur even in small towns such as Oshkosh. In metropolitan areas they are the rule rather than the exception. The history of the past 40 years in Europe has given eloquent proof of the ability of metropolitan communities to survive not only physical destruction but also the disappearance of those functions on which their existence had been based in the past. They developed new functions and survived. Vienna and Leningrad are only two particularly striking examples.

It is worth noting that this is a new phenomenon. The capitals of Oriental empires soon turned into dust once a new ruler transferred his court to a different location. Even Rome was little more than a village after the Western Empire had been destroyed. These cities were mainly centers of consumption, based on the concentration of "power and wealth." The modern metropolitan area is primarily a center of production, based on a concentration of productive forces. It is qualitatively different from the city as it has been known throughout history. It is a genuinely new form of human settlement, and, contrary to predictions of its approaching transformation into "necropolis," it is showing a greater vitality than any previous form of settlement. As far as this writer is aware, no community that during the last century has passed the half-million mark — a truer borderline for the metropolis than the 50,000

[42] *Ibid.*, p. 276.

adopted by the U.S. Census—has fallen below that population level.

The bases of this amazing stability are the business and consumer services and other industries supplying the local market. They are the permanent and constant element, while the "export" industries are variable, subject to incessant change and replacement. While the existence of a sufficient number of such industries is indispensable for the continued existence of the metropolis, each individual "export" industry is expendable and replaceable.

In any common-sense use of the term, it is the "service" industries of the metropolis that are "basic" and "primary," while the "export" industries are "secondary" and "ancillary." The economic base of the metropolis consists in the activities by which its inhabitants supply each other.

Professional Résumé
of Hans Blumenfeld

Mr. Blumenfeld received his professional education at the Polytechnic Institutes of Munich, Karlsruhe, and Darmstadt, from 1911 to 1914 and from 1919 to 1921. He was graduated from Darmstadt in 1921. He studied the history of city planning with Dr. A. E. Brinckman.

From 1921 to 1930 he worked as an architectural draftsman and designer in Germany, the United States, and Austria, where he worked for Joseph Frank and Adolf Loos.

In 1930 he was invited to work in Russia. From 1930 to 1933 he served under an appointment to the Russian State City Planning Institute in Moscow and in Gorki. His work in Russia includes the towns of Vladimir and Vyatka (now Kirov), architecture and site planning in Makeevka and Moscow, and projects for the Commissariats of Public Health and Education in Moscow. Mr. Blumenfeld worked in Russia until 1937. From 1938 to 1940 he worked as an architect and site planner in New York City and Jersey City.

From 1941 to 1944 he was Research Director for the Philadelphia Housing Association. In Philadelphia he served as senior land planner from 1945 to 1948; and Chief of the Division of Planning Analysis for the Philadelphia Planning Commission from 1948 to 1952. In 1949 he returned to Germany as a Visiting Expert in City Planning for the U. S. Department of Defense. From 1953 to 1955 he served as a planning consultant in the city of Philadelphia.

In 1955 he became an Assistant Director of the Metropolitan Toronto Planning Board, in which capacity he served until 1961. Since 1961 he has served as a consultant to the Metropolitan Toronto Planning Board and since 1962 to the Service d'Urbanisme of the city of Montreal. He has been a Senior Lecturer in the Division of Town and Regional Planning, University of Toronto, since 1964.

Mr. Blumenfeld has lectured at many universities and to other agencies in Canada and abroad.

List of Other Articles Published by Hans Blumenfeld

I. On the Metropolis:

"On the Concentric-Circle Theory of Urban Growth," *Land Economics* (Madison, Wisc.), May 1949, pp. 209-212.

> An analysis of data from the 1940 census for the City of Philadelphia, demonstrating the regular concentric distribution of significant qualitative as well as quantitative data.

"The Dominance of the Metropolis," *Land Economics* (Madison, Wisc.), May 1950, pp. 194-196.

> A discussion of the book *The Structure of the Metropolitan Community* by Don J. Bogue, indicating the possibility of a different interpretation of the data presented therein.

"The Tidal Wave of Metropolitan Expansion," *Journal of the American Institute of Planners,* Winter 1954, pp. 3-14.

> An analysis of the dynamics of population movement in the Philadelphia Metropolitan Area, 1900-1950, developing the new concept of the "crest of the wave of metropolitan expansion" as a tool for prediction of population distribution.

"The Exploding Metropolis," *Monthly Review* (New York), April 1959, pp. 476-486.

> A critical review of the book written by the editors of *Fortune* magazine under this name, pointing out contradictions between the analysis of the problems and the remedies proposed.

"The New York Metropolitan Region Study," *Journal of the American Institute of Planners,* February 1961, pp. 91-93.

> A review of the first two volumes of the study bearing the same name, emphasizing the importance of its concepts and methods for understanding of the metropolis.

"L'habitation dans les métropoles." *Architecture, Batiment, Construction* (Southam Ltd., Montreal, May 1966).

> An analysis of the changes in the characteristics and in the distribution of various housing types in response to economic, social, and technical changes, with some suggestions for modification of present practices.

"The Role of the Federal Government in Urban Affairs." *The Journal of Liberal Thought* (The Liberal Federation of Canada, Ottawa, Spring 1966).

> An analysis of the impact of past and proposed Canadian federal policies on urban self-government, transportation, land development, housing, and finances, with reference to United States experience.

II. ON PLANNING METHODOLOGY:

"A Neglected Factor in Estimating Housing Demand," *Land Economics* (Madison, Wisc.), August 1944, pp. 264-270.

> A study of the role of nonfamily households, predicting that high national income will lead to a vast expansion of housing demand from this source.

"Correlation between the Value of Dwelling Units and Altitude," *Land Economics* (Madison, Wisc.), November 1948, pp. 396-402.

Demonstration of a consistent positive correlation between these two sets of data in Metropolitan Philadelphia in 1950, with an indication of its general validity in modern metropolitan areas.

III. ON TRANSPORTATION:

"Transportation in the Modern Metropolis," *Queen's Quarterly* (Kingston, Ont.), Winter 1961, pp. 640-653.
An earlier and shorter version of the article with the same title included in this volume.

"A Factual Evaluation of Toronto's Investment in Mass Transit." *Proceedings of the Institute of Traffic Engineers,* 1963.
An analysis of the experience of the Totonto Transit System.

Introduction to a special issue on transportation of *Architecture Canada: Journal of the RAIC* (Toronto, August 1966).
A discussion of the integration of transportation structures with architecture and urban design, with references to the examples presented in the following articles.

IV. ON DESIGN:

"The Integration of Natural and Artificial Light," *Architectural Record* (New York), December 1940-April 1941, pp. 49-56, 69-76.
A study of the relation between light and seeing and of the characteristics of various means of natural and artificial lighting.

"On a Peculiar Feature of the City Plan of Mohenjo-Daro," *Journal of the Society of Architectural Historians,* January 1942, pp. 24-26.
An investigation of the relation of apparent irregularities of street lines to orientation as a possible indication of concepts and methods of pre-Aryan city planning in India.

"The Toronto Civic Square," *Mosaic,* publication of the

Architectural Society, School of Architecture, University of Toronto, 1957.

A commentary on a major new civic plaza.

V. On Russian Planning:

"Regional and City Planning in the Soviet Union," *Task* (Cambridge, Mass.), 1942, Issue No. 3, pp. 33-52.

A presentation of Soviet experience up to World War II.

"Russian City Planning of the 18th and Early 19th Centuries," *Journal of the Society of Architectural Historians,* January 1944, pp. 22-33.

A presentation of the principles, methods, and achievements of Russian city planning during this period.

"Soviet City Planning," *American Review on the Soviet Union* (New York), November 1944, pp. 53-65.

A presentation of the author's work on the replanning of the town of Vladimir.

"Municipal Reconstruction," *The U.S.S.R. in Reconstruction,* American Russian Institute, Inc. (New York), 1944, pp. 72-82.

Soviet activity in this field during the war.

"The Soviet Housing Problem," *The American Review on the Soviet Union* (New York), November 1945, pp. 12-25.

Prewar and war experience and postwar plans.

"Reconstruction U.S.S.R." *Task* (Cambridge, Mass.), Issues No. 7 and 8, 1948, pp. 25-33.

A discussion of the principles, methods, and standards of Soviet city planning in the early postwar years.

Index*

*References to illustrations are in *italics*.